Solaris™ 9
Security

Ashish Daniel Wilfred

WITH

NIIT

Solaris™ *9 Security*

Premier
P
Press

The Premier Press logo and related trade dress are trademarks of Premier Press and may not be used without written permission. All other trademarks are the property of their respective owners.

Press Important: Premier Press cannot provide software support. Please contact the appropriate software manufacturer's technical support line or Web site for assistance.

Premier Press and the author have attempted throughout this book to distinguish proprietary trademarks from descriptive terms by following the capitalization style used by the manufacturer.

Information contained in this book has been obtained by Premier Press from sources believed to be reliable. However, because of the possibility of human or mechanical error by our sources, Premier Press, or others, the Publisher does not guarantee the accuracy, adequacy, or completeness of any information and is not responsible for any errors or omissions or the results obtained from use of such information. Readers should be particularly aware of the fact that the Internet is an ever-changing entity. Some facts may have changed since this book went to press.

ISBN: 1-59200-005-3

Library of Congress Catalog Card Number: 2002106523

Printed in the United States of America

03 04 05 06 BH 10 9 8 7 6 5 4 3 2 1

Premier Press, a division of Course Technology
2645 Erie Avenue, Suite 41
Cincinnati, Ohio 45208

Publisher:
Stacy L. Hiquet

Marketing Manager:
Heather Hurley

Book Production Services:
Argosy

Cover Design:
Phil Velikan

About NIIT

NIIT is a global IT solutions corporation with a presence in 38 countries. With its unique business model and technology-creation capabilities, NIIT delivers software and learning solutions to more than 1,000 clients across the world.

The success of NIIT's training solutions lies in its unique approach to education. NIIT's Knowledge Solutions Business conceives, researches, and develops all of its course material. A rigorous instructional design methodology is followed to create engaging and compelling course content.

NIIT trains over 200,000 executives and learners each year in information technology areas using stand-up training, video-aided instruction, computer-based training (CBT), and Internet-based training (IBT). NIIT has been featured in *The Guinness Book of World Records* for the largest number of learners trained in one year!

NIIT has developed over 10,000 hours of instructor-led training (ILT) and over 3,000 hours of Internet-based training and computer-based training. IDC ranked NIIT among the Top 15 IT training providers globally for the year 2000. Through the innovative use of training methods and its commitment to research and development, NIIT has been in the forefront of computer education and training for the past 20 years.

Quality has been the prime focus at NIIT. Most of the processes are ISO-9001 certified. It was the 12th company in the world to be assessed at Level 5 of SEI-CMM. NIIT's Content (Learning Material) Development facility is the first in the world to be assessed at this highest maturity level. NIIT has strategic partnerships with companies such as Computer Associates, IBM, Microsoft, Oracle, and Sun Microsystems.

Acknowledgments

My parents and my brother Dennis, who have been a strong support to me while I worked long hours to complete this book. They really helped me bring out the best in the book. Thank you, dear parents, for your support.

My project manager, Anita Sastry, has worked meticulously, reviewing and giving valuable inputs to the book. Without her help, the book would not have been in its present form.

Thank you, Ginny Kaczmarek, for editing the book so well. Your valuable inputs on the book make it a wonderful book! I would also like to thank Stacy Hiquet for making this book happen in the first place. She has provided active support in all developmental stages of the book.

My special thanks also go out to Tanuj Jain and Pankaj Sharan who provided valuable technical inputs for the book. I would also like to thank Pallavi Jain and Harpreet Sethi for helping me out with some important chapters of the book.

About the Author

Ashish Daniel Wilfred is a Microsoft Certified Solution Developer. He is also Microsoft certified in Windows NT Server, Windows NT Workstation, and Windows 2000 Professional. He has worked for the past three years at NIIT Ltd. For the past two years, he has been working as a development executive in the Knowledge Solutions Business (KSB) division of NIIT. During his tenure at KSB, Ashish has had the opportunity to work on various technical assignments. His work involves designing, developing, testing, and implementing instructor-led training courses. He has developed learning materials for audiences with profiles ranging from network administrators to programmers. He developed learning materials on a wide range of technologies, such as Windows 2000, Windows XP, SQL 7, Cisco, and Office XP. The learning materials were developed on different media such as Instructor-Led Trainings (ILTs), Computer-based Trainings (CBTs), and Web-based Trainings (WBTs). He has also written books for various clients of NIIT such as Microsoft, Course Technology, and Premier Press. Ashish also possesses one year of experience in networking at NIIT Ltd. Before joining KSB, he was the network administrator at the School for Employee Education and Development (SEED), a division of NIIT. When not at work, Ashish enjoys reading and acting in plays.

Contents at a Glance

Contents

Chapter 4   **Network Security Tools 91**

Chapter 5   **Implementing System Security 123**

Introduction

Goal of the Book

Solaris is one of the most widely used operating systems. One of the main reasons for its popularity is its enhanced security. Solaris 9 protects systems from internal and external security threats by restricting access to system data, authenticating and encrypting interactive sessions with the Solaris operating environment, and supporting protocol for password updates, regardless of the platform. With the enhanced security mechanisms in Solaris 9, you select the technologies you want to implement and the level of security of your network.

The intended readers of this book are network administrators whose job responsibilities include setting up security, monitoring, security maintenance, and other advanced management and maintenance tasks. The book starts by covering basics and then moves on to discuss the intricacies of securing Solaris systems and networks. It also includes tips, notes, and review questions to make reading fun for you, as well as real-life examples that enable you to easily relate to situations in your working environment. The book provides you with comprehensive knowledge about the security features available in Solaris 9. At the end of each chapter, detailed explanatory concepts and questions help you to check your understanding.

This book will be of immense help for both novice users who have a basic knowledge about the Solaris platform and experienced administrators who wish to efficiently handle their roles. This book is for people managing the following positions:

◆ Network administrators
◆ Web administrators

Chapters 1 through 4 provide you with an overview about security. They discuss the need for security, basic security guidelines, and cryptography. These chapters discuss the available cryptographic techniques and particularly focus on the cryptographic techniques implemented in Solaris 9, such as PDP, SHA, and MD5. The earliest chapters also cover auditing, Role-Based Access Control (RBAC), and the network security tools available in Solaris, such as NIS+, ASET, and Solaris Fingerprint Database.

The next few chapters, Chapters 5 through 7 discuss how you can implement security for users and applications in Solaris. You'll learn about file and directory permissions and network security tools available in Solaris. These tools include Tiger, Tripwire, COPS, and `lsof`. The chapters also discuss the information security tools available in Solaris, such as `TCP wrappers`, `rpcbind`, and `Crack`.

The last few chapters, Chapters 8 through 10 cover how security can be implemented on networks using Solaris. They cover concepts such as Kerberos V5, Sun Enterprise Authentication Mechanism (SEAM), Internet Security Scanner (ISS), Security Administrator's Tool for Analyzing Networks (SATAN), IPSec, and Simple Key Management for Internet Protocol (SKIP). They also discuss implementing security for Web and e-mail services.

The Appendices section in this book gives you real-life relevance about Sun Solaris 9 security concepts and their implementation. These appendices include an overview about some of the additional security tools available in Solaris 9, such as Yet Another Solaris Security Package (YASSP) and Toolkit for Interactively Toughening Advanced Networks and Systems (TITAN). Separate appendices cover FAQs, tips and tricks, and disaster recovery.

How to Use This Book

This book has been organized to facilitate a better grasp of the content covered. The various conventions used in the book include the following:

◆ **Tips**. Tips provide special advice or unusual shortcuts with the operating system.

◆ **Notes**. Notes give additional information that may be of interest to the reader but is not essential to performing the task at hand.

◆ **Cautions**. Cautions are used to warn users of possible disastrous results if they perform a task incorrectly.

◆ **New term definitions**. All new terms have been italicized and then defined as a part of the text.

Chapter 1

Security:
An Overview

In today's networking environment, companies want to achieve all of the benefits of networking. They want faster internal networking, better services for remote users, efficient communication, and a share of the global market. If a company is involved in e-commerce, a faster and more secure network becomes a necessity. Years ago, when the scope of computer networks had not fully evolved, all the computers were confined to one physical location. It was easy to administer a network and to ensure security because only the physical security of resources had to be ensured. With the introduction of Large Area Networks (LANs), Metropolitan Area Networks (MANs), and Wide Area Networks (WANs), the reach of computers has widened. This increase in the scope of computers has created a requirement for securing the servers that are critical to your business or are a part of your network.

Security plays an important role in protecting the integrity of information on your network. However, what exactly is security? This chapter will guide you through the need for security, the principles behind security, and the intricacies of implementing security.

Need for Security

The first question that comes to mind is, What is security? It is important to understand what security means before implementing it in your network. Implementing security means creating a comprehensive security plan that determines which resources should be protected and the measures that you need to take in case the plan fails.

Security plans fail due to their inherent weaknesses, which lead to attacks on the network. The primary source of information about the attacks can be gathered from the history of previous attacks. When these attacks are detected, they help you to identify the weaknesses in the existing security measures. You can then implement the appropriate measures to eliminate the weaknesses. You must properly document the information about each attack and the solutions implemented to protect the network from the attack. This documentation provides a warning to others who might otherwise face similar attacks. All of these measures help to formulate an effective security policy. However, you must also remember that implementing a security policy is only a first step. Once the policy is implemented, you need to regularly audit the implementation of the policy to detect any loopholes. The Solaris operating system provides the facility for logging the activities of a user or the system at the basic level. It also provides the facility to log the result. You could also audit instances of successful and failed read-write operations or deletions.

A workstation is the lowest level at which you can implement security. A workstation might store confidential information, and multiple workstations can connect to create a network. Therefore, the security of an individual workstation may be critical for the security of the network. Most workstations require the proper application of user rights and permissions. You need to ensure that only authorized users have the right to log on to the workstation. You also need to ensure that if multiple users need to log on to a workstation, each authorized user has a valid user account. You can then apply separate levels of user rights for each login based on the security requirements of your organization. In the same way that you need to secure access to a workstation, you also need to secure access to the documents stored on a workstation.

You can implement document-level security by assigning appropriate access rights. A document or folder can have any combination of the three access permissions: Read, Write, and Execute. You can assign any combination of these rights to different users. These rights restrict or provide access to users for documents or folders. You can assign different rights to different user accounts for a folder or document. For example, user A might have the Read access to the Accounts folder but might not have the right to update the information. However, user B might have all three access rights to the folder.

At the network level, you need to ensure the security of *network servers*. Some examples of network servers are application servers, database servers, Web servers, and other business-critical servers that are essential for the successful functioning of a business. The main services provided by network servers are application and data storage. They provide these services to the other computers on the network by allowing them restricted access. They also provide authentication and e-mail services for the network. Due to their centralized location on the network, the network servers also store confidential information related to the organization. Authorized users can readily access this information. If the security of the information stored on these servers is not ensured, it can lead to the loss of confidential information. Therefore, the security of these servers should be a part of your security policy.

While ensuring the security of data on the network, you need to primarily ensure three things: the integrity, availability, and confidentiality of data. The following sections discuss these requirements in detail.

Ensuring Data Integrity

Data integrity implies verifying that information remains unchanged when it is transmitted from one computer to another. When information is transmitted over insecure media, its integrity may be questionable. Therefore, it is critical to secure transmitted information from unauthorized users who might want to alter or delete the information for unscrupulous purposes. A hacker can alter data by using various means, such as session hijacking. *Session hijacking* is a technique by which a hacker can gain unauthorized access to a computer.

Since information is often used in multiple locations, if a hacker is able to tamper with the primary copy of data, the false information is replicated across all the locations. This can lead to a collapse of the entire system. For example, a hacker who hacks into a banking system and manipulates critical account records can use the hacked accounts to make large withdrawals. If the information is linked, the amount in the bank account will appear to be different from that in other sources. If the activity is repeated for multiple accounts, it could lead to a collapse of the banking system.

You also need to keep a constant watch on the network to track which user is making modifications to the data and at what time. Only authorized individuals should have the right to change or delete information. Certain services require the use of anonymous accounts to work. For example, the nobody account is a non-interactive user account that can be used by Web servers. You need to ensure that these accounts are properly secured and are not assigned additional rights to access confidential information.

Not all damages to data integrity are deliberate. Some inconsistencies can be accidental. For example, a data-entry operator might accidentally enter incorrect information due to unfamiliarity with the system, fatigue, or oversight. However, the result in both cases is the loss of data integrity.

Ensuring Data Availability

Ensuring data availability implies providing authorized users access to information at all times. If hackers can gain access to the information, they might alter it for their own advantage. They might also set up barriers that will not allow authorized users to access the information. This process is known as *Denial of Service (DoS)* attacks. DOS attacks involve:

◆ Denying authorized users the ability to use their own computers or the network resources

◆ Flooding a network with unnecessary data packets, thereby preventing authorized users from accessing the network

◆ Disrupting the connection between computers so that a computer cannot access a service running on another computer

◆ Preventing individual users from accessing the resources or services running on other computers

Therefore, a hacker can detect the weak points of a network and use them to prevent legitimate users from accessing the resources on the network. For example, a telnet server is configured to provide access to only a limited number of users. A hacker can obtain multiple connections to the server and prevent authorized users from initiating a telnet session.

Another danger to data availability is *sniffer programs*. These programs use network cards to gain access to data packets at the same time they are transmitted over the network. For example, a remote user connects to an internal network to share confidential information with a user on the internal network. If hackers want to gain access to the information, they can install a sniffer program on either of the computers. The hackers can then easily access the information passed between both the users. Some common examples of packet sniffing programs are `Tcpdump` and `Ethereal`.

You can ensure the availability of data by taking regular backups and presenting the information in an easily readable format. You can also use failover or clustered servers to provide constant access to business-critical data. If the data is replicated across multiple servers and if one server fails, another server can take its place. The data should also be regularly backed up so that if it is hacked or corrupted in any way, you can easily restore the information to its original state.

Ensuring Data Confidentlality

Ensuring the confidentiality of information is also critical for its security. Confidentiality means that only authorized individuals can access information from the system or the network. One of the ways to secure data is by using user accounts with passwords and permissions to restrict access to information. Sometimes, a piece of information is only confidential for a certain period of time, such as in the case of online polls in which individuals give their opinion anonymously. Once the data has been collated, it is released to the public and is no longer confidential. However, you still need to protect the identity and opinions of individuals.

You also need to ensure data confidentiality while transmitting data over the network. If you have not secured the data, a hacker might gain access to it by using hacking techniques such as packet sniffing. Packet sniffing allows the hacker to view all the packets traveling on the network. You can prevent this type of hacking by using encryption techniques, such

 NOTE

To implement security in online transactions, you need to use a trusted operating system, such as Sun Solaris. In the previous version of Solaris, the trusted version (Trusted Solaris 8) was different from the Operating Environment (OE) version. The OE versions contained provision for basic security while the Trusted Solaris version was used for implementing additional security. In Solaris 9, all the functionalities that were available separately in both the versions have been combined in a single version.

as Public Key Infrastructure (PKI) and Secure Shell (SSH), to encrypt information during transit. SSH is a standard for securing remote access to computers over an IP network. The technology encrypts a data packet before it is transmitted over the network. PKI can be used for both encryption as well as signing the contents. Signing the contents is analogous to sealing a letter that contains confidential information. As long as the seal is intact, you are assured of the confidentiality of the information contained in the letter.

Let's look at some of the security principles that you need to keep in mind while creating a security plan.

Security Guidelines

If you ask network administrators how they secure a network, you might get different replies from each administrator. The answer to this question depends on the security policies implemented in a network and the security budget approved by an organization. All network administrators have their own methods of ensuring network security. Some believe in implementing strict security practices, while others install security tools to secure the network. However, none of these measures are complete in themselves. In order to implement effective security, you need to create a comprehensive security plan.

Before you create a security plan, you must know what needs to be secured. It is at this point where security principles come into focus. Security principles are a set of rules that give a complete overview of the resources that you must secure on a network. As an administrator, you should incorporate the following security guidelines that will help protect your networks from hackers and other intrusions:

- ◆ Secure the network from non-employees
- ◆ Implement multilayered security
- ◆ Secure the connections to trusted networks
- ◆ Ensure system security before connecting to the network
- ◆ Plan the network security requirements for the future
- ◆ Disable any unnecessary services and uninstall applications that are not needed
- ◆ Ensure disaster recovery

The following sections review each of these points in detail.

Securing the Network from Non-Employees

Most hackers might be people you already know. Before securing your network from outsiders, you need to secure the network from the people in your own network. These people might want to access information without proper authorization. You might be working with them every day and, therefore, might trust them with a critical password in an emergency. For example, as a network administrator, you might face a situation in which you are in the midst of an important assignment and someone requires access to certain files. To save time (and sometimes even because you trust the person's capability), you might give the person the root password. If your trust is misplaced, the person might use the password to make changes to his or her rights and permissions or modify confidential data. In case a mishap occurs, you would most probably shoulder the blame. Another danger is that these individuals might not restrict their activities to only destroying information. Why restrict yourself when you have the key to the network? A hacker might also destroy data that has been backed up or alter the security settings to prevent you from accessing the information. The hacker might also damage the original software and system files so that you are unable to correct the problem.

In certain cases, the actions of the individual to whom you give the password might not be intentional. For example, the person could be new to the software or the operating system. Therefore, certain system files or program files might be deleted accidentally. Although the possibility of error exists, almost all hackers are individuals who have malicious intent and want to create havoc on your network and delete critical information.

Implementing Multilayered Security

With the growth of the Internet in recent years, the scope of businesses has also expanded. Nowadays, businesses have clients and business partners all over the world. With an increase in the scope of business, the threat of outsiders gaining access to the confidential information of an organization has also increased. Besides the threat to information security, Internet viruses pose another threat. These viruses gain access to a network via the Internet and spread across the network through loopholes in programs. They can infect the files on a network and corrupt information. You need to protect your network by implementing security. Security can be either single-layered or multilayered.

Single-Layered Security

Single-layered security is also known as single-dimensional security. As the name suggests, it involves implementing security for a network by using only one layer or one type of security measures. The drawback is that if the defense fails, the network is left defenseless and open to attack. Mostly, in single-layered security, firewalls are used to act as a defense for the network. Since the firewall is the only way to enter and exit the network, it is easier to secure access to the network. With an increase in the use of the Internet, both for accessing information and for using services, such as remote access and file transfer, the need for security has increased. Each service and application that connects to the Internet has its own inherent weaknesses. The firewall is unable to protect the network from all these weaknesses and sometimes fails, which then leads to the need for multilayered security.

Multilayered Security

Implementing multilayered security involves setting up multiple firewalls or implementing multiple measures to secure a network. This involves creating a security plan that takes into account the security requirements of the network, the tools available, and the measures that can be implemented for security. Determining the security requirements involves exploring all the security options available and deciding which options are the best fit for the network's security requirement. There are many tools available for implementing security on a network: Some tools are for intrusion detection, while others are for preventing intrusion. You also need to devise a plan in case of an intrusion and determine the locations (such as individual workstations, on the server, or directly on the firewalls) where the plan will need to be implemented.

Securing the Connection to Trusted Networks

To misquote a line from Shakespeare, " . . . to trust or not to trust, that is the question. . . ." This question has plagued network administrators everywhere since the scope of a network increased beyond geographical boundaries and the need to connect to multiple networks has become much more prevalent. In the contemporary networking scenario, no network can afford to remain in total isolation. Administrators need to set up trust relationships between networks, but these relationships can cause security problems. For example, if the login, which has been provided for a trust relationship has not been properly secured, a hacker can crack this login and gain access not only to the trusting system but also to all the computers on the trusting network.

 NOTE

A *trusting* network is a network that provides access to another network, whereas a *trusted* network is the one that accesses resources from the trusting network. The relationship between these networks is called a *trust relationship*. This trust relationship can be either one-way or both ways. In a two-way trust relationship, both the networks act as trusted and trusting networks interchangeably. However, in case of a one-way relationship, one network always acts as the trusted network and the other as the trusting network.

Network administrators have to ensure that they follow all the security practices because they have the ultimate control over the network. With an increase in the size of a network and the growth of network traffic, the responsibilities of network administrators have also increased. They have to ensure that they assign appropriate rights to individuals and groups. They also need to ensure that all the administrative tasks are performed and that nothing is left to chance.

NOTE

In Solaris 9, administrators have the facility to implement Role-Based Access Control (RBAC), which allows them to assign specific rights to different users. RBAC distributes the system administration tasks among multiple user roles, and each user role has a separate task.. Therefore, even if an unauthorized user is able to become a superuser, the user's rights are still limited. The other utilities available for implementing security are Mandatory Access Control (MAC) and Java-based tools.

Ensuring System Security before Connecting to a Network

Another area of security weakness is a computer with a newly installed operating system. After installing an operating system on a computer, you must ensure that the system is secured before you connect it to a network. Securing a system involves implementing all the security measures, such as securing all the services and applications running on the system. It is a network administrator's responsibility to ensure that all the applications and tools being used on the system are secure. It is advisable to ensure that an application is secure before it is used on the network.

Planning the Network Security Requirements for the Future

Network administrators face an initial problem in introducing security measures on existing networks. The networks may not have any provisions for the implementation of these security measures. Another major hurdle is that the users may be unfamiliar with the security measures. Therefore, they feel these measures are a hindrance to their productivity. Try to explain to a person in the Sales department that in the new system, access to the Accounts records will be restricted only to the managers. If the department's employees are in the habit of accessing any data they want, they will not appreciate the new security system.

Another problem in configuring the security on an existing system is that it might require changes to the operating system files and other utilities. This might disrupt the normal functioning of the system, the network, and the users connected to the system. For example, everyone on the network prints to a network printer. After security is set up for this printer, access to the printer is restricted to the groups that have the specific print rights. Imagine if the system administrator forgets to add a manager who is supposed to be assigned to the group and given print permissions on a priority basis. The manager might not be able to print and might not even realize the problem until the network administrator rectifies it.

Disabling Unnecessary Services and Uninstalling Needless Applications

As a network administrator, you might already know that not all the services that are installed on a system are necessary for the system to run effectively. Many of these services, especially those that provide network access, are prospective threats to network security. You should disable all the services that are not required by the system. This is especially important in the case of network servers since the users on both the internal and external networks access them. A hacker can gain access to the network by exploiting these unsecured services. Certain software also comes in the category of prospective security threats. Software itself might not be a security threat; however, when placed on a network, it might provide a convenient opportunity for hackers to gain entry to the network. You must stop all the unnecessary services and remove the software that creates a security problem for the network.

To determine whether a service or an application is a security threat, list all of its advantages and disadvantages. Once the information is listed, you can easily determine the usefulness of the software and whether its existence on the network is justified. All the services and applications that are not required should be immediately terminated and access to them should be restricted.

Ensuring Disaster Recovery

Despite all preparations, the fact remains that hackers are just as clever asnetwork administrators. While you are closing one loophole in network security, hackers are busy finding other loopholes and weaknesses in the network implementation. Therefore, as a network administrator, you should always be prepared for the worst. You should periodically make backups of the critical data and software, maintain multiple copies of this software, and ensure that it is accessible at all times.

Securing Physical and Network Resources

A workstation is one of the first resources that you should secure on a network. It might contain important information, which might be required by the other users on the network. If a workstation is secure, the information being transferred on the network is also secure. Most vendors provide a default configuration while providing different hardware and software components. Unfortunately, most of the time, the default configuration is not very secure since selling the features of the component and not the security aspect is a vendor's primary concern. Therefore, you must always reconfigure the software and the hardware to provide adequate security for your workstation. This is also true while setting up operating systems that start their own services and applications. As explained earlier in the chapter, all unnecessary services and applications should be removed from the network.

When securing physical resources, you must first plan how they will be located on your network. The plan should take into consideration the security requirements for each resource and its accessibility. For example, the server room of the organization should be locked, and access should be allowed to only the administrator. Finally, network users should also be made aware of the concerns regarding security and the measures to resolve these concerns.

 NOTE

The support for device allocation that was available in Trusted Solaris 8 continues in Solaris 9. Administrators can assign certain tags to devices to indicate whether these devices should or should not be used. The use of device allocation is not restricted to only hardware devices but also extends to software-emulated devices.

The following are some of the steps that you can take to ensure the security of physical resources:

◆ Build a comprehensive security plan
◆ Secure user accounts
◆ Secure access to physical devices and files
◆ Maintain system logs and back up regularly
◆ Monitor intrusion detection
◆ Secure remote access

Each of these steps will be discussed in detail.

Building a Comprehensive Security Plan

A well-defined security plan will take into account the cost of resources, minimizing the disruption of work, ensuring that the applications installed on a network are secure, and ensuring that users are adequately trained. A well-defined security plan helps to avoid security problems by listing all the measures that you need to implement to counter all the security problems that you might face. The plan is a look at the prospective problems you might face and lists all the measures available with you to resolve these problems. Creating a comprehensive security plan involves determining the following issues:

- ◆ The purpose of each computer
- ◆ The available network services
- ◆ The type of prospective users
- ◆ The user authentication
- ◆ The use of intrusion detection strategies
- ◆ The data backup and recovery procedures
- ◆ The installation of operating systems
- ◆ The network topology
- ◆ How computers should be administered
- ◆ How to identify the unused services, software, and resources
- ◆ How to ensure the deployment plan is regularly updated

The following sections discuss some of these issues.

Determining the Purpose of Each Computer

Each computer on a network should have a purpose. For example, computers might be data servers, applications servers, or simply client computers. The purpose that a computer serves on the network determines its security requirements. For example, it might be more important to secure remote access on servers whereas security of data might be more critical on workstations. You must also determine the type of information that will be transmitted from and to these computers and the security measures required to secure this information during transit. The network services running on a system should be taken into account while determining the security requirements.

Determining the Available Network Services

While determining the security plan, you must also take into account the services available on the computers. For example, a computer might have access to the Internet (the Web service), the e-mail service, the DNS, the database service, or the file transfer service. The computer will have to be secured for each of these services. However, the way in which the computer is secured will be based on whether the computer is a server or a client. If the computer is a client, you need to determine the access permissions, the type of access, and the extent to which users are to be allocated rights. If the computer is a server, the service must be properly configured to ensure that no hacker is able to access the service.

Determining the Type of Prospective Users

Next, you need to identify the users or the type of users that will use a specific computer. Generally, users can be classified into administrators and system users. Administrators can be further classified into network administrators and database administrators. A classification is also known as a user role. A *user role* determines the authority level of a user. Users are allowed to work on a computer based on their rights. In the case of network servers, you need to determine the types of users who should be allowed access to them. For example, an administrator would have all the rights to a file server, while a standard user would only have the right to read information. You also need to ensure that only the administrator has the right to work on the servers. A server should never be used as a regular workstation due to the risk involved in unsecured access. Similarly, you should never configure workstations with the ability to administer network services. Each user role should have its own set of rights and duties. These rights are usually assigned at the group level instead of to individual users.

Determining User Authentication

You also need to determine how a user will be authenticated on a system or a network. Authentication determines if the user, who is attempting to log on to the network, is an authentic user. When users access a computer or a network service, they are authenticated based on their logins and assigned the appropriate rights based on the group to which they belong. Users can be authenticated based on a password or by using a physical device, such as smart cards and tokens.

Determining the Use of Intrusion Detection Strategies

The type of intrusion detection strategy that you should specify in your security plan depends on the type of dangers faced in your network. The risk of intrusions is determined based on an analysis of the system logs. The auditing tools that determine the vulnerability of your system implement this analysis, and you can use this analysis to determine which intrusion detection tools you will implement on your system.

Determining Data Backup and Recovery Procedures

You also need to document the procedures for backing up and restoring data. There are many ways to back up data, such as normal and incremental backups. If a proper backup procedure is followed, you can easily recover any data lost due to data corruption. Sometimes, the data also contains confidential information, such as details about user logins and passwords. You can encrypt the backed-up data to ensure that hackers are unable to retrieve information from it. Before restoring backed-up data, you must ensure that the data has not been tampered with. One commonly used method is to transfer all the backed-up data to a secured server and only restore the data from this server. This not only ensures the authenticity of the data but also ensures that you restore the latest version of the backed-up data.

Determining the Installation of Operating Systems

In the security plan, you also need to specify a setup procedure for installing and securing an operating system. A setup procedure ensures that all the systems installed in a network have the same basic security settings and are installed in the same manner. The security plan also defines the services that should and should not be running on the network. You can specify these conditions in scripts that can be run on a newly installed system. These scripts automatically configure the services and assign a specific level of rights on the system. The security plan should contain a detailed list of all the steps that need to be followed while installing an operating system. You could list all the steps in the form of a checklist that the administrators can follow during installation.

Determining the Network Topology

The security plan should contain a detailed account of how a network is to be configured and how the computers are to be connected to each other. A network can be a LAN or through external access by using the Internet. In a LAN, since all the points on the network are authenticated computers, information may be transmitted on the network without encryption. However, while using the Internet, computers are not connected directly but pass over several other networks. Therefore, you cannot be sure that the connection between two computers is not viewed or changed.

Determining How Computers Should Be Administered

The administration of a network is determined based on the network size. If a network is small, you can administer the servers and workstations individually and perform all the administrative tasks from a central computer. However, in case of a large network or a network spread across a large geographical area, administrative activities can be distributed among multiple network administrators. You can assign one administrator to each site.

Identifying the Unused Services, Software, and Resources

The security plan should also contain information about the services, software, and resources that are not used by a system. All such services, software, and resources should be disabled.

Ensuring Constant Updation of the Deployment Plan

The deployment plan should not be a static document and should regularly be updated with any security change. You need to make changes to the security plan in case of any change in software or due to new security threats.

Securing User Accounts

As mentioned earlier, you need to secure a network from unauthorized users. To do this, you must set up certain authorization mechanisms on the network that validate the credentials of users the moment they try to log on. You might need to make certain changes in a system's configuration to ensure this. In case of a network, you can set up a server that will contain information regarding the logins of all the valid users. When a user tries to log on to the network, the server will first validate the specified login ID and the password. Only when the information matches an entry in the list of valid users will the user be able to log on to the network.

Another way of validating a user's credentials is by using physical devices, such as tokens and smart cards. A smart card is a simple card that contains information about a user, such as the user ID and the PIN. When a user needs to be validated, the smart card is entered into the system. The system then validates the information stored on the smart card with the information stored in a central database. If the information is found, the user ID is validated, otherwise, the user is not allowed access to the network.

The following are certain measures that you can take to secure user accounts:

◆ Eliminate or disable the unnecessary user accounts

◆ Use the security options available in the hardware

◆ Enforce a strong password policy

◆ Secure idle systems

Let's look at each of these measures in detail.

Eliminating or Disabling the Unnecessary User Accounts

Almost all operating systems contain certain default user accounts and groups that are created at the time of installing the operating system or particular software. You should ensure that all these user accounts and groups are deactivated until they are required. For example, the user account is available in Solaris for use by daemons and is available for services that do not require the use of a regular interactive user account. This account should not be made interactive, especially for computers on which confidential information is stored. On such servers, you must ensure that all the unnecessary user accounts are removed and all the administrative accounts are adequately secured. In addition to removing unnecessary user accounts, you can also rename the administrative accounts, which will prevent hackers from identifying the administrative accounts and from hacking them.

You must also keep changing the passwords for administrative accounts at regular intervals. This ensures that hackers are unable to determine the current administrative password even if they are able to crack an old one.

Using the Security Options Available in the Hardware

The computer hardware device also has certain built-in security options that you can use to physically secure the system. For example, you can set up a BIOS or EEPROM password on the system. This password is stored on the hardware and a user must specify the password to access the system. Since this option is hardware-based, the security measure is invoked even before the operating system is loaded.

 NOTE

A drawback to this system is that if a password is lost or forgotten, the hardware needs to be reconfigured. Although changing the jumper settings on the pins for the battery powering the Real Time Clock can break this password, this method requires the physical manipulation of hardware. You have to change the jumper settings and then restart the system. The BIOS settings, including the password, are reinitialized. This is not an effective strategy because if someone who does not know about the hardware performs the activity, the computer can crash.

Enforcing a Strong Password Policy

Another way to ensure that only authenticated users gain access to the network is by ensuring a strict password policy. A strict password policy will prevent hackers from cracking a valid user's password. A password should be of a specific length, should not be very simple or intuitive, and should be changed regularly. You must also restrict users from reusing the same password while changing the existing password. A password set by a user must meet the criteria of the maximum and minimum number of characters in a password. For example, the tool in UNIX checks this compliance. In addition, you must advise users to set a complex password that cannot be cracked easily. A common option is to use a combination of upper- and lowercase alphanumeric characters along with numbers. You can also assign rights to a user group and not to individual users. This not only saves administrative hassles but also ensures that a uniform level of rights is assigned to users. You must document this password policy properly, and users should be instructed to follow the policy conscientiously. The operating system should also be configured to lock out a user account in case of repeated incorrect logins. This is similar to what happens when you forget your ATM pin number. If you try a few incorrect combinations, the system freezes your account and you cannot access your account until it is activated again.

NOTE

There is a drawback in configuring a computer to lock out a user account after a number of incorrect logins. A hacker can deny valid users the ability to work on the network by using this method to continuously get a user's account locked. Therefore, this process should be used judiciously and only for a certain time period. You also need to differentiate between incorrect remote logins and the logins from a console. The incorrect use of one should not disable the other.

Securing Idle Systems

You can implement security measures to ensure that an unauthorized user cannot gain access to your computer while you are away. This is especially true in the case of network servers. You can also configure the operating system to prompt for the user ID and the password after a period of inactivity. This ensures that only you or an authorized user gains access to the system. As a practice, you must either shut down or lock the system if you are away for a long time period. You can also implement the same feature for remote logins. A connection should be discontinued if it is inactive for a specific time period. You need to ensure that hackers are not able to manipulate the discarded remote connections.

Using Encryption Technologies to Secure Passwords

You can use physical security devices, such as smart cards, to ensure the validity of user information. This is especially important in the case of a remote login as information is sent across the network to a central computer to be validated. If the information is not encrypted, hackers might be able to intercept it while it is being transported across the network and use it to access the network in future.

Securing Access to Physical Devices and Files

You can also implement security by using certain features available in operating systems. These features allow you to secure access to files, directories, and the other physical resources available on your system or the network. Securing files and other physical resources ensures protection from unauthorized access. This ensures that users don't make changes to the system security and do not access files for which they have not been authorized. You can also secure both local and remote access to physical locations.

You can implement the following measures to ensure that only authorized users have access to resources.

Assigning Access Based on User Accounts

You need to create specific groups, which should be assigned rights to access specific files, directories, and resources. You can add any user who needs to access the file or resource to a specific group. For example, suppose you make a user a member of the sysadmin group. The user could abuse the granted rights by using the `admin` tool to modify another user's settings. You can also implement other restrictions to ensure security. For example, only the administrative users should have the right to make changes to system files by using the supplied administrative tools. This will enable only authorized people to have access to the files. In operating systems such as UNIX, you can ensure security by mounting a partition as read-only. Mounting a partition as read-only prevents all users, including administrative users, from making changes. You should also implement auditing and maintain log files. These files should contain up-to-date information in case of a system failure. You can use these log files to rectify any problem.

Maintaining a List of User Accounts and Rights

You need to document all the user accounts and their corresponding rights. The documentation should clearly state the user ID, the user group, the level of rights, and the name of the resource. You can use this documentation to keep track of the level of rights provided to each user. You can assign each user group the rights to different categories of information. You can also differentiate between a user's local rights and a user's network rights. For example, a user might have the right to locally access certain confidential information stored on a server but not the right to access it over the network. If the information is transmitted over the network, it might be hacked. One solution is to encrypt information before it is transmitted over the network and decrypt it at the destination. Sometimes, certain software might require additional rights in order to run on the network. The users who use this software might inherit these rights. You might need to control this inheritance and limit it to a selective number of users.

Encrypting Confidential Data

As mentioned earlier, you might need to encrypt information before it is sent to remote users. Sometimes, this feature is available in the operating system, and at times, you might need to use third-party utilities to ensure this security. This is especially true when the information is of a complex nature and you cannot depend only on user authentication to ensure its security during transmission. A drawback to using encryption for ensuring security is that it places an additional load on the processor, which might affect system performance. You need to weigh the security requirement with the cost and make an appropriate decision. Despite the information being encrypted during transit, it can still be hacked at certain other weak points where it is not encrypted. The data can be hacked before it is encrypted, when it is left on the destination computer after decryption, and when it is residual data derived from the encryption process.

Maintaining System Logs and Making Regular Backups

You need to identify all the resources that need to be audited and store the information in log files. The resources to be audited depend on the security requirement of your organization and the policies implemented in it. If you don't log the proper information, you will not be able to detect intrusions and risk attacks by hackers.

You can implement the following measures to ensure that all the required resources are being audited. The following list contains certain requirements for maintaining system logs and making regular backups:

◆ Verify the dependability of logged information

◆ Use third-party utilities to facilitate logging

◆ Document the security plan to secure the log files

◆ Ensure a file backup and restore plan

The following sections discuss these points in detail.

Verifying the Dependability of Logged Information

A danger posed by the use of logging tools is that hackers can also use them to retrieve confidential information from the system. You can prevent this by ensuring that only the authorized users have the right to view the logged information available on the network. Therefore, only the root user should have the right to create, modify, and extract data from the log files. Another reason why it is necessary to secure these log files is that hackers might make changes to the unsecured log files to hide traces of their presence.

One way of securing these files is to store that data on a removable storage device to which you can write only once. For example, you can store the information on a CD-ROM that can be written to only once. Although this is an easy method to store the information, you must ensure the security of these devices once they have been written to. Another method is to store the information on a central server that is kept exclusively for this purpose. You must also secure access to this server by using security measures such as passwords and other security devices. In addition, you must ensure the security of the information while it is transmitted between the client computer and the server. Hackers can try to disable the logging services by filling up the log files so that logging cannot continue. Once this happens, the logging activity stops. You can prevent this problem by allocating separate disk space or partitions for the log files and regularly monitoring the size of the log file. If the size increases beyond an acceptable level, you can truncate the file from the partition after backing it up, which will allow the administrator adequate time to ensure the security of the system.

Using Third-Party Utilities to Facilitate Logging

Many third-party utilities exist in the market that can be used to facilitate the logging process. You can also enable certain logging mechanisms already available in your operating system. These mechanisms can either run constantly or may need to be restarted every time the computer restarts. Any utility you choose for logging should be set up to log information at a certain location. (Some of these tools can log information at a default location, while others can be configured to store the information at a specific location.) Any location you specify should be adequately secured and should contain adequate disk space for the file size to increase. You must also remember that multiple tools can use the same log file to store information; therefore, you should allocate disk space appropriately.

Documenting the Security Plan to Secure Log Files

You must maintain a detailed plan of how the log files should be secured. In addition, you must ensure that adequate information is logged in the log files. Although it is an expensive option to store all the information, it is very difficult to anticipate which information will be required to detect an intrusion or solve a problem. Therefore, you must log as much information as possible and compress the log file to save on disk space. You can also have a single log file that contains information about multiple computers. This ensures that you can detect an intrusion on the network by determining if any pattern exists in accessing files and resources. The log files should also be backed up regularly. Before these files are backed up or while they are stored on a computer, you can encrypt them, which will protect them from unauthorized access by hackers. You will learn about encryption in Chapter 2, "Introduction to Cryptography."

Ensuring a File Backup and Restore Plan

You need to maintain a detailed plan of how you will back up the log files and then restore them. Since the backup has to be done on a weekly, monthly, or annual basis, you need to plan accordingly. The time duration after which the log files should be backed up is based on your requirements and the growth of the log files versus the available disk space. As mentioned previously, you need to maintain a balance between the cost incurred in logging and the advantages derived from it. The plan must be exhaustive and cover all types of computers. Once the files have been backed up, they should also be encrypted. When restoring these backed-up logs, you must ensure that they have not been tampered with. Mostly, these log files are stored on a separate computer that is then secured. The batch files are then periodically appended with any changes that might occur on the servers. If the information stored on a server is ever hacked, the latest information stored on the backup server can be used to bring the information up-to-date. In the case of workstations, the files can be backed up either on the same computer or on another computer on the network. In case you use an external computer, you need to ensure that the information is secured during transit. Only the administrator should have the rights to access the computer locally and all the network services should be disabled.

Monitoring Intrusion Detection

You need to analyze all the resources and maintain a log of their usage. You can then analyze these log files and identify any changes from the normal activity.

You must log the system state immediately after all the system configuration changes are complete. At this time, all the necessary services would be running, and the system state can act as a benchmark for any future comparisons, or analysis. This analysis might occur when you need to compare the current system state with the baseline system state. You can compare both the states and determine if the system is performing as per your expectations.

You need to log all the suspicious activities on the network, detect any intrusions, and create recovery plans. In addition, you can identify any other measures that you can take to prevent intrusion. Although a log file contains an exhaustive store of information, it is possible that you will not find all the required information to detect an intrusion. Therefore, it is necessary that you know what to search for while trying to detect an intrusion.

The following is a list of certain types of information that you need to collect to detect an intrusion:

◆ The system performance, including the CPU, memory, and disk usage
◆ The file-system-related changes
◆ The errors encountered by the system or the hardware
◆ The successful detection of new services or devices on the system or the network
◆ The encryption of files and directories
◆ The changes to the access rights of specific users
◆ User information

The following sections contain some of the points that you need to consider for detecting intrusion. These points are as follows:

◆ Monitoring the system for suspicious data
◆ Determining what needs to be logged
◆ Classifying the accepted network and system performance
◆ Classifying accepted directory and file information
◆ Gathering information about the hardware installed on the system

Let's look at these points in detail.

Monitoring the System for Suspicious Data

Monitoring the network implies continuously observing the network traffic to identify any suspicious activity. This is a continuous event and unlike logging, this is done as events are occurring. It is preferable to enable monitoring because in this case, a vast quantity of information does not need to be stored and analyzed later. You can use monitoring tools to check the network for hacker presence and to raise alerts as soon as any suspicious activity occurs. This is different from checking the logs for such activities. In the case of logs, an alarm is raised after the event has occurred. What is the use of locking the barn door once the horse has bolted? However, this is not always true; you can learn from experiences and ensure more security. You can implement intrusion detection systems to detect hacker attacks. These intrusion detection systems act as tripwires for hackers and are triggered the moment a hacker is detected. The system then sends a message to the network administrator informing the administrator about the hacker's presence. Intrusion detection systems are of two types: system-based and network-based.

System-based intrusion detection systems are placed on computers and check the information being processed for traces of intruders. In *network-based* intrusion detection systems, the system keeps a watch on the network traffic and triggers an alarm the moment an intruder is detected on the network. An intrusion is detected in two ways: Either the detected intrusion maps to an intrusion signature, or the network is searched for any abnormal activity. Abnormal activities could include the use of ports that had not been used earlier or the unauthorized use of network services. However, there is no definite rule as to what can be classified as suspicious activities. Each organization needs to create a policy for itself that documents the security needs of the organization and its policy for the same.

Determining What Needs to Be Logged

As mentioned before, you can log data in order to detect intrusion attacks. However, the question remains, What should be logged? This information primarily depends on your organization's requirements and the type of information that is transmitted over the network. Generally, you need to determine whether hardware is so important that it warrants the logging of its activities. If the system is a network server, you might need to log the activities of the users who connect to the server. You can also audit the resources accessed by different users. You might also log all the services running on a server. The decision regarding what should and should not be logged also depends on your organization's capability to process the data. If your organization has limited capability, it is advisable to limit the amount of data that is being logged. Another way to determine what should be logged is to analyze the trends. These trends are visible over a time-period but once they are documented, they help in narrowing down your search criteria. However, you need to remember that these requirements are not static and change over a time-period. Therefore, you need to constantly monitor the trends and make the appropriate changes whenever required.

Classifying the Acceptable Network and System Performance

You also need to document the acceptable performance of your network and the individual systems. To determine this, you first need to document the adequate system and network requirements. For a network, you need to classify what you consider as the satisfactory working of the network and the acceptable performance of the network. Once these requirements are in place, you can always measure the current performance of the system and the network against these defined benchmarks.

Classifying the Acceptable Directory and File Information

Certain system files have a constant file size. If the size of these files increases for no apparent reason, this warrants a check on the system. Another check could be for the content of certain directories to see if the change in any file might cause a danger to the stability of the system. Many third-party utilities are available to check for these differences. You will learn about these tools in Chapter 6, "Securing the File System." All the tools check certain features in the files and directories. These files include application files, system files, access control lists, user files, reports, and Web pages.

Gathering Information About the Hardware Installed on the System

You also need to gather and document all the information for the hardware installed on your system or the network. All this information should be properly documented for future reference. In addition, any changes made to this information, such as the addition and removal of hardware devices, should be updated in the documentation. The documentation should contain information such as the architecture of the network, the topology implemented, the connectivity for network devices, the domains available on the network, the location of the devices on the network, and the security of the connection between the network and the Internet.

Securing Remote Access

Nowadays, the concept of people working from home is no longer unusual because organizations allow their employees to work from home. The security of these remote connections to the corporate network needs to be ensured. For example, the Sales team of an organization needs to be in constant touch with the corporate office. The Sales personnel require constant access to the information stored in the corporate network. However, because they access the corporate network over the Internet, the connection might not always be safe. A hacker might use an unsecured remote connection to gain access to the network. Let's look at how you can ensure the security of logins by remote users.

The Use of Extranets

With the introduction of e-commerce, the business world has undergone tremendous change. Nowadays, businesses need to interact with their customers and partner organizations by using the Internet. Certain businesses also set up their private networks, such as intranets and extranets, for exchanging information in a secure manner. Businesses use an intranet and the Internet to provide services to authenticated users in a simple manner.

The Use of Encryption

Solaris also supports third-party utilities for securing remote access. A *digital token* is one such technology that provides security to users who log on from remote locations. The technology provides the advantage of a single login that allows a user the appropriate access. When a remote user logs on, the user is assigned a token and the access to resources is determined based on the user's token. These tokens can also be stored on the remote device, thereby overcoming the danger of the token being hacked during transfer over the network. A commonly used version of the digital token used to provide encryption is the S/Key.

The Use of Firewalls to Secure a Network

You need to ensure the full security of the network. The security should be so tight that only authorized users should have access to the network. You also need to conduct periodic checks to ensure that there are no weaknesses in network security. You also need to implement security tools that raise an alert the moment an intrusion is detected.

A *firewall* is a method of restricting external access to a network. It has three components: the internal gateway, the external gateway, and the filtering mechanism. The external gateway is directly exposed to the Internet and is known as the *bastion host*. The filtering mechanism or filter blocks all the restricted traffic on the network. The internal network acts as a barrier between the data traffic on the internal network and the information between the firewalls. The publicly accessible network between the internal network and the outside world is known as the *demilitarized zone* (DMZ). The firewall is the only point on the network from which information can enter and exit the network. Therefore, this is the best point for implementing authentication and authorization. This is also the best point on the network for implementing auditing and logging any unauthorized access and security threats.

Filtering mechanisms can be implemented on routers. A firewall can consist of only a single router or of multiple routers that identify and filter out unnecessary data packets from the network. Firewalls are mostly used to segregate an internal network from the servers that provide access to external users. Firewalls are of three types: routers, application-level proxy firewalls, and stateful packet filtering firewalls. The routers are the simplest types of firewalls; however, they have many shortcomings. Routers are ineffective against attacks like TCP SYN flood attacks and IP spoofing. Routers also lack some of the advanced-level security features, such as the use of VPNs and authentication.

Summary

In this chapter, you learned about the basics of security. You learned that you need to implement security for ensuring data integrity, data availability, and data reliability. Next, you looked at the security principles. These principles serve as guidelines for implementing security on the network. This chapter also covered the need for securing resources on both the local computer and the network. It also covered the use and importance of maintaining a detailed security plan. Next, you learned how to secure user accounts. You learned about the importance of removing unnecessary accounts, having a strong password policy, and using encryption for securing passwords. Then you learned about securing access to physical devices and files using user accounts and encryption. Next, you learned the importance of maintaining system logs and making regular backups. Then you learned how to detect intrusion on your computer or the network. You learned about the types of information that need to be logged and the type of information you need to be able to detect intrusion. Finally, you learned about securing remote access and the use of firewalls.

In the next chapter, you will learn how to implement security by using cryptography. Cryptography involves securing information while it is being transmitted over the network.

Check Your Understanding

Multiple Choice Questions

1. Which user account can a Solaris Web server use for anonymously accessing a service available on the network?

   a. root

   b. nobody

   c. sys

   d. adm

2. Select the option(s) that can be classified as Denial of Service attacks.

   a. Utilization of scarce resources

   b. Changing file properties of user created files

   c. Changing of system information or user rights

   d. Alteration of network components or services

3. Which of the following are encryption techniques that are used for encrypting information during transit?

   a. VPN

   b. SSH

   c. Firewalls

   d. PKI

4. Which are the two versions of Solaris that ware available separately in earlier versions and have been combined into a single version in Solaris 9?

   a. Trusted Solaris version

   b. Operating System version

   c. Trusting Solaris version

   d. Operating Environment version

5. Which of the following statements are true in the case of trusting and trusted networks?

   a. A trusting network provides access to another network.

   b. A trusting network is allowed access by another network.

   c. A trusted network provides access to another network.

   d. A trusted network is allowed access by another network.

6. Which of the following is a new type of access control model available in Solaris 9?

   a. Record-Based Access Control

   b. Role-Based Access Control

   c. Rights-Based Access Control

7. Which of the following are valid pieces of information that you need to collect for intrusion detection?

   a. Detecting changes made to system files

   b. Detecting changes made to user files

   c. Detecting new services and devices on the computer

   d. Collecting information about the system performance

8. Which of the following are valid Intrusion Detection Systems (IDS)?

   a. File-based IDS

   b. Machine-based IDS

   c. System-based IDS

   d. Network-based IDS

9. Which of the following measures can hackers use for trapping an authenticated user's password?

    a. Attaching a snooping device to the LAN cable

    b. Changing the existing password

    c. Intercepting lost data packets on the network

    d. Creating a program disguised as a logon screen

10. You are the network administrator of a large organization and you need to provide secure Internet access to the users on the network. To deal with the threats posed by the Internet, and to make sure that only authorized users have access to the Internet, which of the following measures do you need to implement?

    a. Install antiviral software that would protect your network

    b. Change the network passwords frequently

    c. Encrypt all information transmitted through and received from the Internet

    d. Install firewalls that would protect the network

11. Which of the following statements are true?

    Statement A: Ensuring data availability is providing authorized users access to information at all times.

    Statement B: Ensuring data confidentiality is making sure that once information is termed as confidential, it always remains confidential.

    a. Both statements A and B are false.

    b. Statement A is true while Statement B is false.

    c. Both statements A and B are true.

    d. Statement A is false while Statement B is true.

Short Questions

1. What is a network sniffer and explain how it is able to extract information from the network?

2. Discuss the benefits of remote backup and how it is more secure than local backup?

Answers

Multiple Choice Answers

1. **b.** The nobody user account can be used to access a service available on the network. The user account has limited access rights; it is therefore considered secure.

2. **a, c,d.** Utilizing scarce resources, changing system information or user rights, and altering network components or services are the correct options. Changing the properties of files does not cause denial of service unless it involves system files.

3. **b,d.** Both Secured Socket Layer (SSL) and Public Key Infrastructure (PKI) are valid encryption techniques for encrypting information being transmitted over the network. Although VPN encrypts information being transmitted over the network, it uses technologies such as SKIP or IPSec for the actual encryption process.

4. **a,d.** The two versions of Solaris that were available until Solaris 9 were the Trusted Solaris and the Operating Environment (OE) version. The OE version was the basic version of Solaris and had limited security features. The Trusted Solaris version was used where additional security features were required.

5. **a,d.** A trusting network is a network that provides access to another network, whereas a trusted network is a network that is allowed access to another network.

6. **b.** Solaris 9 provides a new access control model called, Role-Based Access Control. This model allows administrators to assign specific rights to different user roles.

7. **a,c,d.** Intrusion detection involves collecting information about changes made to system files, detecting new services and devices on the computer, and collecting information about system performance. However, collecting information about changes made to user files is not part of intrusion detection.

8. **c,d.** The two valid intrusion detection systems available are, the system-based IDS and the network-based IDS. The system-based IDS is placed on the local system and searches for traces of intrusion on the local system, whereas, network-based IDS searches for intrusion on the network.

9. **d.** A hacker can create a program that is disguised as a logon screen. A user enters the login name and the password without knowing that the program sends the information to the hacker. The hacker can then use the same information to logon to the network as a valid user.

10. **d.** The best option for making sure that only authorized users have access to the Internet is to install firewall software. Firewalls ensure that only users who have the appropriate right can access the Internet.

11. **b.** Statement A is true while Statement B is false. Ensuring data availability is providing authorized users access to information at all times. While ensuring data confidentiality, it is important that access to data should remain restricted. However, this restriction cannot be permanent for all information. Sometimes, after a specific time-period this restriction can be removed.

Short Answers

1. In a networked environment, information and services are freely available and distributed. Since information is sent from one computer to another over the network, hackers can read data packets meant for other computers by tapping into the network. The task of intercepting data packets meant for other computers or users is called *sniffing* and programs that provide this service are known as a *network sniffer*. Hackers use a network sniffer to capture the account information of a valid user. Then, they use the information to gain access to another computer and retrieve the address of the computer. The header information of all data packets being transmitted over the network contains the address of the recipient computer. Hackers can then replace the original address of the data packets with their own address and gain access to all data packets addressed to the authenticated computer.

2. Nowadays most administrators prefer backing up business-critical data on remote or separate computers. You only require an automated backup system and network connectivity to set up an automated remote backup system. Such a system ensures that the data is backed up periodically, without the need of an administrator. Since the data is stored on a separate computer, you only need to implement the data-security measures on a single computer. Security of data is also ensured during transit since all files sent over the network are encrypted using encryption algorithms, such as Blowfish or DES.

Chapter 2

In the previous chapter, you learned about security and its requirements. You also learned about some of the measures you can implement to ensure security. One such measure is implementing cryptography, or encrypting information. In this chapter, you'll learn about the need for cryptography, the types of cryptography, and ways of implementing cryptography.

Need for Cryptography

Cryptography is the conversion of information available in a readable format to a format that is undecipherable without decryption. This technique was first used in ancient Egypt. Many etymologists maintain that even the word *cryptography* is derived from the Egyptian word *crypt*, which means to keep a secret. The technique of cryptography involves converting unencrypted or plaintext into encrypted text. Only those who have the appropriate key can decrypt the encrypted information. *Plaintext* is information that has not been encoded. After encryption, the information is known as *cipher text*. The process of changing plaintext to cipher text is known as *encryption*. A *key* is used to change plaintext into cipher text. Most keys are mathematical algorithms or values that are used to change the content of plaintext. These keys can be used in many ways, which will be discussed in a later section in this chapter.

A *cryptosystem* is a method that is used to implement cryptography. A cryptosystem contains multiple methods for ensuring encryption. Each method is based on the use of a particular key for implementing encryption. The use of multiple methods in a cryptosystem ensures a robust system, which is difficult to hack.

Security of information is required primarily for three reasons:

◆ **To ensure integrity of information.** Ensuring integrity implies verifying that hackers are unable to make modifications to the information being passed over the network. This information can be passed between servers or between servers and clients.

◆ **To ensure authentication.** Cryptography is most commonly used in the process of authenticating users. When a user logs on to a network, a user ID and a password are given to the user. This information is checked against a database of valid user IDs. The information stored in the database is encrypted to ensure the confidentiality of the information. Even the data sent for authentication is encrypted so that it is not snooped on during transmission.

◆ **To ensure privacy of information.** As mentioned in the previous chapter, you also need to ensure the privacy of data. This data can be either stored or transmitted over the network. In the latter case, hackers could use techniques such as IP spoofing and sniffing to retrieve information stored in data packets. Information also needs to be secured on mobile computers. For example, data stored on a laptop computer should always be encrypted. This way, even if the laptop is stolen, the security of data stored on it is not compromised.

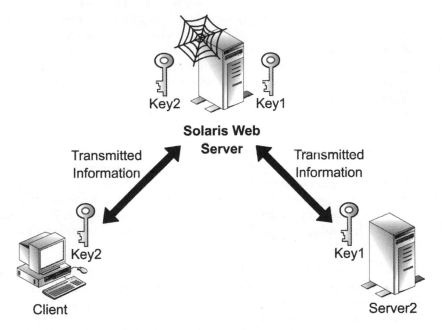

FIGURE 2-1 *Transmitting information over the network*

Figure 2-1 shows the exchange of information between a Solaris Web server, Server2, and a Client. Both the servers and the client shown in the figure have a key. These keys are used for encrypting and decrypting the information. These keys can be either the same or different. When you use the same key, the process is known as *symmetric encryption*, and when you use different keys, the process is known as *asymmetric encryption*. You will learn about both these encryption technologies in a later section in this chapter.

When information is transmitted over the network, it must be encrypted to guarantee its security. After it is encrypted, only the individuals who have the decryption algorithm or the key for decryption can read the data. In the preceding figure, if Solaris Web Server sends data encrypted using Key1, then only Server2, which has the corresponding decryption key, can decrypt the information. Anyone else who tries to access the data will view only encrypted information. Similarly, the client can view only the information that is encrypted by Key2.

The security and effectiveness of an encryption algorithm depend on three factors:

◆ **Complexity of the algorithm.** The effectiveness of an encryption algorithm depends on its complexity. If the algorithm is so complex that hackers are unable to decipher it, the algorithm can be considered effective. The actual effectiveness of an algorithm is established only after it has been put to field trials and has been exposed to hackers.

◆ **Privacy of the key.** The privacy of the key is very important because it is an essential component of an encryption algorithm. The security and integrity of data stored on the computer and the data packets being transmitted over the network depend on whether the key has been encrypted. If a hacker is able to get access to the encryption key, the encryption algorithm falls apart. A hacker can easily use the key to decrypt all information encrypted using the algorithm. Therefore, it is important that the key should be secured both on the sender's side and on the recipient's side. You also need to ensure the security of the key, if it is being transmitted over the network.

◆ **Key length.** The security of the key depends a great deal on the length of the key. The number of possible key combinations also depends on the size of the key. A large number of key combinations can possibly dissuade novice hackers from trying to attempt to break the key. The measure of the size of a key is in bits. Therefore, if the key size is x bits, there is a possibility of 2^x key combinations. Increasing the size of the key reduces the chance of hackers decoding the key.

Cryptography has emerged as one of the leading ways for ensuring security of information. Cryptographic techniques are of two types, based on the number of keys used for encryption: symmetric and asymmetric key encryptions. Each has certain advantages and disadvantages. The next section will consider these two types of cryptographic algorithms in detail.

Types of Cryptographic Algorithms

Cryptography can be implemented using one of the following methods:

◆ **Symmetric cryptography.** This is a simple method where the text is encrypted using a simple key such as a numeric or an alphanumeric string. The same key is used for both encryption and decryption.

◆ **Asymmetric cryptography.** This is a more complex form of cryptography. In this case, two keys are used. One key is used to encrypt the data, and the other key is used to decrypt the data.

The following section discusses these types and their uses in detail.

Symmetric Cryptography

Symmetric cryptography is simpler than asymmetric cryptography, as it encrypts information using a single key. The same key is used to encrypt and decrypt the message. For example, Julius Caesar, the great Roman general, used to send messages to his generals in an encrypted form. He used a very simple method to encrypt the messages. He simply replaced each letter in the message with the third letter from it. Therefore, *A* was replaced by *D*, *B* by *E*, *C* by *F*, and so on. In this way, he ensured that only the people who knew this "shift technique" were able to read the messages. The code only needed to be explained once, and because nothing but the message was transferred, the content remained secret. Disclosing the code to a third person was the only way of breaking the code. The success of this encryption technique depended on the secrecy of the key, which is why this type of cryptography is also known as secret key encryption.

Figure 2-2 graphically displays the process of cryptography by using symmetric key encryption.

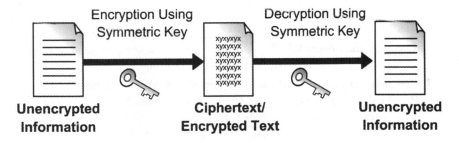

FIGURE 2-2 *Implementing cryptography by using symmetric keys*

Some of the common examples of symmetric key encryption are explained in the following sections.

Data Encryption Standard (DES)

Data Encryption Standard (DES) was one of the first encryption standards in use. It was developed in the 1970s and was officially adopted by the government of the United States as a security standard in 1977. In the case of DES, the algorithm takes blocks of 64-bit plaintext and returns blocks of 64-bit encrypted text. The algorithm uses a 56-bit key for encrypting the data. DES offers a large range of encryption keys, and the key is chosen at random for encrypting the information. Both the sender and the receiver should have a copy of the key. You can decrypt the encrypted text only by using the same key that encrypted the information. It is difficult to determine one piece of information from another because all the blocks are of the same length. Encrypting data by using DES involves 16 rounds of encryption. Each round consists of mixing the information and the key by using an encryption algorithm. The encrypted information that you get finally bears no resemblance to original data.

DES may appear secure and reliable, but hackers and other intruders can use available technologies for decrypting the encrypted information. The first drawback to DES is that the same key is used to encrypt all messages. If a hacker is able to gain access to the key, the information can easily be deciphered. Another drawback is the small size of the key. Because of the small size of the key, only a small number of possible combinations exist, so hackers can decrypt the keys. One of the first successful attacks on DES was made possible by using differential cryptanalysis. In this attack, the hackers decrypted 2^{47} bit encrypted data packets. Although the attack was considered successful, it was inconclusive because of its limited scope. Hackers performed the next attack by using linear cryptanalysis. In this attack, hackers were able to retrieve a DES by analyzing 2^{43} key combinations. Although the key was decrypted successfully, the decryption process required 12 computers working simultaneously for 50 days. Therefore, the attack was still considered impractical.

Certain measures that you can implement for improving the security of DES keys include:

◆ **Changing the DES keys regularly.** The only way a hacker can hack information encrypted using a key is by attempting different possible combinations of the key. If the key is changed periodically, the hacker will be unable to gain access to the current key. In addition, if one key is compromised, the information secured by using another key will still be secure.

◆ **Ensuring the security of the transmitted key.** While sending the DES key from the sender to the receiver, you should also ensure the security of the key. Encrypting the key generally does this. The algorithm creates a different key for each session. Hackers are unable to decrypt the key because it is inconsistent.

The frequent change of DES keys is a cumbersome process. When you change a DES key, you first need to decrypt the information by using the old key and encrypt it again by using the new key. A simpler solution is to have a single primary DES key that is used to encrypt DES keys. These keys are the ones that are used to encrypt individual files. Therefore, you only need to change the primary DES key to ensure security. In addition, because the key does not directly encrypt the information, hackers are focused more on decrypting the keys than on the original information.

Because of the availability of new hacking techniques, the time required by hackers to decrypt the keys has decreased. Therefore, DES keys can no longer be considered secure. Better and more secure encryption technologies are required. The technologies require the use of longer keys for ensuring better security. A possible solution is the implementation of triple encryption by using Triple DES.

Triple DES

Triple DES is DES implemented thrice. It contains certain advancements that were previously not available in DES. As it is based on DES, it is reliable and can be easily implemented. The Triple DES standard uses long keys, which is an improvement over the limitation of DES, which uses short keys.

The Triple DES standard uses three keys of 64 bits each to encrypt the information. The standard uses all three keys together to create a single key of 192 bits. It does not implement each key separately. The process of encryption is done the same way as in the case of DES. The data is encrypted by first key. It is then encrypted by the second, followed by the third key. The information is secured three times, which explains why it is called Triple DES. The process of decryption is the same as the process of encryption, except in the reverse order. It is like keeping a valuable object in a box, putting the box in a bigger box, locking the bigger box, and finally keeping both the boxes in another box. If you need to extract the valuable object, you will need to open all the boxes in the reverse order in which you closed them. This concept is depicted graphically in Figure 2-3.

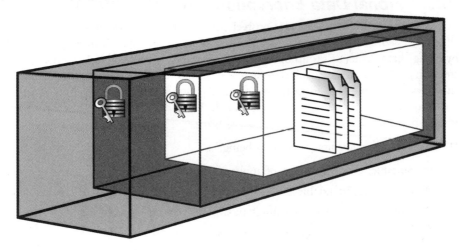

FIGURE 2-3 *Security in Triple DES*

 NOTE

While using the 64-bit DES key, you need to keep in mind that the actual length of the key is only 56 bits. This is because the last bit of every byte, which is at the extreme right of the key, is a parity bit. This bit ensures that the number of 1s in every byte is always odd. However, when calculating the actual size of the DES key, these parity bits are ignored. Hence, the DES key is 56 bits in length.

In the long run, even Triple DES is not able to provide adequate security for information. As DES is implemented three times over, it is three times slower. Therefore, it is necessary to replace the standard with a better one. Advanced Encryption Standard (AES) is an improvement over Triple DES.

Advanced Encryption Standard (AES)

AES is an improvement over Triple DES because the encryption it provides is better and faster than the encryption provided by Triple DES. The shortcomings of DES and the limited utility of Triple DES gave rise to the need for formulating a better encryption standard. In 1997, the National Institute of Standard and Technology (NIST) organized a competition for identifying these standards. Fifteen entries were received originally, but only five were short-listed. The winners were Vincent Rijmen and Joan Daemen of Belgium. This standard, which was named Rijndael, forms the basis of AES.

International Data Encryption Algorithm (IDEA)

IDEA is one of the latest encryption technologies that is secure and reliable. The algorithm is based on known mathematical operations and involves 16 rounds of encryption by using three different group operations. The length of the key is 128 bits. This key is then divided into eight, 16-bit sub-keys. These sub-keys are then used to create 52-bit sub-keys. The same algorithm is used for encryption and decryption. The 64-bit blocks are used to create four 16-bit blocks: A1, A2, A3, and A4. These blocks form the input for the first round of encryption.

IDEA has certain advantages, such as being:

◆ Suitable for a wide range of applications

◆ Easily understandable

◆ Not restricted to any specific type of information

◆ Dependable for a high level of security

◆ Acceptable worldwide

◆ Used efficiently and economically

Symmetric keys have certain advantages; however, they have a couple of disadvantages too. For example, symmetric keys stand the chance of being compromised if the secret key is discovered. Another shortcoming of symmetric key encryption is that you always need to exchange the secret key securely before you can use it to encrypt information. The solution is to use asymmetric cryptography, which provides solutions to overcome these shortcomings.

Asymmetric Cryptography

Asymmetric cryptography is also known as *public key cryptography*. Asymmetric encryption differs from symmetric encryption in that asymmetric encryption uses a pair of keys for encryption and decryption. One key, known as the *public key*, is typically used for encryption and the other key, known as the *private key*, is used for decryption. Only the corresponding private key can decrypt any information encrypted by using the public key, and vice versa.

NOTE

It is also possible to use the private key for encryption and the public key for decryption. This is a common use of the key pair, as it helps to verify the identity of the sender.

Asymmetric cryptography has certain advantages over symmetric cryptography, including:

◆ **Nonrepudiation.** This means that a sender cannot deny sending certain data. The data is encrypted using the sender's private key and can only be decrypted by the sender's public key. The benefit of nondeniability makes this a better option than symmetric cryptography. In the case of symmetric cryptography, the key can easily be hacked. If the keys are hacked, accountability for the transmitted information cannot be established. Therefore, asymmetric cryptography is a better option when compared to symmetric cryptography.

◆ **Key sharing not required.** The most important advantage with asymmetric cryptography is that you do not need to share the key over an insecure line, providing for greater security.

◆ **Enhanced security.** Because asymmetric cryptography uses a combination of public and private keys for encryption, it is more secure than symmetric encryption. As the private key is not shared with anyone, the information is kept secure. In case of symmetric cryptography, the same key is used for both encryption and decryption. If the key is hacked, all the data can be easily accessed.

The only disadvantage in using public key encryption is that it is slower than symmetric key encryption. This is because the algorithms used for public key encryption are more complex and involve keys of greater length than those used by symmetric encryption. Some of the commonly used algorithms in asymmetric cryptography are discussed in the following sections.

Public Key Infrastructure (PKI)

The most popular encryption technique that uses asymmetric cryptography is *Public Key Infrastructure (PKI)*. As mentioned earlier, the information encrypted using the public key can only be decrypted by the corresponding private key. Therefore, anyone can use the public key for encrypting data that has to be sent to the recipient. In addition to being used for encryption, the key pair of public and private keys can be used for creating and verifying digital signatures. When this technology is used along with the encrypted messages, it can be used to authenticate the source and destination of the messages.

In addition to creating public and private keys, you also need to create security policies that determine how the security should be implemented on the network. These policies discuss issues, such as:

◆ Mechanisms for generating and managing keys

◆ Procedures that specify how the keys should be generated and implemented

PKI provides support for both of these issues. It also includes support for different components, policies, and applications. PKI successfully bridges the gap caused by lack of security. It ensures that all information being transmitted over the network is adequately secured.

Another utility available in Solaris for securing information transmitted over the network is GnuPGP, which will be discussed in detail.

GnuPGP

Solaris provides many utilities for providing security of communication between computers. Some of these utilities are out-of-the-box or are available by default in Solaris. Others are third-party utilities that need to be installed separately. GnuPGP is one such utility that is used for securing communication between clients and servers. The utility provides facility for:

◆ Creating public and private keys

◆ Exchanging keys

◆ Encrypting and decrypting information using the keys

◆ Verifying the originality of the keys

◆ Attesting to the authentication of the document or information received

GnuPGP uses asymmetric cryptography for ensuring the security of transmitted information. The utility creates a pair of public and private keys, which are used for encryption and decryption. The owner of the pair of keys keeps the private key secure while the public key is distributed to anyone who wants to communicate with the owner of the key.

Generating Keys

You can create different types of keys by using GnuPGP. GnuPGP provides certain options for creating keys. Following is a list of these options:

1. **DSA and ElGamal key pairs.** These are used for signing and generating digital certificates.

2. **DSA key pair.** This is only used for signing information.

3. **ElGamal key pair.** This key pair is used for signing and generating digital certificates.

NOTE

You may have noticed that option 3 has not been mentioned in the preceding list. GnuPGP uses this option for creating an ElGamal pair of keys. However, this key pair cannot be used for creating digital signatures.

The first option provides the facility of creating two pairs of keys. GPG creates one pair by using DSA, which is used for creating digital signatures. The second pair of keys is created using the ElGamal encryption algorithm. This key pair does the actual task of encrypting information.

The second option creates only a single pair of keys that provide the facility of both creating digital signatures and encrypting the information.

The next option also creates only a single pair of keys. However, Solaris creates this key using the ElGamal encryption algorithm. This key pair also handles both the tasks of creating digital signatures and encrypting the communicated information. The default option creates two pairs of keys; one pair of keys is DSA, and the other is ElGamal. However, you can change the option based on the security requirements of your organization.

The DSA key pair, which is generated in GnuPGP, is between 512 and 1,024 bits in length. As explained earlier, the length of a key adds to the strength of the algorithm. However, the increase in the size of the key causes the encryption and decryption process to become slower. Your choice is between speed and security, and you need to keep this in mind while deciding on the length of the key. The ElGamal key pair that is generated is of variable size. However, GnuPGP has a restriction that the size of its keys cannot be less than 768 bits in length. Therefore, the DSA key pair has to be at least 1,024 bits in length, whereas the ElGamal key pair can be of 768 bits in length. You can never change the size of the keys after the size has been selected. After selecting the size of the keys, you need to specify an expiry date for the keys. This ensures that the keys are changed at regular intervals. Although the expiry date can be changed in future, it is difficult to provide this information to everyone who has used your public keys. The same expiry date is used for both pairs of keys. You also need to provide your personal information to personalize the keys. The option `--gen-key` is used to create the keys.

```
norman% gpg --gen-key
```

The process of encrypting information by using these keys is relatively simple. Consider an example: User A wants to send encrypted information to User B. User A encrypts the information by using B's public key. When B receives the information, B uses the private key for decrypting the information. In the same way, when B wants to send information back to A, B uses A's public key for encryption and A uses the private key for decryption. The `encrypt` option is used for encrypting the information. You need to provide the public key of the recipient and the name of the document to be encrypted as parameters. The command will appear as shown in the following code.

```
norman% gpg -output report.gpg -encrypt -recipient anorman@asc.org report
```

Only someone who has the corresponding private key can decrypt the encrypted document. You cannot decrypt the encrypted document unless you are one of the recipients. The –decrypt option is used to decrypt the encrypted information. The option takes the private key as an input parameter and returns the decrypted information. The syntax of the option is shown in the following code.

```
norman% gpg -output report -decrypt report.gpg
```

After you have created a pair of public and private keys, you must immediately create a revocation certificate. Suppose that you misplace your private key or forget your password. You may think that you cannot use the key anymore for encrypting information and all the encrypted information is lost, but that is not absolutely true. Although you cannot use the key anymore, you can still decrypt the encrypted information, provided you have created a revocation certificate. A revocation certificate, as the name suggests, is used for revoking or deleting a key. This key can be used to inform all your clients that the key is no longer in use. You can decrypt previously encrypted information, but you cannot encrypt any additional information. The -gen -revoke option is used to generate a revocation certificate for a primary key.

```
norman% gpg -output revoke.asc -gen --revoke sourcekey
```

The sourcekey is supplied as a parameter to the option, and the generated certificate is stored in the revoke.asc file. If you do not supply the output parameter, the output appears as standard output. The security of the revocation certificate is critical for ensuring the security of the encrypted information. If hackers are able to gain access to the certificate, they can easily decrypt the encrypted information. They would no longer require the private key.

Encrypting Information

Suppose a user needs to send certain confidential information to another user. The sender first needs to find the receiver's public key. The sender can find all the public keys available on the network by running the command-line option --list-keys. The command is specified as shown in the following code.

```
norman% gpg -lists -keys
```

Before a public key can be sent, it first needs to be exported. The -export command is used for exporting the key. The public key is passed as a parameter. The command appears as shown in the following code.

```
norman% gpg -output clients.gpg -armor -export anorman@asc.org
```

Generally, the output of the export command appears in the form of a binary file. It is difficult to send this file through e-mail or publish it on the Web. You can use another option available in GnuPGP to convert this binary file into a file of ASCII characters, the -armor option. This option can be used to convert any output derived from GnuPGP into a file of ASCII characters.

You can use the import command to add a new public key to the list you viewed earlier. After this key has been imported, it needs to be validated. You can do this by first authenticating the key's fingerprints and then signing the key. You will learn about fingerprints in a Chapter 4, "Network Security Tools." This task certifies the key as authentic. The following commands are used for including a new public key and then verifying its authenticity.

```
norman% gpg -Import antho.gpg
norman% gpg -list -keys
norman% gpg -edit-key anormon@acs.org
command> fpr
```

The next section will review Pretty Good Privacy (PGP).

Pretty Good Privacy (PGP)

Philip Zimmerman originally created *Pretty Good Privacy (PGP)*. PGP is another algorithm that is used for encrypting and decrypting communication between computers. The algorithm uses the RSA encryption mechanism for encrypting information. PGP is primarily used for encrypting information stored on the computer, encrypting information transmitted between computers, and ensuring confidentiality of e-mails sent by clients to one another. PGP is also used for ensuring security of financial information being transmitted between a server and clients. For example, in case of e-commence, the algorithm can be used for encrypting a user's credit card information that is passed to a Web server for validation. The encryption facility provided by PGP helps online shoppers feel secure about sending their credit card information over the Internet. Similarly, you need to ensure the security of e-mails being transmitted over the network. If these e-mails are not encrypted, hackers or anyone who has access to your computer can access these e-mails. PGP acts as a container that secures the information by locking it in using a key. Only the person who has the proper key can open the container to access the information.

PGP uses the public key encryption technology for implementing cryptography. PGP creates a pair of public and private keys for encrypting the information. Suppose I want to send encrypted information to you. I'll send a request to you asking for your public key. You will then e-mail your public key to me. I'll then use the public key to encrypt the message. In this way, only you can read the message because only you have the corresponding private key. The public key can be freely distributed, because the private key is secure with the owner and only the private key can be used to decrypt the information. PGP provides support for different operating systems such as DOS, Windows, UNIX, Macintosh, and OS/2. When you use it on Solaris, you can communicate securely with computers running other operating systems.

PGP can also be used for creating digital signatures. Suppose you send an e-mail to a friend. How can your friend be sure that the e-mail is authentic? A hacker can easily replace the e-mail during transit and send another e-mail impersonating you. PGP is an effective way to protect you from such deception. You can use PGP to attach a digital signature to a message. The system can use digital signatures for validating users, because hackers cannot easily replace digital signatures. The sender's public key is used to validate the authenticity of the digital signature attached to a message. A digital signature is created using both the public and the private keys. The authenticity of the transmitted information is guaranteed because the access to the private key is restricted to the owner of the keys. If your public key can decrypt the information, your private key must have encrypted the information. Thus, the sender's identity is established. A *one-way hash function* is used to ensure that the information has not been tampered with during transit. A one-way function acts on the message to produce a message digest or hash, which is unique. When the same function is applied at the receiver's end, the result must be the same. This guarantees that the message has not been tampered with.

Next, I'll discuss how hash functions are used for providing encryption.

Hash Functions

The hash functions work by taking information strings as input and converting them into equal-length strings. The equal-length strings created by using the functions are known as *hashes*. After the information has been converted, it becomes virtually impossible to differentiate between one piece of information and another. The most basic of hash functions involves clubbing all the bytes in the information together and then dividing them into packets of 256 bytes each. This creates the encrypted text. Although it is the simplest method, it is the weakest. The function works on the principle that two encrypted messages will not have the same hash value, which is not always true. Some of the better and more advanced hash methods are Message Digest 2 (MD2), Message Digest 5 (MD5), Secure Hash Algorithm (SHA), and HAVAL. Asymmetric cryptographic methods generally utilize hash functions to create digital signatures. Some of the commonly used hash functions are discussed in the following sections.

Hashing is a reliable method of securing data as compared with encryption. The drawback of an encryption algorithm is its encryption key. If a hacker is able to gain access to the key, the encrypted test can easily be converted back to the original plaintext. Hashing only happens in one direction. The following is an example to determine how hashing is different from encryption and how it is more secure.

Consider the statement, "A mod B = C". Here, C is the resultant value when the value B divides the value A. In itself, value C is meaningless, because it is mathematically impossible to determine the original values of both A and B. Therefore, many combinations will produce the same result.

Consider another example. You want to encrypt the string "SECRET". The first step will be to create hash values. You decide to do so by using the corresponding ASCII values of the characters in the string. The values will appear as follows:

```
S = 83
E = 69
C = 67
R = 82
E = 69
T = 84
    454
```

You can see that the sum of all the ASCII values is 454. This is the hash value. In itself, the value 454 is meaningless. You will not be able to determine the original text from the hash value even if you knew that it was derived by the sum of the ASCII values of the string. Other strings can produce the same hash value. For example, either of the words ECSTER or RESTEC will produce the same hash value 454. Even if you change the sequence of characters, the final sum of ASCII values remains the same. Multiplying or adding the ASCII values of each character with its position in the original text can be one solution. The position of each character is shown in the following code.

```
Original Text        SECRET
Position             123456
```

The next step is to multiply the ASCII values of each character in the string with its position in the string.

```
S = 83 * 1 =  83
E = 69 * 2 = 138
C = 67 * 3 = 201
R = 82 * 4 = 328
E = 69 * 5 = 345
T = 84 * 6 = 504
           ====
           1599
```

Note that it would be hard for anyone to determine the original string.

You can use this concept to secure passwords. Suppose that before you stored the passwords in a database, you encrypted all the passwords by using this hash algorithm. Even if hackers were able to gain access to the database and see the passwords, they would be unable to decipher the hashed passwords to retrieve the originals.

The question that arises is how you can retrieve the original passwords from the hashed values. How can you authenticate a password entered by a user with the hashed values stored in the database? The answer is simple, you don't. You only need to match the hashed values. Hashing follows a different methodology compared with encryption. In the case of encryption, the password stored in the database first needs to be decrypted and then compared with the value provided by the user. This is a longer, insecure process. In case of hashing, the password supplied by the user is first hashed and then compared with the password stored in the database. If both the hash values match, the password is correct and the user is authenticated.

The next section will review some of the hashing functions available.

Secure Hash Algorithm (SHA)

The NIST developed the Secure Hash Algorithm (SHA). The algorithm pads the stored information by passing through a hashing process consisting of four rounds. The algorithm finally creates the hashed information packets of 160-bit length. It is generally considered more complex than the MD5 hashing algorithm.

An advanced version of the algorithm was published in 1994 and was named SHA-1. The new algorithm solved some of the security issues that were present in SHA. The algorithm creates a message digest of 160 bits and is considered secure. However, it sacrifices speed and can encrypt a plaintext message of a maximum of 2^{64} bit length.

MD5

Message Digest 5 (MD5) is a hashing algorithm that was developed by RSA Data Security, Inc. The algorithm produces a 128-bit unique digest of data. The algorithm also ensures that no two pieces of information produce the same message digest. MD5 is generally used to convert passwords into hash values. MD5 is the most popular hashing technique available in Solaris.

Secure HTTP (HTTPS)

With the introduction of the Internet, information on the network has been exposed to a new set of dangers. The primary danger is that hackers can access the network by camouflaging themselves as authentic senders or recipients of information. This danger was also present in the past, but the advent of the Internet has increased it immensely. Therefore, you need to implement measures to secure the information on the network. One of the ways of ensuring security is to encrypt all confidential information before it is transmitted over the network. The following sections discuss how to implement security on the network.

As the name suggests, Secure HTTP (HTTPS) is an extension of the commonly used HTTP protocol. The HTTPS protocol usually functions at the application layer level. It provides privacy and authentication of all data being passed over the network. The protocol provides support for a wide range of cryptographic algorithms for ensuring data security. For example, RSA is used for initial key generation.

Now that you know about the various types of cryptography mechanisms, you can look at some of the ways of implementing these mechanisms.

Implementation of Cryptography

In the earlier sections, you learned about the different methods that are available to implement cryptography. These methods can be used to encrypt information in many ways. The use of cryptography ensures that the information has not been tampered with in any way.

Some of the applications of cryptography are digital signatures and smart cards, which will be discussed in detail.

Digital Signatures

The use of the Internet opened tremendous opportunities for e-commerce. Most of the business transactions are over the Internet and involve supplying confidential information. This information includes personal and credit card information, which can be hacked during transit if it is not secured adequately. Therefore, you need to ensure that the information being passed is correct and from an authentic source. Digital signatures are one such mechanism that can be used to ensure the authenticity of information. Digital signatures provide the following functions:

◆ Services for authenticating users

◆ Assurance that the contents of data packets have not been tampered with during transit

◆ Assurance that only the authentic users have sent the information

Digital signatures are similar to handwritten signatures that uniquely identify an individual or an organization. Digital signatures also ensure security of exchanged information. Unlike handwritten signatures, digital signatures cannot be easily copied. However, as these signatures can be stolen, they should be kept in a secure location. In the case of handwritten signatures, a person can have only one signature; however, in the case of digital signatures, you can use multiple signatures for the same purpose. For example, you can use different signatures for authentication depending on circumstances or users.

In organizations, you can implement role-based digital signatures. Role-based digital signatures ensure that only a person with a certain level of rights can digitally sign the information to validate its authenticity. This also prevents users who do not have the adequate rights or who do not belong to the departments from trying to make changes in the information.

Digital signatures are based on public key encryption and use both public and private keys to digitally sign information. When a digital signature is used, two keys are generated: one is a public key, and the other, a private key. The private key is always kept secret and its use is restricted only to the owner. The public key is for general use and is used by anyone. Both the keys need to be used together to digitally sign a piece of information.

To digitally sign an electronic document, the encryption software produces a message digest (or a hash value) of the source document. The algorithm then uses the owner's private key to encrypt this message digest, creating the digital certificate. After the digital signature has been created, it is sent to the recipient along with the encrypted message. The message is encrypted using the public key of the recipient. The recipient decrypts the message with the private key. The recipient then uses the public key of the sender to decrypt the message digest, validating that the original sender had sent the message. The recipient then runs the same hash algorithm on the message. Using the same hash algorithm on the message should yield the same hash value as the decrypted message digest, which confirms the integrity of the message.

Digital signatures ensure that the recipient has received the message without any tampering. They also ensure the authenticity of the sender, which is important because hackers can always hack the information during transit and can then modify the packet and substitute their own message digest. One method to verify the sender's credentials along with the authenticity of the message is by using *Certificate Authorities (CAs)*. CAs are authorized organizations that can attest to the authenticity of known users. CAs either can be external to an organization or can be an internal part of it.

Using digital signatures also ensures that only authorized individuals can send the data packets. As digital signatures are not transferable, you can easily pinpoint the source of the message based on the digital signature that was used to sign the message. Digital signatures are conclusive proof that an individual or an organization has sent a particular piece of information. They are valid proof that certain information has been sent from a particular recipient or received by a particular recipient.

Certificate Authorities (CAs)

Certificates are a specific type of digital signatures that are used in e-commerce. They are created by using a combination of public and private keys and are used to categorize and assign the activities that a certificate holder can and cannot perform. They are also known as *Digital IDs* and can be considered the electronic equivalent to a driving license or passport. Just as a driving license identifies you and gives you the right to drive, digital certificates identify you as a valid network user with a certain level of rights.

A digital certificate contains details about the owner's name, owner's public key, and the CA who issued the certificate. The certificate also contains information about the expiry date of the certificate, the serial number, and any other information related to the certificate. A recognized CA issues a digital certificate. A CA is a reputed organization that certifies that the information is authentic. The CA signs the digital certificate by using its private key, attesting that the information secured by using the digital certificate is also secure. Two of the commonly found CAs are VeriSign and GlobalSign. You can obtain a digital certificate by visiting the Web site and submitting a request. After your identity has been verified, the request is processed. Because requesting for a digital certificate is a time-consuming process, as it generally takes three to five days to be processed. In addition, there are different classes of certificates that you can obtain from a certification authority. Certificates can primarily be divided into three classes: Class1, Class2, and Class3. Class1 certificates are the least secure. Hackers can use these certificates to impersonate valid CAs. Class2 and Class3 certificates provide a higher level of security as compared to Class1 certificates. You can use the class of certificates that best suits the security requirements of the network.

Because a CA provides the digital certificate, the CA also verifies that the organization or individual is indeed a trusted source. As digital certificates are based on public key cryptography, it uses both public and private keys for ensuring encryption. Only the owner of the key pair has access to the private key and can use these keys to create a digital signature. The public key is accessible by all and is used for verifying the digital signature. Both the public and private keys are independent of each other and are only bound together by the use of the digital certificate. Digital certificates help authenticate a user's right to use a key and protect the network from people pretending to be authentic users. Because digital certificates also uses encryption, they provides a comprehensive solution for ensuring data security and the identity of valid users.

The use of digital signatures provides a tremendous scope for increasing business prospects on the Internet. Because security is a major concern while transmitting information over the Internet, digital signatures provide the security of information as it is being transmitted between different locations. Previously, security was restricted to controlling access by using passwords. However, passwords have become insufficient. Digital signatures provide a better security option. The use of digital signatures is not restricted to only online Web sites. It also extends to e-commerce servers that need to access confidential information. Because the CAs validate the authenticity of the servers before signing digital certificates, businesses are assured of the authenticity of the recipient or the sender.

Using Smart Cards

Many of the authentication protocols used on the network require long keys for authenticating users. Because it is difficult for users to always remember the keys, the key is generally attached with the password. However, some passwords can be easily hacked, as they are easy to decipher or too simple. In such a case, even if the authentication mechanism is reliable and effective, the weak password makes it ineffective. Because the information is also stored in central servers, a weak password makes the security of the server weak. Single password authentication is not always effective because users may not always remember the password. Smart cards offer an easier solution.

A smart card is similar to a credit card in size. It is used for physically authenticating users in a system. It contains a chip that can be used to store a user's information, which is critical for authenticating the user. The card also contains a unique key that is used for encryption, which is stored in the card. Because the key is available on the card, the physical security of the card is important to guarantee the security of the information. Smart cards actually use dual authentication. As a physical component, you possess the smart card that authenticates you on the system. Along with the physical component, you have a password that you need to remember and provide at the time of authentication. Both of these components need to be provided for you to be successfully authenticated by the system. Thus, if somebody stole your smart card, they would have to know your password, as well. Similarly, if someone knows your password, they would still require your smart card to obtain access.

The growth of the Internet has led to an increase in the use of smart cards. They are especially useful in the field of e-commerce. They help to ensure authenticity of the transaction and maintain integrity and confidentiality of all information being transmitted over the network.

Smart cards are of two types:

◆ Contact smart cards
◆ Contactless smart cards

Contact smart cards, as the name suggests, need to be inserted directly into the system. A smart card reader reads the information stored in these cards and validates it with the information stored in the system. The information is stored on the card in the form of chips. The reader provides the interface for the application to send and receive information.

Contactless smart cards do not require any physical access to the reader. The card is held close to the reader, and information is transmitted with the help of an antenna. The power for the chip in the card is derived from an electromagnetic force.

Smart cards also ensure that nobody tampers with the information and that the information is authentic. The card is a physical medium and is used to provide the valid information. Even if hackers were able to get your password, without the smart card, the password would be useless. Besides authenticating information, smart cards are used for ensuring the physical security of the information.

Pluggable Authentication Modules (PAMs) can be used to provide the authentication portion of using smart cards. PAM provides a single integrated module that provides authentication facility for multiple authentication mechanisms. Because all the authentication mechanisms use the same password, the users need to remember only a single password for authentication. All the details required for authentication are stored on the smart card. The `use_smart_card` function is used to provide the authentication interface. The services implemented in the client system can then use this interface for providing authentication.

I'll now discuss PAM in detail.

Pluggable Authentication Modules (PAMs)

PAM was originally developed by Sun Microsystems as a pluggable module. This framework was created for independently plugging in authentication modules. These modules can be used dynamically without disturbing the existing setup and services running in the Solaris system. The framework provides services for user, password, and account authentication. A few examples of these services are given in the following list:

- ◆ `ftp`
- ◆ `rsh`
- ◆ `rlogin`
- ◆ `login`
- ◆ `dtlogin`
- ◆ `telnet`

PAM implements the security mechanisms in the form of dynamically available and loaded programs. Administrators install these programs without the awareness of other applications. PAM loads the authentication libraries (APIs) on the client computers and the authentication programs on the servers. PAM uses the Service Provider Interface (SPI) to connect the libraries and the authentication programs. The applications write to the PAM APIs while the authentication programs write to the PAM SPIs. PAM can be used to integrate UNIX authentication programs with other security mechanisms, such as Kerberos.

The services running with the applications access the PAM APIs. These APIs load the suitable authentication program. The information about the authentication program to be loaded is available in the configuration file. The information is then sent to the authentication program for further processing. When the authentication is complete, the PAM API returns the result back to the calling program.

Advantages of PAM

Some of the common advantages of PAM include:

- ◆ **Ease of use.** In PAM, authentication mechanisms can use the same password for authenticating users. PAM can also be configured to avoid the requirement of retyping passwords used in different authentication mechanisms. The users are queried about the authentication mechanism to be used if multiple mechanisms exist on the system.

◆ **Flexibility.** PAM allows the implementation of separate authentication policies for each application installed on the system. You can also set a default authentication program that Solaris should use in case the user doesn't select any authentication mechanism.

◆ **Integration with authentication services.** PAM also has the facility for passing certain parameters that are not compulsorily required by the authentication mechanism to function.

You need to understand the modules available in PAM, because these modules determine the functionality provided by PAM.

Modules Available in PAM

Each PAM module provides certain interfaces that can be used by the services through the PAM API to perform certain actions. The following points discuss these modules:

◆ **Authentication module.** This module is used for providing user authentication services and for setting user rights. It serves as an user account administration tool. The `pam_authenticate()` function is used for authenticating users, whereas the `pam_setcred()` function is used for setting and destroying a user's credentials.

◆ **Account module.** The account module is used for implementing a check on user accounts. These checks include checking for account expiry, age of the password, and logon hour restrictions. This module is implemented after a user has been authenticated. It is used to specify that the user currently has the right to access the network or system. The `pam_acct_mgmt()` function is used for checking these rights.

◆ **Session module**. This module has the responsibility of handling the task of opening and closing an authentication session. The session module contains tasks for logging activities and performing cleanup actions when the session is over. The `pam_open_session()` function is used for managing the opening of the session, and the `pam_close_session()` function manages the closing of the session.

◆ **Password module**s. This module is used for changing user passwords. The `pam_chauthtok()` function is used for this purpose.

PAM provides complete functionality for implementing authentication on a Solaris system. An important part of implementing cryptography is generating random numbers for creating keys. The next section discusses this concept in detail.

Generating Random Numbers

In the case of both public key encryption and private key encryption, the most important requirement is to have a ready supply of random numbers. These numbers are important for creating keys. The most important requirements for generating random numbers are that the numbers should be picked in random order and their sequence should be unpredictable. These requirements are the only security available to protect the keys from being decrypted by hackers. The computer can generate the numbers by using physical devices that generate numbers randomly or based on chance. They can also be generated based on the physical performance of the computer, such as the speed with which the hard disk is revolving or the processor speed. However, the best option is to use hash functions to create these random numeric values, because not all other methods are definite.

You can also use pseudorandom numbers to generate random values. The difference between random numbers and pseudorandom numbers is that pseudorandom numbers are generated based on a specific algorithm while random numbers generated based on variable components, such as processor speed or disk speed. Since the values generated by random numbers cannot be easily duplicated, they are considered more secure.

You must remember that random numbers are not required in all situations. For example, in the case of RSA, when the private numbers have been generated and the modulus value calculated, the public key is calculated based on an arbitrary value. The public key is then used to create the private key. Therefore, the determination of both the public and private keys doesn't require any random number to be generated.

Cryptography software requires the use of random numbers for generating keys that encrypt information. One way in which the system can retrieve these numbers is by utilizing the unpredictable events thrown out by the kernel during processing. These numbers can then be read as characters. One solution for solving this problem is loading a separate kernel module. This module is available in `/dev/random`.

Summary

In this chapter, you learned about cryptography, its history, and its requirements for ensuring security of information. Cryptographic techniques are of two types, symmetric and asymmetric. Symmetric cryptography uses one key for both encryption and decryption. Some examples are DES, Triple DES, AES, and IDEA. Asymmetric cryptography uses separate keys for encryption and decryption. One key is known as the public key while the other is known as the private key. Some examples are PKI, GnuPGP, and PGP. You also learned how to generate keys and how to use them for encryption. Then, you learned about hash functions and how they are more reliable than simple encryption. Then, you learned about some of the hash algorithms such as SHA and MD5. Next, you learned about some of the way in which you can implement cryptography. You learned about digital signatures, certificate authorities, smart cards, and PAM. Finally, you learned how to generate random numbers that can be used for creating hash messages.

In the next chapter, you'll learn about securing system startup and shutdown. Then you'll learn how you can implement auditing in Solaris. Finally, you'll learn about the different access control models available in Solaris 9.

Check Your Understanding

Multiple Choice Questions

1. What are the actions performed while digitally signing a document? (Select all that apply.)

   a. You require a cryptographic application.

   b. You need to create a private key.

   c. You need to create a public key.

   d. The cryptographic algorithm uses the public key to encrypt the information.

   e. The cryptographic algorithm uses the private key to encrypt the information.

2. What are the features of a good hashing technique? (Select all that apply.)

   a. A hash algorithm should not be easily decipherable.

   b. A hash algorithm should be consistent and should only change if a large number of changes are made to the document.

   c. A hash algorithm should create a hash value for a document the first time the document is checked and then reuse the same hash value for subsequent checks.

   d. The hash value for every document should be unique.

3. You are encrypting a message using PGP. Suppose that you encrypt the same message on multiple machines. Will the output be similar?

   a. The output will be similar for the message every time it is encrypted.

   b. The output will only be similar on the same machine and not on multiple machines.

   c. The output can never be the same, regardless of the number of times you encrypt.

   d. The output can be the same if the message is encrypted multiple times using a specific sequence.

Short Questions

1. What is a digital key? Explain its use.
2. Define a digital signature.
3. How can you verify an individual's digital signature?
4. How important is the security of digital keys?
5. Is it possible to crack a PGP algorithm? Can hackers use a lost or stolen key to read encrypted messages?

Answers

Multiple Choice Answers

1. **a, b, d.** The first step in digitally signing a document is to ensure that you have installed cryptographic software. Some examples of commonly used cryptographic softwares are PGP and Triple DES. The next step is to create a private key by using the encryption algorithm. The final step is to use the private key to digitally sign the document. The algorithm ensures that the information remains secure and unaltered.

2. **a, c, d.** Effective hashing algorithms should generate numbers randomly and create an encryption key using these numbers. Even a minor change in the document should change the hash value, and an error should be raised the next time the value is checked. The algorithm creates and stores the hash value for a large document when the document is encrypted. The current hash value is checked against the stored hash value, and any change is immediately reported. The hash value generated for each document should be unique and therefore cannot be shared between two files.

3. **c.** The output can never be the same, regardless of the number of times you encrypt the data. A different session key is created every time the information is encrypted by using PGP. When the key changes, the entire header and body information stored along with the message also changes. Therefore, you cannot get the same encrypted message twice, regardless of the number of rounds of encryption. The algorithm cannot produce the same hashed value twice, even if the source machine is the same.

Short Answers

1. A digital key comprises a group of numbers that are arranged in a specific sequence. This sequence is based on mathematical calculations. The resultant key is used for encryption information that is sent over the network. The

size of the key depends on the encryption algorithm used for encrypting the information.

2. A digital signature is created using a cryptographic algorithm and verifies that the document or information it signs is authentic. The information is stored in the form of a time stamp and is created by using an encryption key.

3. The first step is to retrieve the individual's public key. As the private key is used to create digital signatures, only the corresponding public key can verify the authenticity of the private key. This information can be verified either by using the Fingerprints database or by checking the certificate with the Certificate Authority responsible for issuing the certificate.

4. It is very important to ensure the security of your digital keys. The key is used to sign documents and attests that the documents have been sent by the owner of the key. Therefore, if the owner loses the key or if crackers gain access to the key, the crackers can impersonate the valid user and send messages containing user's digital ID. They can also use the key to decrypt messages delivered to you. You would be held responsible for any damages caused by such activity. If your digital certificate is lost or stolen, you must immediately report the matter to the Certificate Authority. The Certificate Authority can then revoke the certificate so that it can no longer be used.

5. Although PGP is a quite stable and secure, it is possible to crack PGP encryption by using a dictionary attack. The attack involves sequentially checking the stored password against words in the dictionary. Because users sometimes specify simple words or popular phrases as their passwords, hackers use different combinations of words found in the dictionary to decrypt the encrypted password. Most cracker programs are able to decipher common phrases, names, and quotes that are used by users as passwords. Therefore, it is essential to use a password that is not only easy to remember but also difficult to crack.

Using a stolen secret key to read encrypted messages is not possible, unless the hacker also processes the corresponding password. Both the key and the password are only effective together and are useless without each other. However, the hacker can always use the secret key to revoke the earlier certificate and create a new secret key containing a different password. In the case of lost keys, administrators use this method to create a new pair of keys. The administrator also needs to inform all the users about the loss of the old key and distribute the new key for encrypting information in future.

Chapter 3

This chapter covers the steps for ensuring security at system startup and shutdown. You'll learn about auditing and how auditing can be used to keep track of the activities that occur on the network. You'll also learn about the different access control models available in Solaris.

Configuring Security at System Startup

You need to perform certain steps during system startup and shutdown to secure a Solaris computer. Following are some of the steps that a computer has to take for ensuring its security during startup:

◆ Securing Programmable Read-Only Memory (PROM)

◆ Removing unnecessary accounts

◆ Using the init command to change run levels

I'll now discuss each of these in detail.

Securing PROM

When a system boots, it loads the PROM and its environment variables into the memory. The PROM retrieves information about the system variable autoboot and boot devices from the system files. These variables contain information about the settings that should be implemented during startup. They also contain information about the boot device. *OpenBoot* is the memory chip that handles all the system startup settings of PROM. OpenBoot contains information about the booting procedure as well as other system commands for checking hardware during system startup.

 NOTE

The version of OpenBoot referenced here is OpenBoot version 2.0.

The OpenBoot system is activated the moment the system is switched on. It is based on the system settings specified in the OpenBoot that the computer boots either from the local hard disk or over the network. By default, all systems boot from the local hard disk and don't display the OpenBoot prompt.

You need to ensure that users do not have access to OpenBoot. Any user who gets access to OpenBoot can change the startup option. Users can make the system boot from a different media and gain complete control over the computer. Users can also alter the environment variables managed by OpenBoot.

Securing the system by using security levels with OpenBoot can solve this problem. OpenBoot supports three levels of security: none, command, and full. The default option set for OpenBoot is none. The following list explains each of the security levels in detail:

◆ **none**. At this level, neither the authentication facility nor any security measures are available. Anyone who has physical access to the computer can change the OpenBoot settings.

◆ **command**. At this level, authentication is implemented by using passwords for all commands except boot and go. The boot command is used to specify the boot device from which Solaris needs to be loaded. The go command is used when the computer is in break mode.

◆ **full**. At this level, which is also the highest security level, a password is required for using any OpenBoot command except the go command. You need to provide the OpenBoot password to access all the commands available in Solaris.

The recommended security levels are command or full. The essential difference between the command and full security modes is that the system will not start in the latter without the correct OpenBoot PROM password. Thus, the full security mode requires operator interaction to start the system. The next step for ensuring security is setting the OpenBoot PROM password. You must change the PROM password regularly to ensure that hackers are unable to gain access to the current password. You need to take the steps given in the following commands to set the OpenBoot password on a Solaris SPARC computer:

 CAUTION

The eeprom command only works on SPARC systems.

```
# eeprom security-mode=full
Changing PROM password:
New password: xxxxxxxxx
Retype new password: xxxxxxxxx
```

In the preceding code, the security mode has been set to full with the eeprom command and the current password has been changed to a new password. If the OpenBoot password is not currently set, eeprom prompts the administrator to set the password. This usually happens in cases where the security level is increased from none to full or command.

 CAUTION

You should be cautious while setting the security level to full. In this state, the computer will be inaccessible if the OpenBoot password is lost. The only way you can retrieve the password is by running the eeprom command from the user's root.

If both the PROM password and the root passwords are not available, the entire PROM will have to be changed.

You need to configure regular auditing for the PROM setting to find out whether hackers have changed it or not. The audit log keeps track of the current security settings and host IDs. This information is later compared with the system's current security settings. However, this method is not entirely secure because a hacker can physically break into the system to reset the settings. The hacker can then replace the current PROM with another PROM, which has a different set of security settings but the same host ID. In such a case, the system will be unable to recognize the change, and even the audit will not reflect the change.

Removing Unnecessary Accounts

The next step in securing a system is removing unnecessary accounts from the system. These accounts are uucp, listen, smtp, and nuucp and are available in the /etc/shadow and the /etc/passwd files. You can easily lock these accounts by putting *LK* in the password field of the /etc/shadow file. The following command is used to remove a user account from the system:

```
# passmgmt · d uucp
```

The cron command and the at command are used for executing a set of commands at a specific time in future. You may consider logging all cron activities by setting CRONLOG=yes in /etc/default/cron file. Access to all the commands related to cron can be controlled using the files available in the /usr/lib/cron directory, such as cron.deny, cron.allow, at.deny, and at.allow. These files are used to provide or deny access to the commands. If the files do not exist, only the root has the right to access the commands. The Solaris operating environment includes scheduled cron events for the lp, adm, and root accounts. These should not be included in the deny files. Any additional system or software-specific accounts that do not require cron or at access should be added to the deny files.

Using the init Command to Change Run Levels

The init process starts when the kernel is loaded into the memory and the file system has been mounted. If the run level of the system is a single user, the system boots to the command prompt and waits for further instructions. If the root password is entered, the root shell opens and allows the administrator to perform any administrative task. When the administrator's work is done, the shell needs to be closed.

The init command is used to change the run levels of a system. The run level indicates the services currently available on the computer. The next section discusses some of the system run levels available in Solaris.

System Run Levels Available in Solaris

The system run levels are the various levels at which the Solaris operating system can run. Knowledge about the system's current run level is critical for ensuring security. It is also important to know how to change this level based on your requirements. The startup and shutdown procedures involve changing the operating system's current run level.

A run level indicates the services available to users and the number of users who can access the system. For example, the computer starts at the basic level (level 0). The computer moves to run level 2, which is a multiuser level, as soon as it finishes booting. If you need to put the computer in the maintenance mode, you need to change the run level to 1, which is a single user mode. Table 3-1 lists all the system run levels available in Solaris and their use.

Table 3-1 Run Levels in Solaris

Run Level	Description
S	Used for the single-user mode where all the local file systems are mounted
0	Shuts down the computer and brings the OS to the PROM prompt, where it is safe to switch off the computer
1	Brings the system to the single-user mode for administrative and maintenance purposes

continues

Table 3-1 (*continued*)

Run Level	Description
2	Brings the system to the multiuser mode, where all the facilities are available, except for NFS
3	Brings the system to the multiuser mode, where all the facilities are available, including NFS
4	Is also a multiuser state, but currently not used by Solaris
5	Used when you want to power down the computer to a safe level before actual switching the power off
6	Reboots the system; however, the system reboots to the default run level, which is 3

Before changing the run level, you must first know the system's current run level. The who command is used to determine the system's current run level. The following code displays the output of the who command:

```
# who -r
 . run -level 2 May 6 20:30      2      0      S
#
```

Generally, the administrator boots a system to the single user mode for performing administrative tasks. In all other instances, the system opens in the multiuser mode. When the system boots, the init process searches the /etc/inittab file to determine its next task.

Securing Shutdown

Security is required during both startup and shutdown. The system uses two commands to implement security during shutdown. These commands are the init command and the uadmin commands. You can shut down a system by changing the system's run level to 0 or by using the shutdown command. When the computer shuts down, the init command runs the /etc/rc0 shell script. The script, in turn, executes other shell scripts, which are available in their respective directories. These shell scripts include /etc/shutdown.d, /etc/rc0.d/S*, and /etc/rc0.d/K*. The /etc/rc0 shell script then tries to kill all processes currently running on the system. The script uses the killall command and does not kill each process individually. The uadmin command is used for executing administrative commands.

After securing the startup and shutdown of the computer, you need to implement auditing on the system. Auditing helps to keep track of the activities that are performed on the network. The next section explains auditing in detail.

Implementing Auditing

Solaris provides numerous utilities for network administrators that log all the activities that occur on the system and the network. The logging utility can be used to track system activities at the lowest (granular) level. Since the utility is part of the Solaris *Business Security Module (BSM)*, the security module of Solaris, the utility is also a part of the operating system. Solaris is at the security level C2 because it fulfills all the auditing requirements specified by the *Trusted Computer System Evaluation Criteria (TCSEC)*. The C2 level provides security by tracking all system events back to the users who raised the events.

Objective of Auditing

The first and foremost objective of auditing is to determine what needs to be audited. Detecting intrusions involves recording all user activities and detecting any suspicious activities. Suspicious activities are activities that do not ordinarily occur on the network. These activities can include unauthorized attempts to access resources and unauthorized use of certain critical services, such as FTP. Administrators should be able to differentiate between common network activity and any suspicious network activity. Administrators need to be very careful while determining which activities should be audited and which should not. However, hackers will not always use the same intrusion method. It is also impossible for network administrators to audit all the activities. If administrators implement auditing for all services, it will create a long log file. It may be impossible to track details of all suspicious activities in the log file. In addition, logging all activities may lead to performance degradation and disk constraints.

Another critical factor that is influenced by what is being audited is the system performance. An increase in the number of activities that need to be audited puts an additional load on the computer. Therefore, administrators need to be cautious about what they are auditing and the size of the log. If the auditing plan is prepared carefully, it reduces the load on the system processor and provides administrators with logs containing selective information. This helps to narrow down the search for suspicious activities.

Most administrators do not perform an exhaustive or in-depth study of network activities. They only examine the commonly audited services or the ones that are relevant. There is no test of the effectiveness and usefulness of the audited information. Even at the client side, auditing is left until the end or as the final task while configuring auditing. It is generally implemented as an additional action and is, therefore, not effective. Now that you are aware of the objective of auditing, I will explain how to implement auditing on Solaris. You need to begin by understanding the principles behind auditing.

Principles of Auditing

Auditing is merely another tool available to administrators for ensuring the security of the network. In the end, it depends on the administrator's analytical skill to determine that an intrusion has occurred or is about to occur. The first principle for auditing is ensuring accountability. This is critical for ensuring security on the network. All users must be accountable for their actions, and constant monitoring of their activities is performed to ensure safety. Regular auditing also serves as a deterrent for potential internal hackers. If users know that the network is regularly checked for unauthorized access of resources, they may not attempt to perform such activity. However, the constant monitoring of the logged information causes certain problems. The main problem is evaluating the vast quantity of logged information. The other problem is determining that a user's activity is a security threat. The implementation of appropriate auditing provides a solution to this problem.

Administrators need to analyze the logs minutely to detect any suspicious trail of activities. They also need to analyze past attacks and determine the types of activities that took place at that time. They can then constantly monitor the network for such events.

Implementing Auditing

In Solaris, auditing is not enabled by default. The facility to enable auditing is available in BSM. To implement auditing, you need to perform two steps. The first step is to bring the system to run level 1. As explained earlier, this mode is a single user mode and is used only by the administrator for administrative and maintenance purposes. You use the following command to perform this action:

```
# /usr/sbin/init 1
```

This command boots the system into the system maintenance mode. The next step is to enable BSM. You can do this using the following command:

```
# /etc/security/bsmconv
```

You are then prompted to reboot the computer. When the system is rebooted, a message, which indicates that auditing has been implemented, is displayed. A log file is created in the /var/audit directory, which stores all the audit entries. You can verify the presence of the file by using the following command:

```
# ls -l /var/audit
```

When you no longer need to implement auditing, you can use the `bsmunconv` command to disable auditing.

Key Terms in Auditing

There are certain key terms you need to know before you implement auditing in Solaris. These terms are listed below.

◆ **Audit flags**. Audit flags are used for defining the event selection.

◆ **Audit Preselection mask**. Audit Preselection mask is a 32-bit field that indicates the logical sum of the classes being audited. A user connects to a computer by using the `login` command, which calls the `audit_control` file. This file contains information about the `audit classes` that needs to be enabled. You can also add additional audit classes by specifying their `Audit UID`'s in the `audit_user file`. This information is then added to the audit mask. Inheritance is practiced while using audit masks. Therefore, a child process inherits its audit mask from its parent. The only exception to this rule is if the child is explicitly assigned a new audit mask.

◆ **Audit trails**. Audit trails contain all the logs created by the system. You can analyze audit trials by using the `praudit` command and `auditreduce` command. You use the `dir:` parameter in the audit control file to indicate the location where the audit files should be saved.

Using Audit User ID (AUID)

Audit User ID (AUID) is a user ID that is enabled along with BSM during setup. The AUID is set once during installation and remains the same throughout the life of the session. Even users such as `superusers (su)` who have administrative access cannot change the AUID. The audit log contains the AUID along with the corresponding event. In this way, administrator can keep track of the activities that take place on the network and track the user who authorized the activity. The log contains the AUID irrespective of the execution of any `setuid` command.

An AUID contains the following components:

◆ `audit_class`
◆ `audit_control`
◆ `audit_user`
◆ `audit_event`

Let's consider these components in detail.

audit_class

An audit class contains a set of audit events. Audit classes are defined in the /etc /security/audit_class file. Audit events are assigned to audit classes in the /etc /security/audit_event file. Enabling the classes globally by using the audit_control file helps to keep a track of these audit classes. You can also use the audit_user database to assign these classes to individual users. Other files, such as audit_user, audit_event, and audit_control, use these classes for implementing auditing.

A typical entry in the audit_class file appears as shown in the following code:

```
mask:name:description
```

The mask value can contain unsigned integers that signify the class mask. A mask can contain 32 different types of classes. The name contains the reference to the class names that are used in other files that are used for configuration. The description contains a method for storing the class definition. Figure 3-1 shows a sample of the audit_class file.

FIGURE 3-1 *Sample entries as they appear in the* audit_class *file*

audit_control

The `audit_control` files store the parameters that are used for auditing. These parameters include information such as the location where audit logs are stored, the flags indicating events that are to be audited, and the flags indicating the events that are not to be audited. The file also contains information about the amount of disk space that must be available for auditing to continue uninterrupted. An example of how entries appear in the `audit_control` file is shown in Figure 3-2.

FIGURE 3-2 *Sample entries as they appear in audit_control*

You can also restrict the type of events that are logged. You can configure the computer to only log failed or unsuccessful events. For example, the information stored in the log may be restricted to only contain information about all unsuccessful attempts. The `audit_control` and the `audit_user` files are not the log files themselves. They are used to configure the audit settings.

audit_user

The `audit_user` database is used for storing audit event settings for specific users. The database is stored in the `/etc/security` directory, and the rules for accessing this database are stored in the `/etc/nsswitch.conf` file.

audit_event

An audit_event corresponds to a specific action in the operating system. You can audit the different events that occur on the system by assigning different audit events to them. Some of these audit events are low level, such as the ones that access the kernel, while others are high level and involve auditing of complex tasks, such as logon events. You can also assign the same audit event to multiple audit classes. Figure 3-3 shows sample entries in the audit_event file.

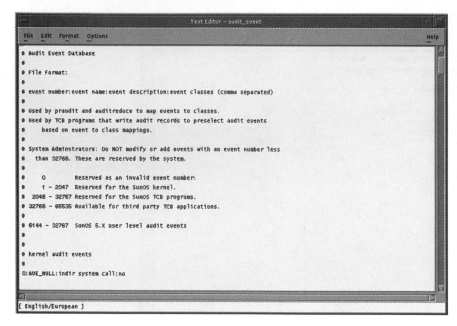

FIGURE 3-3 *Sample entries as they appear in the audit_event file*

Audit events can be divided into two types, user level and kernel level. At the user level, the events occur in the range of 2048 to 65535. In case of kernel level events, these values range from 1 to 2047. You can also assign values to third-party events. The values of these events range for 32768 to 65535.

The audit_events are stored in the audit_event file. This file is located in the /etc/security directory and can be used for assigning events to audit classes. The same audit event can be assigned to multiple audit classes, and you can also create your own audit events. These user-defined events are stored in the /usr/include/bsm/audit_kevents.h or /usr/include/bsm/audit_uevents.h files and are created only for user level events and not for kernel level events.

After implementing auditing on the computer, you need to restrict access to resources as the next step in implementing security. You can restrict access based on the implemented access control models. Broadly speaking, Solaris offers three kinds of access control models, Role-Based Access Control (RBAC) model and Mandatory Access Control (MAC) model. Discretionary Access Control (DAC) model is another access control model used in relation to MAC. The following section focuses on these models.

Access Control Models

When you talk about accessibility, you refer to the rights that a user has to access certain resources. These rights can include the ability to use, change, or view the information. These rights need to be explicitly provided or removed. You can do this by using the controls available on the computer. You can also specify the rights that are assigned to these users or services. You can assign these rights both for internal as well as external computer devices.

Solaris provides three types of access control models. These models are:

- ◆ RBAC model
- ◆ MAC model
- ◆ DAC model

Let's discuss these access control models in detail.

RBAC Model

RBAC model is a new feature that is available in the Solaris 9 OE version. Earlier, this feature was only available in the Trusted version of Solaris and not in the OE version. RBAC provides administrators the facility to create privileged accounts. These accounts provide addition resource access privileges as compared to the default privileges provided to standard users. These rights are similar to the ones available to the superuser accounts. A *superuser account* is also known as the root account in a Solaris or UNIX system.

This account has the facility to read or write to a file, execute programs, and kill processes. However, these accounts created by administrators do not have all the rights that are by default available to superusers. For example, an administrator can create a user account that provides a user the right to backup files and access certain restricted services, such as FTP. Although the user may have the right to make backups, the user may not have all the other rights associated with a superuser. The earlier versions of Solaris didn't have a standard way to assign different levels of systems administrator access. The user had either all the rights or none at all.

Advantages of RBAC

If RBAC is implemented correctly, it provides the users with the ability to execute a range of authorization activities. System administrators can control access to resources by assigning specific rights to selective users. They can do this by creating roles, hierarchies, relationships, and constraints. These methods of assigning rights are better than using Access Control Lists (ACLs). With ACLs, rights have to be set for individual objects, whereas with RBAC, roles can be created with specific rights. Individual users can then be assigned roles and uniformly assigned rights to access resources. As an analogy, you can consider the methods available in the Object Oriented Programming System (OOPS) model. A method can be used multiple times by different classes after it has been created. Similarly, a role can be assigned to many users after it has been created.

In case of distributed applications, the administration of the RBAC model can be divided into central and local domains. The policies created in the central domain are implemented at the enterprise level, whereas the local domains handle security of local resources. For example, in the case of an enterprise-level sales application that is implemented over a large geographic region, the administration of the sales transactions can be handled from a central domain. On the other hand, the administration of users, such as the addition and deletion of user accounts and assigning rights, can be handled at the local domain level.

Implementing RBAC

In Solaris, when the user logs on to the system, the user is assigned a certain set of rights that are based on the user account. In case of the RBAC model, users are assigned certain restricted rights that allow the user to access certain administrative tools and services. The RBAC model is fully integrated with the auditing facility available in Solaris. When a user logs on, the auditing mechanism includes an entry in its logs containing information such as user ID, role, and any other ID used to override the security policy. The RBAC model contains three elements. These elements are:

◆ **Role**. This implies that a user who logs on to the network by using a specific ID assumes a certain ID or role.

◆ **Authorization**. This implies that a certain role or user can be assigned the right to perform certain actions that are otherwise restricted by the implemented security policy.

◆ **Rights associated with certain profiles**. This implies that you can also assign access to specific packages based on user roles. A user can be assigned the permission to access packages, to change *user IDs (UIDs)* and *group IDs (GIDs)*, and to override security measures that are implemented by the security policy. You can also specify certain additional rights to the user profile.

The various elements of RBAC are integrated with the administrative facility available in Solaris for user administration. You can assign a role to a user providing the user with all

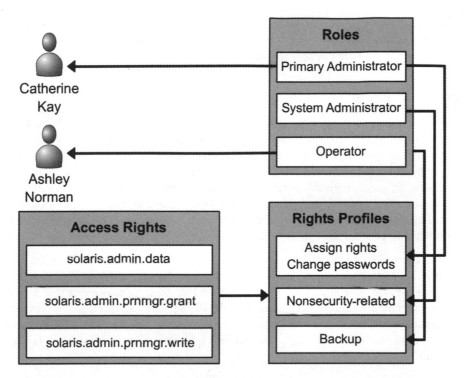

FIGURE 3-4 *Assigning rights to RBAC elements*

the rights associated with the role. If you assign certain additional administrative rights to the roles, the user gains ability to perform the administrative tasks. These tasks are similar to the ones that are available with user accounts, such as the root. Therefore, a root account can perform all the tasks that can be performed by an RBAC user. However, the reverse is not possible. A user profile contains both access permissions and commands that contain certain security attributes. These access permissions and rights can be assigned directly to users. However, this is not a safe security practice. You must assign these rights to users by using roles. Figure 3-4 represents this graphically.

Using Privileged Applications

You can configure certain applications to override default system controls based on user ID or the group ID. These applications are known as *privileged applications*. These applications form a part of RBAC elements and use permissions and administrative commands to override default security measures. Some of these applications are:

◆ Solaris Management Console

◆ Commands used to execute batch files, such as `batch()`, `at()`, and `crontab()`

◆ Commands used for allocating devices to the system, such as `deallocate()`, `allocate()`, and `list_devices()`

The root user account already contains all the access rights and the use of commands for performing administrative tasks. These access rights and the use of administrative commands can be delegated to appropriate users.

Using Roles

Roles are similar to user accounts and contain their own set of rights, path to the home directory, group information, and password information. The information about each role is stored in databases such as the user_attr, audit_user, and passwd. Multiple users can log on by using the same role. All the users who log on using a specific role share the same access rights, access the same home directory, and work in the same environment. A user can log on using one role and change the role by using the su command at the command line. The user also needs to provide the appropriate password along with the command. Another way of changing the user role is by using the *Solaris Management Console tool*.

Users cannot directly log on by using the role information. They can only log on by using their individual user accounts. The roles are lined to the user account. Therefore, when a user logs on, the user is assigned the rights based on their role. When a user logs on by using a specific role and then changes the role, all the rights assigned to the previous role are replaced. A user can only be audited based on the user's UID. When a role is audited, the log file contains all the actions performed by the user along with the role ID and the user ID.

By default, Solaris does not contain any roles. The administrator creates all roles after considering the network requirements. Nevertheless, an administrator should always create three roles. Using the predefined rights profiles available in Solaris, administrators can create these roles. These roles are:

◆ **Primary administrator**. This role provides administrators the right to perform administrative tasks, grant rights, and change rights related to administrative roles. The role also provides the rights to create other primary administrators and grant rights available to these administrators.

◆ **System administrator**. This role is used for creating roles that are used for performing administrative tasks not related to security. A system administrator may be able to create a user account but may not have the right to change the password or grant rights to users.

◆ **Operator**. This role is used for performing simple administrative tasks. These tasks include making backup, restoring backup, and administering print operations.

An administrator can use any of the earlier mentioned administrative roles instead of creating a user account and then assigning different rights profiles.

Using Authorization

Authorization is the right assigned to individual users or roles. These assigned rights are checked by applications that use RBAC for providing access. These applications provide access to themselves or their subprocesses based on these rights.

Authorization contains a name by which the right is referred and a short description of the right. As a convention, an authorization name is specified in the reverse order of the Internet name of the provider. The name begins with the provider's name. The subject area, subarea, and the function follow the provider's name. All these values are separated using a dot. A sample authorization name would be `com.asc.drivers.access`. Exceptions to this rule are authorizations that are provided by Sun, where the prefix `solaris` is used instead of the Internet name. Therefore, the example would appear as `solaris.asc.drivers.access`. Administrators can also use wildcards for specifying multiple authorization strings available in a hierarchal fashion.

As mentioned earlier, users or roles can be configured to delegate their right to other users. To do this, the authorization should end with the word *grant*. Therefore, a role that has the authorizations `solaris.admin.prnmgr.grant` and `solaris.admin.prnmgr. write` can also delegate the right to other users. In case the wildcard (*) is used with an authorization, you can delegate any of the rights contained in the role. Therefore, if the authorization is `solaris.admin.prnmgr.*`, then the role can be used to delegate all authorizations beginning with `solaris.admin.usermgr`.

Using Rights Profiles

As mentioned earlier, rights profiles provide administrators the ability to delegate certain rights to other users. These rights provide the users the ability to evade certain security settings implemented using security policies. The users are provided just enough authority to perform the job related to their role. Following is a list of some of the typical types of rights profiles:

◆ The Basic Solaris User rights profile uses the `policy.conf` file for assigning tasks to users. However, these tasks are not related to security.

◆ Each of the rights profiles mentioned earlier is created to perform specific roles. For example, the primary administrator profile is used for creating administrators that perform administrative tasks related to security. The system administrator is used for creating administrators that perform administrative but nonsecurity-related tasks. The Operator profile is used for creating administrators to handle simple administrative tasks.

◆ All the rights profiles provide access to commands without setting specific security attributes.

All information about rights profiles is stored in the help files. The help files are in HTML format and are stored in the `/user/lib/help/profiles/locale/C` directory. You can also store the help files in other locations.

You can use the Solaris Management Console Rights tool for examining the rights profiles. The Console Rights tool provides a collection of utilities that you can use for managing RBAC tools. These utilities are:

◆ **Administrative Roles tool**. This tool is used for creating roles and associating users to specific roles. The Administrative Roles tool is similar to the User Accounts tool except that it does not provide you with the provision to set passwords and configure mail. These tasks are not applicable to roles and are only set for individual users. You can also configure a profile shell for each role. This shell provides certain default settings for the role.

◆ **Rights tool**. This tool is used for creating or modifying rights profiles. These rights profiles contain commands, access permissions, and other rights that can be assigned to a profile. You can explicitly set security attributes to commands by using the Commands tab in the Rights tool.

◆ **User Accounts tool**. This tool is used for assigning rights profiles and roles to individual users. By using this tool, you can preview both the assigned rights and the rights that can be assigned to the user. You can also change the order in which the assigned rights profiles are implemented for a user. The order in which the rights profiles are implemented determines which command takes final precedence.

As you know, there are different types of roles for creating users. Similarly, there are different types of rights profiles that you can create for each type of user. These rights profiles are the *primary administrator*, *system administrator*, and *operator rights* profiles. These are predefined profiles, which only need to be enabled. I'll now discuss each of them in detail.

◆ **Primary administrator**. The primary administrator rights profile is used for creating users with superuser rights. All the authorization rights available in Solaris can be assigned to users by using the `solaris. *` authorization. A user can be given the right to delegate authorization to other users by being granted the `solaris.grant` authorization. When this right is granted to a role, the role can delegate authorization to any role, user, or rights profile.

◆ **System administrator**. As the name suggests, the system administrator rights profile is used to assign rights to the system administrator role. Unlike the primary administrator rights profile, the system administrator rights profile can only be used to assign specific, nonsecurity-related rights to roles. These rights profiles do not contain any access permissions related to specific roles, rights profiles, or password.

◆ **Operator**. This profile is used to provide role-specific rights. These rights are related to simple administrative tasks, such as administering printers and making backups. As the task of restoring files from backup is of a more secure nature, this right is not available in the operator rights profile.

As shown in Figure 3-4, an individual user is assigned a role and rights profiles are assigned to roles. For example, the user Ashley Norman is assigned the operator role. This role has its own set of rights that are assigned by using the rights profiles. One of these rights is to modify print operations.

RBAC supports a number of databases that are used for storing information about RBAC elements. There are four databases that store information about RBAC elements. These databases are:

◆ **prof_attr**. This stands for *rights profile attributes* database. The information is stored in the `/etc/security/prof_attr` file. This file contains information about profiles, such as the name, description, and attributes of the profile. The file contains five fields. Three of the fields are `profilename`, `description`, and `attributes`. The `profilename` is a reference to the profile name and is used to reference the profile. The `description` field provides a short description of the profile. This information is also visible in the help file. Therefore, the description should not only be short, but also be meaningful. The `attribute` field provides information about access rights and reference to the help files. This information is stored in the form of keys, such as `key=value`. The `helpfile` information is stored in `/usr/lib/help/auths/locale/C` directory. By default, this file provides information about the resource to which the role is being granted access. However, you can even configure the file to provide general information about the resources. Both the pieces of information stored in the key, the access rights, and the link to the help documentation need to be separated by using a semi-colon. You can also store multiple values in a key by separating each value using a comma. The following is a sample entry:

```
profilename::::description:attributes
```

◆ **exec_attr**. This stands for *profile execution attributes* database and stores all information about profile execution. This database contains all the attributes related to privileges that are assigned to specific profiles. The database is stored in the `/etc/security/exec_attr` file. The first field in the database is the `nameofprofile`. This is a case-sensitive value and refers to the name of the profile. Although the value can be left blank, it is preferable to provide a valid name that describes the profile. The next field contains information about the security policy. The field either contains the value `suser` or `superuser`. The next field is the `string` field that contains the location of the resource to which privileged access is being provided. The last key is the `attributes` field, which stores information in the form of keys. This field contains information such as numeric user ID, numeric group ID, the group name, and user's name. The following is a sample entry:

```
nameofprofile:securitypolicy:type:::string:attribute
```

◆ **auth_attr**. This stands for the *authorization attributes* database. This database is used for assigning rights to individual users. The information about the rights is stored in the `auth_attr` file. When a user tries to access a certain application or a resource, the user's rights are checked. The user is allowed to access the resource only if the user has the appropriate right. The information about the implementation of these rights is stored in the file `user_attr`. The `auth_attr` file contains information about setting up a resource group, which has a selective set of rights. The file contains fields such as `authname`, `shortdescription`, `long description`, and `attributes`. The `authname` field is used for uniquely identifying a resource. The field uses a hierarchical tree-like structure for storing information and the caveat forms the root of the tree. Therefore, the process of creating user groups involves a hierarchical process. First the root profile is created by the name `solaris`. Then a subgroup can be created, which you can name `solaris.admin`. After the administrator group has been created, you can create a separate group for users named `solaris.admin.users`. After creating the group, you can create separate groups that would contain different sets of rights. For example, you can create `solaris.admin.users.add` or `solaris.admin.users.delete`. The next field is the `shortdescription` field, which, as the name suggests, provides a short name for the application. This name appears in the title bar of the application window. The `long-description` field, on the other hand, provides a more detailed, in-depth description of the application. The attribute field provides information about access rights and reference to the help files. The field stores information in the form of keys and can contain multiple values, each separated by a semicolon. Generally, this field contains information about the location of the help documentation. Following is a sample entry from the file:

```
authname:::shortdescription:longdescription:attributes
```

◆ **user_attr**. This stands for extended *user attributes* database and contains information about additional rights provided by RBAC to individual users. The file contains information in addition to the information found in the `shadow` and `password` files. These additional rights include additional access rights, execution rights, and other security attributes. The `username` field is the first field in the file and contains the user's name. This information is retrieved from the password file. The `attributes` field contains information about the authorization names, profiles, and attribute specific information. It also contains information about roles and the type of profile. The authorization names are retrieved from the `auth_attr` file and can contain multiple values. If a wildcard is used with authorization names, all the authorizations listed in the tree are retrieved. The profile information is retrieved from the `prof_attr` file. If multiple values are retrieved from the file, a comma is used to separate each entry from one another. The sequence in which these values are retrieved and stored is of paramount importance. Based on these values, commands are executed to provide or deny access to users. It is preferable to set the value of this field to `ALL`. This ensures that all users are provided access. However, security attributes have to be set individually. The role information stored in the file is used for assigning a specific role to individual users. However, a single user can be assigned multiple roles. The type key can store either a user value or a role value. If the value is set to user, then the user is assigned the appropriate rights when the user is authenticated. On the other hand, if the value is set to role, the account is set as a role profile. Any user who logs on using the profile is assigned the role and its associated rights. Following is a sample entry:

```
username::::attributes
```

CAUTION

You cannot assign a role to another role.

I'll now focus on how to use the Solaris Management Console tool for creating roles and rights profiles. The first step is to start the System Management Console tool.

Steps for Starting the Solaris Management Console Tool

You need to perform the following steps to start working with the Solaris Management Console tool:

1. There are two ways of starting the Solaris Management Console tool. You can either type smc & at the command prompt or you can click the Solaris Management Console icon. The icon is available in the Tools subpanel in the CDE front panel. The main window appears. However, toolbox is not visible, as shown in Figure 3-5. The toolbox appears only after the user has been validated.

2. Locate the appropriate toolbox where the change has to be made. When the utility is opened for the first time, only one toolbox is available in the Navigation pane. This toolbox is used for administering the local server. You can create new toolboxes by using the Toolbox editor.

3. In the Navigation pane, double-click the This Computer toolbox. The toolbox contains management tools for administering and configuring services on the local computer.

4. From the list of available tools, click on the System Configuration icon to open the System Configuration folder. In the folder, double-click on the Users icon. You are prompted for your username and password by using the authentication dialog box. You need to be authenticated before loading any of the Solaris Management Console tools. The authentication screen appears as shown in Figure 3-6.

5. After you enter your username and password, click OK. If no role has been created yet, you will need to use the root login and the password. The root account can be used to load any of the tools. If you have logged on as a standard user who has not been assigned any role, you can only access the tools available for standard users.

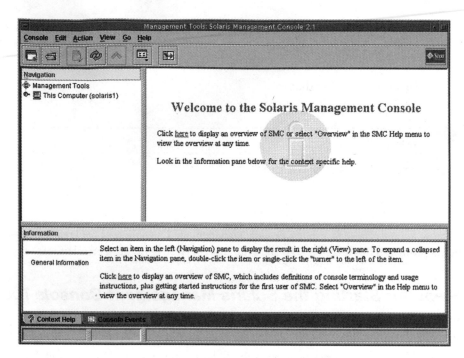

FIGURE 3-5 *The first screen of the Solaris Management Console tool*

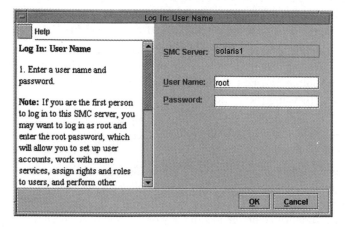

FIGURE 3-6 *The authentication screen of the Solaris Management Console tool*

6. If a role has been assigned, you can log on either with or without the role. Click on the appropriate button after entering the details.

7. You are now ready to create a new role or a new rights profile.

In Figure 3-6, the name of the server appears by default. You need to enter the login name and the password of the root account or of any user who has appropriate rights to configure the system.

Let's now learn how to create a new role.

Steps for Creating a New Role

The new role can be assigned to individual users. As explained earlier, the primary administrator's role is the most important role that you can create. The role has the maximum amount of rights and authorization.

1. After the Users collection has been loaded, double-click the Administrative Roles icon. The Administrative Roles icon is available both in the View pane and the Navigation pane.

2. In the Action menu, click on the Add Administrative Role option. The Add Administrative Role wizard appears, as shown in Figure 3-7. You can use this wizard to create the different types of roles. The first screen prompts you to provide a name for your new role.

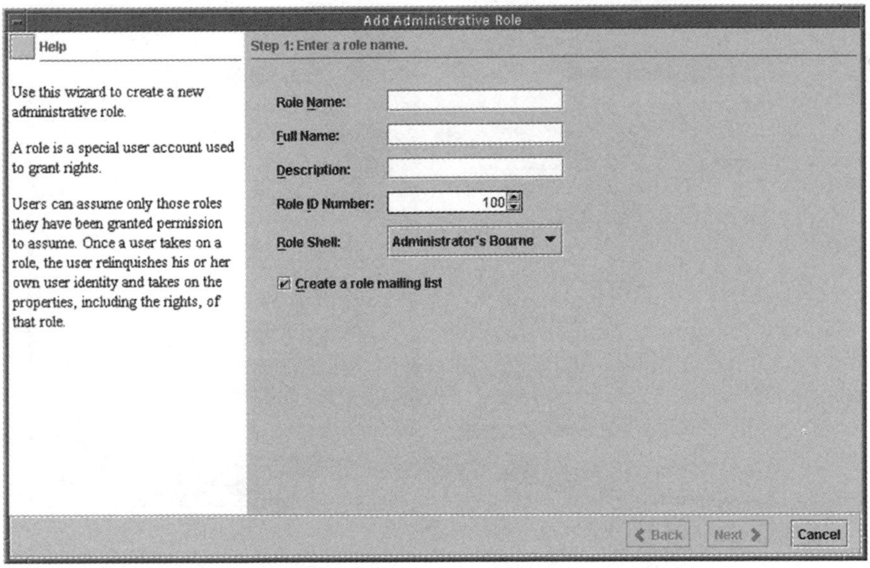

FIGURE 3-7 *The Add Administrative Role wizard used for creating new roles.*

3. Enter ProcessManager in the Role Name box and click Next. The role name should be unique within a single domain but can exist under the same name in separate domains. It should have a minimum of 2 and a maximum of 32 characters. However, a domain name should not contain spaces, dashes, and other special characters. It should begin with an alphabet and at least two of the

alphabets used in the name should be in lower case. You can also create alias names for the users who are assigned this role by using the mailing list option.

4. The next screen prompts you to enter the password for the role. You need to enter the password again to confirm the password. It is preferable to use an easy-to-remember password, since the password has to be provided when the user logs on to use the role. The password should contain a minimum of six characters, of which at least two should be alphabet letters and one should be either a special character or a number.

5. In the next screen, you need to assign the appropriate rights to the role. You can select the appropriate rights profile from the Available Rights column. When a right is assigned, it appears in the Granted Rights column. It is advisable to use the rights profile with the role containing the same name. For example, you should apply the Primary Administrator rights profile to the Primary Administrator role. Figure 3-8 shows all the rights available in Solaris. Select `Audit Review` and click `Add`. The right appears in the `Granted Rights` column. Click Next to continue.

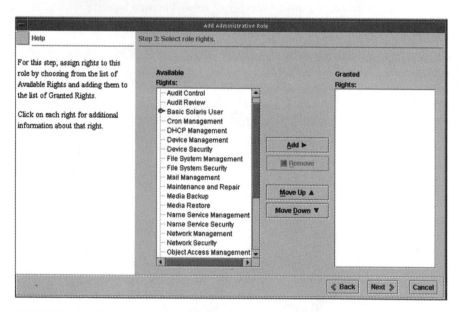

FIGURE 3-8 *All available rights that can be assigned to a new role*

6. In the next step, you need to specify the location of the home directory. The path would include the server name and the absolute path to the home directory. Click Next to continue.

7. In the next step, you can assign individual users to the role. You can do this by specifying the login names of the users. Click Next to continue. You can later

assign new users to a role by using the `Assign Administrative Role` option available in the Action menu.

CAUTION

You can only assign existing users to a role. If you need to add a new user, you first need to create the user account and then add the user to the role by using the `Assign Administrative Role` option.

8. The final step is to review the information as it appears in the Review dialog box. After you have verified the information, click Finish to close the dialog box and confirm the settings.

Your new role is created. You can later add any additional users who might need to be assigned to the role. You'll now learn how to create a new rights profile for the roles.

Steps for Creating a New Rights Profile

In addition to using the default rights profiles available in Solaris, you can create your own customized rights profiles. The following steps need to be performed for creating these rights profiles:

1. Click on the Rights tool to begin creating a new rights profile.
2. From the Action menu, click the Add Right option. The Add Right dialog box appears with the General tab active, as shown in Figure 3-9.
3. Enter `Generate Reports` as the name of the new right. You also need to enter a short description of the right and specify `Myhelpfile.html` as the name of the help file. The information stored in the help file is displayed when the right is assigned to a user. The help file can be created in a simple text editor and saved with an .html extention. The file should be saved in the `/user/lib/help/profiles/locale/C` directory.
4. Click on the Commands tab. The tab contains all the commands that can be assigned and the ones that have already been assigned as shown in Figure 3-10. The Commands Denied column, which is on the left, contains all the commands that can be assigned to the rights profile. As this is a new profile, the Commands Permitted column, which is on the right, would be empty. You can then shift commands between the two columns and assign the required rights to the rights profile. You can also change the order in which the commands are assigned by changing their sequence. You can also add a set of commands stored in a directory by using the Add Directory button.

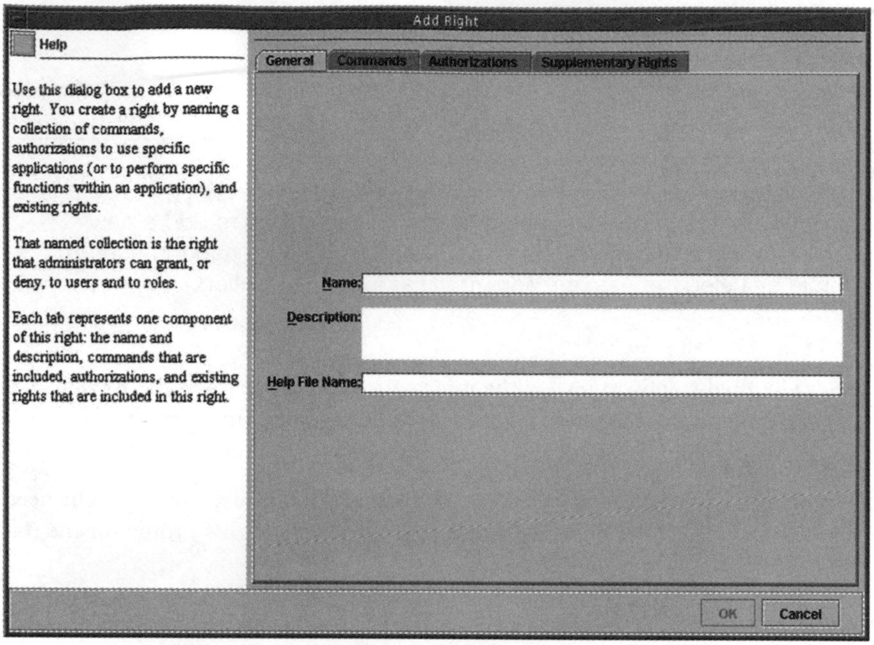

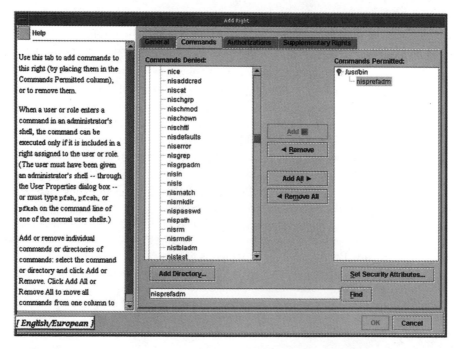

FIGURE 3-9 *The* Add Right *dialog box used for adding and modifying rights assigned to users*

FIGURE 3-10 *The commands that can be assigned and denied to users*

5. In the Commands Denied column, select a command and click Add to add the command to the `Commands Permitted` column.

6. Select the `nisprefadm` command in the Commands Permitted column and click the Set Security Attributes button to set the security attributes for the command. The Set Security Attributes dialog box appears as shown in Figure 3-11.

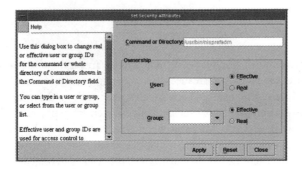

FIGURE 3-11 *The Set Security Attributes dialog box*

7. Next, you need to set the user ownership. Use the Effective button to specify the User Ownership by entering root in the User box. Click Apply to apply the settings and then close the dialog box.

8. The final step is to click OK to close the Add Right dialog box. Your new rights profile is created. You can now use this rights profile to add rights to a role.

The final step is to assign a rights profile to a role.

Steps for Adding a Rights Profile to a Role

1. In the Navigation pane, click on the Administrative Roles icon. The Administrative Roles tool is displayed and all the currently created roles appear in the view pane.

2. Double-click on the ProcessManager role that you had created earlier. The Role Properties dialog box appears. You can use this dialog box to make changes in the role.

3. In the dialog box, click on the Rights tab. All the rights currently assigned to the role are displayed.

4. Find the Generate Report rights profile that you previously created and assign it to the role by double-clicking the rights profile. The right appears in the Available Rights column.

5. After the right has been assigned to the role, the right appears in the Granted Rights column.

6. Click OK to close the Role Properties dialog box and save the changes.

You have now added the right to the role. Any user who logs on by using the role inherits these rights.

In addition to RBAC, there is another type of access control model that is used for assigning access rights for resources. This model is known as MAC.

MAC Model

MAC is used for managing access to information and processes by arranging them at different sensitivity levels. It creates labels that correspond to different sensitivity levels and allows access based on these levels. For example, in a sales application, the managers should have access to all information available, including confidential reports. On the other hand, the sales force should have access only for entering information and restricted access for viewing data. MAC compares the sensitivity or access level of a user with the access rights set on the resource. If these rights do not match, the user is denied access to the resource. MAC is called *mandatory* because the access rights or labels are set automatically by the system and cannot be modified by individual users. The administrators can change these rights, as can users who are delegated the appropriate right from the administrators.

MAC is required in cases where the security policy implemented on the system specifies that:

◆ The right to allow or deny access to resources is not available to the owners of the resource

◆ The right to allow or deny access to resources lies with the system

DAC Model

Another type of access control model available in Solaris is the *DAC* model. This model uses file permissions and ACLs for restricting access to resources. This information is compared with a user's ID or group information. In the case of DAC, users have the right to control access to data or resources. The access control is termed *discretionary* because the rights are assigned based on the discretion of resource owners. The owner of the resource can decide who should have access to the resource and who should not. The owner of the resource can provide any combination of read, write, or execute permissions to the users. As DAC permissions used on system files can only be modified by the administrator, DAC is used with MAC for restricting access to the system files.

When a user needs to read a file, write to a file, or execute a file, a check is required to determine the user's access rights. The level of access is determined based on ACL entries. Generally, the access assessment is executed on ACL entries in the following sequence:

- ◆ The owner of the resource or information
- ◆ The user who is trying to access the resource
- ◆ The group to which the owner of the resource belongs
- ◆ The group to which the user belongs
- ◆ Any other check

MAC and the DAC may appear similar, but they are different. DAC verifies the authenticity of the user information and provides access based on the discretion of the owner. In contrast, in MAC, the user's identity is verified based on parameters that are beyond the user's control. For example, a user ID can be shared across multiple users who can use the same ID to log on. The system cannot differentiate one user from another. MAC checks for the identity of the user by accessing system information such as the system's IP address.

Summary

In this chapter, you learned about implementing security at system startup and shutdown. You also learned how to implement auditing on the system, how auditing can be used to keep track of the activities that occur on the network, and about the auditing models available in Solaris. Additionally, you learned about the benefits of RBAC model and how it can be implemented on the system. Finally, you learned about the MAC model and the DAC model.

Check Your Understanding

Multiple Choice Questions

1. Which auditing tool is bundled along with the Solaris operating system?
   - **a.** Business Security Module
   - **b.** Basic Secure Model
   - **c.** Basic Security Model
   - **d.** Basic Security Module

2. Which script does Solaris provide for enabling BSM support on a computer?
   - **a.** /etc/security/bsmconv
   - **b.** /etc/audit/bsmconv
   - **c.** /etc/security/bsmunconv
   - **d.** /etc/audit/bsmunconv

3. Which script does Solaris provide for disabling BSM support on a computer?

    a. `/etc/security/bsmconv`

    b. `/etc/audit/bsmconv`

    c. `/etc/security/bsmunconv`

    d. `/etc/audit/bsmunconv`

4. Which of the following components are valid methods of an Audit ID? (Select all that apply.)

    a. `audit_class`

    b. `audit_user`

    c. `audit_command`

    d. `audit_event`

5. From the list of security levels available in Solaris, which security level requires authentication for providing access to all commands except the `boot` and `go` commands?

    a. `none`

    b. `full`

    c. `command`

    d. None of the above

6. What are the recommended security levels available in Solaris 9? (Select all that apply.)

    a. `none`

    b. `full`

    c. `command`

    d. None of the above

7. Which of the following user accounts are not required by the system and can be removed safely until they are required again?

    a. `uucp`

    b. `smtp`

    c. `none`

    d. `listen`

8. Which one of the following codes is used for removing a user account from a Solaris computer?

    a. `passmgmt -a <username>`

    b. `passmgmt -m <username>`

    c. `passmgmt -d <username>`

    d. `passmgmt <username>`

9. From the following run levels available in Solaris, which run level is used to bring the computer to the multiuser mode and where all the facilities including NFS are available?

   a. 0

   b. 1

   c. 2

   d. 3

10. From the following run levels available in Solaris, which run level is used to shut down and then reboot the system?

   a. 0

   b. 1

   c. 5

   d. 6

11. Which one of the following codes is used to identify the system's current run level?

   a. `who -b`

   b. `who -d`

   c. `who -r`

   d. `who -q`

12. Which one of the following audit components stores information about the different parameters that are used while implementing auditing?

   a. `audit_class`

   b. `audit_control`

   c. `audit_user`

   d. `audit_event`

13. Which one of the following files stores information about the audit events applicable to specific users?

   a. `/etc/nsswitch`

   b. `/etc/audit/nsswitch.conf`

   c. `/etc/nsswitch.conf`

   d. `/etc/audit`

14. Which one of the following files stores information regarding user-defined events?

   a. `/usr/include/bsm/audit_kevents.h`

   b. `/usr/audit_kevents.h`

   c. `/usr/bsm/audit.h`

   d. `/usr/bsm/audit_kevents.h`

Short Questions

1. You are administering a Solaris 9 computer. You need to change its run level so that the administrator can perform administrative tasks without forcing the currently logged in users to log off. Will you use run level 1 or run level s? What is the difference between both the run levels?

2. You are an administrator of a network containing computers running Solaris 9. Some of the users are complaining that their files are being deleted and you notice that some of the log files are also being modified. How will you enable auditing on the network so that you can identify the user who is making these changes and record the time when the changes are made?

Answers

Multiple Choice Answers

1. **d.** The Basic Security Module (BSM) is one of the auditing tools available by default in Solaris. The related files are stored in the directory location /etc/security. The tool provides Solaris with C2 level security for auditing. It stores information about all the audit events that occur on the computer.

2. **a.** Solaris uses the file /etc/security/bsmconv to enable BSM support on a Solaris computer.

3. **c.** Solaris uses the file /etc/security/bsmunconv to disable BSM support on a Solaris computer.

4. **a, b, d.** audit_class, audit_user, and audit_event are valid methods of an audit ID.

5. **c.** The command security level requires authentication by using passwords for using all commands except the boot and go commands. At the none security level, no security is provided, and at the full security level, authentication is required for accessing any command, including the boot and go commands.

6. **b, c.** The recommended security levels in Solaris are command and full. The command security level provides partial security since authentication is required for all commands except the boot and go commands. The full security level provides complete security since password is asked for accessing all commands.

7. **a, b, d.** From the list of given commands by default only the uucp, smtp, and listen user accounts belong to the list of user accounts not required by the system. The none user account is required to provide access to remote users who only require limited access to the network.

8. **c.** The `passmgmt -d` command is used for deleting a user account from the computer. The `-a` command is used for adding an entry for a new user while the `-m` option is used for modifying the entry of an existing user. Only specifying the password command raises an error.

9. **d.** The system run level 3 is used for bringing the system to the multiuser mode where all the facilities including NFS are available. Level 0 is used for shutting down the computer while level 1 is used for bringing the system to single user mode for administrative tasks. Level 2 is used for bring the system to the multi-user mode but without the NFS facility.

10. **d.** The system run level 6 is used for shutting down the system and rebooting to the default run level of 3.

11. **b.** The system's current run level can be determined by using the `who -r` command. The `-b` option returns the last time and the date when the system last rebooted. The `-d` option displays all the expired processes and the `-q` option displays the name and ID of users who are currently logged on the network.

12. **b.** The `audit control` files store the parameters that are used for auditing. These parameters include information, such as the location where audit logs are stored, the flag indicating the minimum space required by the system, and other flags that are assigned to different users and system processes. You can also restrict the type of events that are logged. For example, you could configure the computer to only log failed or unsuccessful events.

13. **c.** The `audit_user` database is used for storing audit events related to specific users. The database is stored in the `/etc/security` directory, while the rules for accessing this database are stored in the `/etc/nsswitch.conf` file.

14. **a.** These user-defined events are stored in the `/usr/include/bsm/audit_kevents.h` or `/usr/include/bsm/audit_uevents.h` files and are created only for `user level` events and not for `kernel level` events.

Short Answers

1. You need to change the run level to 1 to allow administrators to make administrative changes without logging out the currently logged in users. The run level also allows new users to logon to the network. In contrast, the run level s closes all current sessions and logs out all logged in users. Only the administrator has the right to logon from the console. Administrators use the run level s for performing administrative tasks such as making backups when no user is logged on to the network. The system run level 1 is used while performing simple administrative tasks that do not require users to log off the network.

2. Auditing is one of the first things that you need to implement for ensuring the security of information on the network. Solaris offers a number of built-in tools to enable auditing on the system. Basic Security Module is one such system that you can use to enable auditing. The module helps you keep track of information

about the time when certain files were last accessed, when users or process authentication took place, and when the system calls were made. The bsmconv command is used to enable auditing and the bsmunconv command is used for disabling auditing.

Chapter 4

This chapter focuses on some of the network and system file security utilities available in Solaris. In this chapter, I'll be discussing three major utilities, Network Identification Service Plus (NIS+), Automated Security Enhancement Tool (ASET), and the Solaris Fingerprint Database. This chapter covers the features of NIS+ and how NIS+ differs from the previously available NIS. In addition, the different objects available in NIS+ and how to configure the different types of servers will be discussed. You will also learn why administrators are moving from NIS+ to Lightweight Directory Access Protocol (LDAP). Additionally, this chapter covers how ASET can be used to specify security levels for your computer. Finally, you will learn about the Solaris Fingerprint Database, which you can use to verify the authenticity of stored files by using the information stored in the database.

Network Identification Service (NIS)

NIS was introduced in 1985 by Sun Microsystems, Inc. It is still one of the most commonly implemented enterprise directory services for corporate intranets. NIS was previously called YP. These names are used interchangeably when NIS is discussed, but *NIS* will be used throughout this book. The NIS server provides NIS service for all client computers on the network. You can have multiple NIS servers, but you can have only one *NIS master server*. The NIS master server contains the files that are required for creating NIS maps. The rest of the NIS servers are known as *NIS slave servers*. These servers contain copies of the original NIS maps that are stored on the master server.

 NOTE

The NIS utility is bundled with the Solaris software.

Certain services run on Solaris servers and provide NIS-related facilities. Following is a list of these services:

◆ The YPXFRD service runs on the master server and performs the task of replicating the NIS maps to the slave servers.

◆ The YP server daemon runs on all the slave servers and is responsible for processing all NIS client requests and queries.

◆ The YPBIND daemon is used for providing an NIS client computer access to the NIS maps.

NIS+ has replaced NIS as the default naming service for Solaris. NIS+ performs the tasks of a naming service and provides information about the following items:

◆ Network
◆ Sockets
◆ Home directory
◆ Remote Procedure Call (RPC) program names
◆ Protocols

However, NIS+ is not an improved version of NIS with additional capabilities. NIS+ is an entirely new service and is not related to NIS. The commands and architecture of NIS+ are very different from those of NIS. For example, in NIS+ the information about the network, sockets, and RPC program names are stored in the /etc directory. In the case of a small network where this information has to be synchronized, NIS is an acceptable choice. NIS is useful in situations where the network is typically limited to a few servers and a few client computers. NIS also provides support for a limited number of remote users. NIS+ was developed to service the requirements of large networks that consist of 100 to 1,000 or more client computers and 10 to 100 servers providing different services. These servers are typically placed in varied global locations and provide secure connection to unsecured networks, such as the Internet. Therefore, in the case of large networks where a large quantity of information has to be synchronized, NIS+ provides a fair amount of consistency with a small amount of administrative effort. NIS+ provides support for earlier NIS clients by using the YP-compatibility mode. NIS+ tries to resolve some of the problems that were not addressed earlier by NIS. Similarly, most of the commands in NIS+ have a syntax that is different from the syntax of the commands in NIS.

NIS+ secures access to NIS+ servers by using a secure authentication method. The method provides two logins. The first login is a standard user login for users to access their local computers. The second login is the network login, or *Secure RPC Login*. This login provides a user with access to the NIS+ service. Typically, both logins have the same password. In this case, the user only needs to log on once to access the NIS+ service. Sometimes different passwords are used for the local user login and the network login. In this case, the user needs to log on by using the network login (KEYLOGIN) for accessing the NIS+ service.

NIS+ reuses some of the services that were previously available only in NIS and *Domain Name Service* (DNS). Like NIS, NIS+ provides name service for various types of information on the network. However, NIS+ arranges the information in a hierarchical manner, similar to the way information is stored in DNS. Arranging information in a hierarchical manner enables subdomains to inherit their administrative rights from the parent domains.

The security that NIS+ offers is better than the security that NIS and DNS offer. You can specify the authority that would service a particular type of request. For example, you can configure DNS, NIS, or NIS+ to service network requests. NIS+ uses data encryption technologies, *Data Encryption Standard* (DES) and *Diffie-Hellman key exchange*, to ensure the security of information transmitted over the network. When a program requests the NIS+ service, the user is thoroughly authenticated before the program is provided any access. Solaris provides three shell scripts that can be used for setting up NIS+. These scripts are `nisserver`, `nisclient`, and `nispopulate`. You will learn more about these commands when you use them later in this chapter.

The next section focuses on the differences between NIS and NIS+.

Differences between NIS+ and NIS

Following are some of the key differences between NIS+ and NIS:

◆ **Server binding.** NIS and NIS+ differ significantly based on the type of server binding available in both the services. In the case of NIS, the clients are directly bound to a specific server, which is known as *hard binding*. The ypbind process performs this binding during startup by connecting a specific server to a client. When the client queries for certain information, the query is directed to a predefined server. This is a major drawback of NIS servers, because if too many clients query the same server simultaneously, load on the NIS server increases. However, in the case of NIS+, this is not so. The client query can be serviced by any of the available NIS+ servers, which is known as *soft binding* because all the servers have the same updated NIS+ maps. Therefore, the ypwhich command that is used to determine to which server a specific client is bound cannot be used in the case of NIS+.

◆ **Namespaces.** NIS supported the concept of *flat namespaces*. This means that only one domain that could be accessed by the host or the client was available in NIS. In contrast, NIS+ supports hierarchical domains. This concept is somewhat similar to the one followed in UNIX. UNIX has one root directory, which comprises several other subdirectories. The hierarchical structure of the NIS+ namespace can be based on the logical hierarchy implemented in the organization. This structure helps in providing meaningful names for and administration of the network. You can also create separate domains for each level or division of the organization.

◆ **Automatic replication.** In NIS, any change made to the NIS maps means that the master server has to resend the complete NIS map updates to each of the slave servers. In the case of NIS+, the master server only needs to update any changes made to the NIS+ maps stored on the master server to the copies stored on the slave servers. This is called *incremental updation*, which leads to a more efficient and faster system of replication. The master server can easily synchronize its information with the information available on the slave servers.

◆ **Support to other groups.** NIS provides support to all UNIX groups and other groups on the network. This support also continues in NIS+. In addition, NIS+ allows you to group multiple NIS+ clients in a single NIS+ group. Each NIS+ group can be assigned its own set of rights and access permissions.

◆ **Better security.** NIS+ provides authorization, authentication, and RPC facilities. These facilities are not available in NIS.

◆ **Complete search facility.** NIS provides a search facility for maps that is limited to a single predefined column. In contrast, NIS+ extends the search facility to multiple columns.

◆ **Reuse of DNS domain names.** NIS+ provides you with the facility to reuse the domain names that you may have specified for DNS. This ensures consistency and easier transition from DNS to NIS+. Except for the sharing of names, there is no similarity between the utilities. You cannot exchange information between a DNS server and an NIS+ server.

◆ **Computer and username.** In NIS, you can use the same name for the computer name and the username. In case of NIS+, this is not so. Both the names need to be unique and should not contain a period (.) in NIS+. This is because the period symbol is used for separating objects in NIS+.

◆ **Case sensitive.** In NIS, the commands and the names are case-sensitive. In NIS+, the commands and the names are not case-sensitive.

◆ **Data storage.** In NIS, all information is stored in the form of a two-dimensional table. In NIS+, all the information is stored in the form of a multicolumn table.

◆ **Maximum size of a record.** In an NIS record, you can have a maximum of only 1,024 bytes. In contrast, there is no such restriction in the case of NIS+ records.

◆ **Authentication.** In NIS, there is no facility for authentication. In contrast, NIS+ uses DES authentication for ensuring security of information as it is transmitted over the network.

In NIS+, certain objects are required for the smooth functioning of the service. The next section explains these objects in detail.

NIS+ Objects

The NIS+ object consists of a range of five objects that are used for running the NIS server and providing its functionalities. Following is a list of the various objects available in Solaris:

◆ **Directory object.** The directory structure in NIS+ is similar to the directory structure in UNIX. You can use the directory object to store different types of objects, such as group objects, table objects, entry objects, and link objects. The directory object stores information in an inverted hierarchical structure, which is shaped like a tree. The root domain forms the first node of the structure, and the subdomains form the branches. Each main directory object contains a copy of the domain's `org_dir` and `group_dir` directory objects. The `org_dir` directory object contains information about all the tables in the domain, whereas the `group_dir` object contains information about all the administrative groups available in NIS+. For example, the root directory of Bukbuz, Inc. can be `buk-buz.com` and the subdomains would be named `org_dir.bukbuz.com` and `group_dir.bukbuz.com`.

◆ **Table object.** The table objects are similar to the NIS+ maps and store network information. The tables can contain either an entry object or the value zero. The value zero indicates that the object is empty. There are 17 predefined table objects, which are administered using the `nist blodm` command and the `nisdetect` command. Each entry object forms a row in the table and is known as a *record*. An example of a table object is passwd.org_dir.bukbuz.com and an example of an entry object is [name=user1],passwd.org_dir.bukbuz.com.

◆ **Group object.** These objects store information about the administrative user groups available in NIS+. These administrative groups have the right to manage and modify the namespace based on each group's rights. The `nisgrpadm` command is used for performing the administrative tasks. An example of a group object can be admin.group_dir.bukbuz.com.

◆ **Link object.** The link objects serve as pointer objects and are similar to symbolic links. They are usually used to point to tables or object entries and are administered using the `nisln` command.

Now that you know about the different objects available in NIS+, you will learn how to configure NIS+. The first step in the process is to prepare a site for NIS+.

Preparing a Site for NIS+

Before installing NIS+, you need to plan how the service will be implemented on the network. The hardware and software requirements are the first items for which you need to plan. The minimum hardware requirement is 64 MB of RAM and 128 MB of swap disk space. The NIS+ files are stored in the directory location /var/nis, and a directory size of 20 MB is recommended. You also need to provide a domain name for the root server.

In addition to planning for the hardware and software requirements, you need to plan for the domain name, the domain hierarchy, and security levels. As explained earlier, there can only be a single root domain for an NIS+ namespace, which forms the origin of the domain hierarchy. The domain name should contain two labels separated by a period (.). A few examples of valid domain names are abc.org, asd.edu, and abc.com. As you may have observed, NIS+ reuses the DNS convention of using the Internet convention of .com for commercial site names and .org for organizational-specific names. You can also use .edu for educational institutions. The next naming convention you need to ensure is for subdomain names. Subdomain names should be based on the parent domain name and should be unique in the parent domain. Clients to the domain, both individual users and computers, are assigned to the respective domains instead of to the main domain. For example, all the employees working in the sales department would be assigned to the Sales domain and all employees related to the production department would be assigned to the Production domain. This helps in implementing an administration that is more efficient and easier to use for assigning access rights. You will have user groups with names such as `sales.asc.org` and `prod.asc.org`.

The next step is to configure the appropriate security level. By default, NIS+ runs at the security level 2. However, you can change the security level based on your organization requirement. For example, if the NIS+ server provides service to a SunOS system on the network, the server needs to be run in YP compatibility mode. After the security level is determined, you need to set up the user rights and create administrative groups.

UNIX users would know that administrative rights are, by default, available only with the file owner or the folder owner. This can cause a problem in a networked environment where information needs to be accessed over the network. NIS+ provides a solution to this problem by creating an administrative group that has the appropriate privileges for the domain. Any user who requires administrative access can be added to the group and can be removed when the work is finished. This reduces administrative hassles and ensures consistent application of rights.

NOTE

It is preferable to assign the name `admin` to the user group with administrative rights. This makes it easy to identify the rights assigned to the group.

In addition to the root server, there can be multiple master servers and slave servers. As explained earlier, each subdomain will have its own master server and slave servers. The presence of multiple slave servers that will act as replication servers is, however, optional. You need to identify the computers that will be assigned these roles.

CAUTION

The presence of multiple slave or replication servers is optional. All the same, it is advisable to have at least one replication server. This ensures that the replication server serves as a backup if the master server goes down.

Next, you need to configure NIS+ clients to access NIS+ servers. NIS+ clients can be either individual users or computers. The NIS+ servers that are a part of a subdomain are clients of their parent domain. The only exception to this rule is the root domain, which is a client of the base or the original domain. The name of each client should be unique and based on the naming convention followed in Solaris.

Many scripts are available in Solaris that can be used for creating the NIS+ namespace. The next section focuses on how you can configure an NIS+ master as the root computer.

Configuring an NIS+ Master Server as the Root Node

The first step in configuring an NIS+ master server is to log on using the root account or the superuser account. Only superuser accounts have the appropriate rights to create the root node. The nisserver script is used for creating the root domain. Following is the syntax of the command:

```
root-server# nisserver -v -r -d domain_name
```

When the domain is created, the appropriate NIS+ tables are also created along with it. By default, these tables are empty. You can populate the tables by retrieving the information from the appropriate ASCII files.

TIP

A recommended practice is to copy all the files into a temporary directory. You can then edit and customize the files according to your requirements before populating the tables in the NIS+ database.

NIS+ contains a standard list of tables that can be installed on a computer. You can either install all of the tables or configure only selective ones based on the network requirements of your organization. These tables are then used to populate the NIS+ maps. Following is a list of all the available NIS+ tables:

- ◆ auto_master
- ◆ auto_home
- ◆ aliases
- ◆ passwd
- ◆ networks
- ◆ rpc
- ◆ protocols
- ◆ time zone

- ◆ cred
- ◆ bootparams
- ◆ hosts
- ◆ group
- ◆ netmasks
- ◆ netgroups
- ◆ services

The nispopulate script is run to populate the tables with the appropriate files. Before running the file, you need to change the directory information to point to the directory where you stored the edited or customized files. Following are the commands required to change the directory information:

```
root-master# cd /var/tmp/nisfiles
root-master# nispopulate -v -F
```

The default network password for all the users is nisplus. All users should change their respective passwords to ensure security. If a user is a standard user, the user can run keylogin and use the chkey command to change the password.

 NOTE

Users are recommended to use the same password as their network password and their login password. If both the passwords are the same, the user only needs to log in once for authentication on a local computer and for getting network access.

After all the tables have been populated, you need to restart the computer. When the computer restarts, executing the following commands checks whether the files have been correctly configured:

```
root-master%% nisls
root-master%% niscat passwd.org_dir
```

The next step is to configure the NIS client. The next section contains a list of steps for configuring the NIS+ client computer.

Configuring an NIS+ Client

The first step in creating an NIS+ client is to create an entry for the client on the master server. Only the root login has the right to create this entry on the root server. You can use the `admintool` to create the entry if the entry does not already exist. After the entry has been created, you need to run the `nisclient` script for providing the authorization to the client computer. Following is the syntax for the command to create the client entry:

```
root-master# nisclient -v -d domain_name -c client_computer
```

In the preceding code, the `domain_name` is the name of your NIS+ domain, and the `client_computer` is the client computer's name.

CAUTION

After executing the command, you might receive a warning indicating that the client details already exist on the client computer.

After the client entry has been created on the master server, you need to log on to the client computer by using the `root` account and run the `nisclient` script. Following is the syntax for running the script:

```
client# nisclient -v -i -h master_computer
    -a master_ip -d domain_name
```

NOTE

The reader needs to remember that the code has to be typed in a single line.

In the preceding code, `master_computer` is the name of the master server, `master_ip` is the master server's IP address, and `domain_` name is the name of the NIS+ domain.

Configuring the Root NIS+ Replica

After configuring the NIS+ client, you need to start the NIS+ server daemon. This daemon is used for replication. The following command is used to start the daemon:

```
root-replica#rpc.nisd
```

Now you need to run the `nisserver` command on the NIS+ master server. Following is the syntax of the command:

```
root-master# nisserver -v -R -d domain_name -h replica_computer
```

In the preceding code, the domain_name is the NIS+ domain name and replica_computer is the name of the NIS+ slave server where the replication has to take place. The final step is to populate all the tables on the client NIS+ server computer. Following are the commands that you need to execute to populate the tables:

```
root-master# nisping domain_name
root-master# nisping org_dir.domain_name
root-master# nisping groups_dir.domain_name
```

The next section discusses how to configure an NIS+ subdomain master.

Configuring the NIS+ Subdomain Master

You can promote any of the previously configured slave servers as the domain master of the current domain. The current domain can be either directly below the root domain or under a subdomain. The next step is to start rpc by using the following command:

```
subdomain-master#rpc.nisd
```

When the preceding command has been executed, you need to log on to the master server of the domain above the current domain. There you need to execute the nisserver command.

 NOTE

You can log on to either the master server of the domain above the current domain or any other domain higher up in the hierarchy.

After the server has been created, you need to fill all the tables with information regarding the newly created subdomain. The commands are executed as shown here:

```
subdomain-master# cd /var/tmp/nisfiles
subdomain-master# nispopulate -v-F
```

Once the computer is configured, you need to restart the computer for the changes to be implemented.

Securing NIS+

Although NIS+ provides better security, it also involves additional administrative tasks compared with NIS. Using NIS+ also involves additional effort on the part of users who are not accustomed to using security procedures implemented in Solaris. NIS+ might be considered secure but given enough time and resources, any encryption algorithm can be decrypted. Even the security of the shared key is not completely ensured. The shared key that is stored on the master server is not removed if the any other user besides the user logs on in the case that the `root` logs out without using the `keylogout()` command. Even if the `root` uses the `keylogout()` command to log out, the session key is still maintained until the session expires. Despite these drawbacks, NIS+ continues to be more secure than NIS.

NIS+ also provides certain benefits for its users, because NIS+ ensures the reliability of the information that is transmitted over the network. It also secures the information from unauthorized access. As explained earlier, NIS+ provides additional security by specifying a network login for users to log on to the network. However, users do not need to provide the password repeatedly if their account is correctly configured. A client account is considered to be correctly configured if the login password and the client's *Secure RPC password* are the same. In NIS+, users can change their account information and password by using the `passwd` command. This information is automatically updated by NIS+ in the file `/etc/.rootkey`, which stores the root password.

 NOTE

A RPC library can make procedural calls to other computers across the network. To secure this connection, RPC uses the DES authentication encryption technology. This technology is known as *Secure RPC* and is used for authenticating clients.

The use of DES for user authentication provides adequate security for administrators, who do not need to buy third-party applications for this purpose. The administrators need to instruct users on how to use the `passwd` and the `password -r` commands, which is essential for ensuring the security of the user password.

 NOTE

The `passwd` command is used for setting and changing user passwords. A `root` or `superuser` can use the `passwd` command to change the root account password and the passwords of other users. The command can also be used to change the full name details and the type of shell associated with a user account. The password information can be stored either on the local computers or at a central location. If the passwords are stored locally, they are stored in the `/etc/security/password` database. When the passwords are stored at remote locations, they are generally kept in the Distributed Computing Environment (DCE) or NIS+. The `passwd` commands also contain certain parameters. For example, you can use the `passwd -f` command to change the name recorded in the `/etc/passwd` file. Similarly, you can use the `passwd -s` command to change the login shell of the user.

Creating a secure NIS+ namespace involves making sure that the correct information about users and computers is stored on the master server and that the same information is replicated on all the slave servers. You have to check the tables on the master server periodically to ensure that there is not any redundant information in them and that entire obsolete user accounts are deleted.

You also need to determine the security policy that will be implemented in the domain. The content of the security policy depends on the type of clients available in the domain. NIS+ provides three levels of security: 0, 1, and 2. Level 0 is used while configuring NIS+; level 2 is the default security level. You will learn more about these levels in the next section. The security levels dictate the type of NIS+ objects that can exist within the tables. As mentioned earlier, clients can be either computers or individual users. The user groups available in NIS+ are `user`, `group`, `world`, and `nobody`, and the available rights are `read`, `modify`, `delete`, and `create` permissions. Just as in the case of UNIX, in Solaris the rights appear along with the file information. The display follows the sequence of `nobody`, `user`, `group`, and `world`, and displays rights as `rmcd`. By default, NIS+ does not provide the `nobody` group with any rights. It provides the `world` with only the read permission, and the `user` and `group` user groups with all the permissions.

If the network works in a diverse environment, which contains computers of different types, the NIS+ security level has to be changed. After creating NIS+ objects, you need to run the `rpc.nisd` command to run NIS+ in the compatibility mode. Although this causes the security level of NIS+ to be reduced, it does not endanger the security of information on the network. Therefore, all the objects on the network will be able to read the information despite the security implemented by NIS+.

The next section discusses the security levels available in NIS+.

Security Levels in NIS+

NIS+ offers three levels of security. Based on these security levels, users are authenticated on the network. Users need to provide different credentials for different security levels. For example, the user credentials that might work at security level 0 will not work at security level 1. The default security level of NIS+ is level 2. Table 4-1 lists the various security levels available in NIS+ and their descriptions.

Table 4-1 NIS+ Security Levels

Level	Description
0	This security level is primarily used for testing and configuring the NIS+ namespace. At security level 0, the servers allow all clients complete access to any information stored in the domain or transmitted over the network. The security level should be used only during setup and should not be used by standard users.

Table 4-1 (continued)

Level	Description
1	This security level provides AUTH_SYS security. AUTH_SYS is used in RPC for calling remote procedures.
2	This is the default security level of NIS+ and is the most secure level. At this level, authentication is provided by using the DES authorization. If any client doesn't have the proper authorization, the client is assigned to the nobody class and is assigned all rights as defined for members of the nobody class. If the client fails to acquire the DES authorization, the request is rejected and an authentication error appears.

NIS+ has enhanced security features compared with NIS. However, it still falls short in fulfilling certain other security requirements. LDAP fulfills these requirements and provides a more secure environment. The next section discusses LDAP in detail.

Switch from NIS+ to LDAP

NIS+ fulfills most of the requirements for which it was developed. However, most of the enterprise directory services being implemented in today's corporate world prefer using newer technologies, such as LDAP. If the transition between technologies is not carefully planned, it could lead to chaos on the network. Therefore, most network administrators prefer migrating users in small groups while testing new technologies. If the transition fails, only a small section of users are deprived of the service, instead of all the users. You can migrate the currently used legacy servers with gateway servers. The gateway servers can provide all the services that were previously provided by the legacy servers, and the users will not know the difference. One such transition is between NIS+ and LDAP.

What Is LDAP?

LDAP is a client-server protocol used for accessing a directory service. A *directory service* is a database whose primary objective is to provide information, rather than to write the information. A directory is not used for performing complicated transactions and does not provide the facility to rollback incomplete or unsuccessful transactions. A directory performs updates by performing either all the changes or none of them.

Because of their simple structure, directories provide a faster search and lookup procedure. The directories replicate information on multiple servers to ensure easy availability and reliability of information, which also ensures faster lookup of specific information. Although there might be a slight time lag between replication on each of the servers, ultimately all the servers will contain the same information.

You can provide a directory service in different ways. You can store different kinds of information, search for different types of information, and specify conditions about how different types of information should be referenced or updated in the database. Directory services can be either local or global in their scope. A local scope implies that information is stored and searched for on a single computer, whereas a global scope implies distributed storage of information and a broader search scope.

LDAP has now become a recognizable standard for providing access to directory information. It performs the part of a gateway for other electronic information systems configuring their intranet and extranet networks. It has become a standard lightweight database that can be easily used on the Internet. Various companies store information on LDAP servers, which act as central repositories of information for mail servers, Web servers, directories, and other applications requiring centralized access to information. The LDAP database can be used along with existing information repositories, such as SQL server databases, for providing information. LDAP can also be used with Internet technologies, such as Netscape directory software development kits (SDKs). These SDKs provide support for either reusing the existing features or creating totally new clients. Because the source code is free and easily available, you can customize it based on your requirements.

LDAP uses *LDAP Data Interchange Format* (LDIF), which is in ASCII format for transferring directory information between two LDAP directory servers or between a client and a server. You can also use LDIF for working with command-line utilities on the LDAP server. An LDAP file contains information, which is stored in hierarchical order of entries. Following is a sample of what an LDIF file looks like:

```
dn: o=bokbuz, c=NL
o: bokbuz
objectclass: organization
dn: cn:Ashley Norman, o=bokbuz, c=NL
cn: Ashley Norman
sn: Norman
mail: anorman@asc.com
objectclass: person
```

In the preceding code, dn signifies the distinguished name attribute and contains a unique value for each user. The dn attribute contains the name of the entry; it also traces the path of the entry to the base or root of the tree.

Shifting from NIS+ Maps to LDAP Objects

As explained earlier, all information in NIS+ is saved in the form of map entries. These entries store information in pairs, a keyword, and its corresponding value. Whenever the computer requires certain information, it searches for the information in the keys and displays the corresponding value. A drawback of this system is that if you want to search on multiple keywords, you'll need to create a different message map for each search. You could search based on user IDs or by using other pieces of user information.

LDAP stores information in the form of object classes. These classes contain attributes that define the different types of information that an object class can contain. Each individual record in an LDAP server is stored in the form of LDAP entries. LDAP entries contain both attributes and values. An important attribute that is present in all entries is the *distinguished name* attribute. This attribute stores unique information for each record. You can also search for specific information based on this attribute, which ensures fast and correct retrieval of information. You could then search for specific records based on the values stored in the attribute. For example, the attribute `userid` should store unique values for each user. When you search for a specific value, the record for a single user is returned. LDAP has an advantage over NIS+ because you can search on multiple attributes in LDAP. This removes the necessity of maintaining multiple message maps, as is the case with NIS+.

LDAP contains a set of object classes and attributes, including:

- ◆ `ipHost`
- ◆ `posixAccount`
- ◆ `posixGroup`
- ◆ `gidNumber`
- ◆ `uidNumber`

These attributes store similar information as that stored in the NIS+ message maps.

How LDAP Works

LDAP directories follow the client-server model. Information is stored on one or more LDAP servers and is used to create the LDAP directory tree or the backend database. When an LDAP client requires specific information, it connects to the server and queries for the information. The server then searches for the specific information and returns either the information or a pointer to the location where the information is kept. A benefit of replication is that irrespective of the server that the client connects to, the same information is returned from any of the servers, which helps to ensure consistency and reliability of retrieved information.

As mentioned earlier, information in LDAP is stored in the form of a tree. All the similar information or groups should be grouped together under one branch. Similarly, all the divisions of your organization should form different braches in the tree, and the users working in these divisions should form subbranches. The root of the tree is the `Domain-Class` (`dc`), which contains the root attributes. The `dc` is named after the domain and requires a unique name. For example, if the domain name is `asc.com`, then the `dc` would be named `dc=asc, dc=com`. You can then create subdomains or branches for each of the departments of your organization. For example, the LDAP server that would provide information for the sales department could be named `dc=sales, dc=asc, dc=com`.

Automated Security Enhancement Tool (ASET)

Automated Security Enhancement Tool (ASET) is a built-in feature available in Solaris that allows you to specify the security level for a computer and maintains the computer at that level. It allows you to automatically audit security policies by using a simple administration interface. ASET can be used to set the security level of a computer as low, medium, or high. ASET can also be used for checking file permissions and contents of system files and for configuring environment variables in startup files. It checks a computer for security loopholes and cautions the user about future security problems. It also changes the security level of system files according to the current security level of a computer. You need to install the SUNWast package to run ASET on your computer. Following is the syntax of the ASET command:

```
aset [-p] [-d aset_dir] [-l secure_level] [-n user@host] [-u userlist_file]
```

Table 4-2 explains each of the options in detail.

Table 4-2 ASET Options

Option	Description
-p	This option is used for scheduling ASET to run after a set time interval. This information is stored in the /etc/crontab file in the form of an entry. The time interval is set using the environment variable PERIODIC_SCHEDULE, which is available in the /user/asset/asetenv file.
-d aset_dir	This option is used for changing the default working directory of ASET, which by default is /usr/asset. The working directory forms the root directory of ASET and is used to store all the files and utilities used by ASET. Another way to change the default directory is to use the ASETDIR environment variable. The value set by using the -d command line option overwrites the value stored in the environment variable.
-l secure_level	This option can be used to stipulate the security level for ASET to work. The default security level of ASET is low. Another method of changing the security level is to use the environment variable ASETSECLEVEL. Here again the value specified by using the command-line option overwrites the value of the environment variable.

Table 4-2 (*continued*)

Option	Description
`-n user@host`	This option is used to e-mail information about ASET to a user. This user account is created on the host computer. If this option is not specified, the information appears as standard output on the local computer. The displayed information consists mostly of the execution log and any error information.
Maintenance commands	You can use this option to access the maintenance commands that are available in ASET. The maintenance report created by ASET is stored in the directory location `/usr/aset/reports/latest` directory.
`-u userlist_file`	This option can be used to provide a list of valid users to ASET. ASET then performs a series of checks on environment variables for each of the users in the list. The list of users is stored in a text file, and this file is passed as a parameter to the command. The entry for each user is specified in a separate line and contains the username or login name.

As shown in the preceding table, you can determine the current security level of ASET by using the `aset -l` command-line option. You can also change the security level to any of the predefined security levels, which are `low`, `medium`, and `high`. At the `low` security level, ASET doesn't change the computer's performance in any way. It performs a series of security checks and warns the user of probable security problems. At the `medium` level, some of the system files are modified by ASET. User access to certain system files is restricted to reduce the danger of security attacks. Even at this level, ASET performs a series of security tests and warns users of the security problems they may face in future. It also provides information about any changes made to the system files. These changes do not affect the normal functioning of system services, and all system applications retain their original purpose.

At the `high` security level, ASET changes all the necessary system files to convert the system into a defensive system, which is ready to face any type of security threat. All the available security practices are implemented on the computer. However, not all these practices are normally required. The security level on many of the system files is increased to such a level that only a specific computer or a limited number of users can access the files. At this level, the computer's security takes priority over the computer's performance. Most of the system applications and commands perform in the same way as before, however, the performance of some of the applications and commands changes because of their changed security levels. The master files and the `asetenv` file contain information about how ASET performs at each of the security levels and how you can customize the information to suit your needs. Following is a list of some of the checks performed by ASET at the highest security level:

◆ Authenticate the content of the system files

◆ Authenticate the integrity and consistency of information stored in the passwd and group files

◆ Verify that appropriate permissions have been assigned to system files

◆ Stop the IP forwarding service and configure the computer to act as a firewall

◆ Validate the current eeprom settings to prevent standard users from accessing login by using the console

◆ Verify the information stored in the system configuration files

◆ Validate the information stored in the .login, .profile, and .cshrc environment files

You can configure ASET to run periodically when the computer reaches a certain security level. You can use the -p option to set this time interval when ASET is run at a specific frequency and a specific time. If you do not specify the -p option, ASET will execute only once. Table 4-3 lists some of the files that are checked by ASET and the actions that are performed on the files.

Table 4-3 Files Checked by ASET

Option	Description
/etc/vfstab	This file contains information about creating file systems that can be read and written to by all users.
/etc/inetd.conf	This file is checked for the ps, tftp, netstst, and rexd entries.
/etc/default/login	This file provides root-level access by specifying the CONSOLE entry, such as CONSOLE=entry.
/etc/hosts.equiv	This file contains all the '+' entries.
/etc/aliases	This file contains information about all the aliases used by different users and used to match a specified alias with the corresponding user.
/.rhosts	This file is removed if the security level is medium or high.
/etc/dfs/dfstab	This file contains information about files that are shared without any restrictions being assigned to their access.
/var/adm/utmp	This file is used to change the read-write permission for everyone in case of a high security level.
/etc/ftpusers	This file is used to prevent users from accessing the FTP service. You can even prevent the root superuser from accessing the service. This step is generally taken in the case of a high security level.

All information about scripts and reports pertaining to ASET are stored in the /user/aset directory. The files that are used to set security levels are stored in the /user/aset/masters directory. These files also contain information about the owners of the files and the permissions assigned to the file.

Features of ASET

In ASET, every feature is called a task. Except for the tune task, which is executed only once during installation, all the other tasks are executed after a specific interval of time. The following sections discuss various tasks available in ASET.

The tune Task

This task is performed once at the time of installation. The tune task involves adding restrictions or tightening permissions regarding system files. After installation, all the system files and directories have limited security settings on file permissions to facilitate sharing of information. Because security is essential, you need to change the permission on these files and directories to create a more secure environment. You have already learned about the different security levels available in ASET. The low level provides the least amount of security. At the medium level, the security is tightened to ensure a reasonably secure environment. At the high level, the system files are at the maximum level of security and the most restrictive file access policies are applied. The files that are used for setting the different levels of security are tune.low, tune.med, and tune.high.

The cklist Task

The system maintains certain files whose content remains the same over a period of time. These files are compared against a master file and any changes are logged. This information is stored in the /user/aset/masters/cklist.level file, which is created when a computer performs the cklist task for the first time. The information stored in the files is compared with the following pieces of information:

◆ The owner of the files and directories
◆ The group to which the user belongs
◆ The permissions that have been set for the files
◆ The checksum and the size of the file, if the file is being checked
◆ The date and time when the file was last modified
◆ The number of links to the file

ASET also checks specific directories based on the current security level. You will learn more about security levels in relation to directories in a later section, where I'll explain the ASET environment file. This file contains information about different security levels applicable in case of directories.

The usrgrp Task

In this task, ASET checks to ensure the integrity and consistency of user accounts and groups. This information is stored in the groups and password databases, and any changes made are immediately brought to the administrator's attention. Following are some of the typical problems that can occur in the password file:

◆ You may have created a user account by providing a corresponding password.

◆ You may have created duplicate user IDs on a computer. However, if the ID is an alias, it is not brought to the attention of the administrator. Information about all duplicate user IDs are stored in the uid_alias file.

◆ You may have created duplicate usernames in user profiles. Although this may not be a problem, it can cause problems while you are searching for specific records.

◆ You may not have entered the entries for certain records in the passwd file in the appropriate format.

◆ You have to check that the corresponding C2 password, which is stored as encrypted, is in the correct format. This is essential if C2 security is available.

◆ You may have incorrectly stored the information saved in login directories.

Following are certain other problems faced by group files:

◆ Identical group names or entries can exist in the file.

◆ Identical group IDs can exist in the file.

◆ The password for the group may have been set as NULL.

◆ The entries made in the file for the groups may have been entered incorrectly or in an incorrect format.

Based on the value set in the YPCHECK environment variable, ASET checks either the local passwd file or both the local file and the passwd file stored on the NIS+ server. The second option is applicable only if the value of the environment variable is set to true. The discrepancies found in the file are only noted automatically. They are not corrected. All the three security levels are checked, unless ASET is instructed otherwise.

The sysconf Task

As the name suggests, the sysconf task involves checking the system configuration files, which are stored in the /etc directory. ASET evaluates all the system tables based on each of the security levels, except when it is explicitly instructed to ignore the change. Table 4-4 lists some of the tasks performed on each of the system tables.

Table 4-4 Tables Affected During the `sysconf` Task

Option	Description
`/etc/inetd.conf`	ASET checks the information stored in this file for any weaknesses or shortcomings. The entry to be checked is tftp(1). ASET checks whether any authentication is performed and whether the service has started in the correct directory, as shown in Figure 4-1. The way ASET responds to the result depends on the current security level. For example, if the security level is `low`, then only a warning is issued stating that the service has been configured incorrectly. In case of `medium` and `high` levels of security, first a warning is displayed and then the required security changes are made to the file. Other entries that are checked are `ps()` and `netstat()`. These entries appear as shown in Figure 4-2. These entries may provide confidential system information to crackers who might gain access to the computer. If the security level is `high`, then these entries are disabled.
`/etc/hosts.equiv`	This file contains information about all the trusted hosts registered on the computer. By default, the file contains only a single line of + symbol. This implies that all the hosts that attempt to connect to the computer are considered trusted hosts. However, this is an insecure method of security. If the system security level is `low`, only a warning is issued. However, if the security level is `medium` or `high`, in addition to displaying the warning, even the entry is deleted.
`/etc/default/login`	The entry for the `consol=line` is checked to ensure that root login is only available from the administrator's computer. At the `low` security level, only a warning is displayed, whereas at security levels `medium` and `high`, the entry is changed to `CON-SOLE=/dev/console`.
`/etc/aliases`	This entry checks for any weak or unsecured aliases. These aliases are then disabled based on current the security level. Figure 4-3 displays all the aliases registered on the current system.
`/etc/dfs/dfstab`	ASET checks in this file for information about any file system that doesn't contain any restriction on being exported.

`/etc/ftpuser`	At the highest security level, only the `root` has the right to access the FTP service, and `ftp()` is removed from the list of valid users.
`/.rhosts`	Everyone on the network cannot be allowed access to the `.rhosts` file. In the case of `low` security level, only a warning is issued. In the case of `high` security level, the file is renamed `/.rhosts.bak`.
`/var/adm/utmpx`	At `low` security level, only a warning is issued, whereas at `high` security level, the file can only be read and cannot be written to by everyone.

FIGURE 4-1 *Entry for* `tftp` *in the* `inetd.conf` *file*

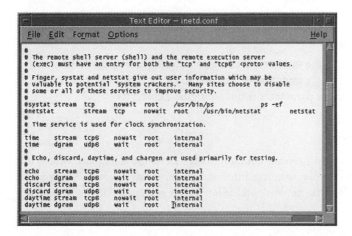

FIGURE 4-2 *Entry for* `ps()` *and* `netstat()` *in the* `inetd.conf` *file*

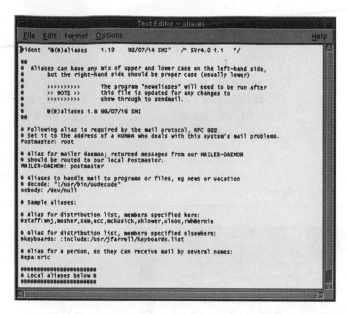

FIGURE 4-3 *Entry displaying all the aliases registered on the computer*

The env Task

As mentioned earlier, you can pass a list of users that ASET validates based on certain criteria. The environment variable for each of these users is checked for any security risks. The user information is retrieved using the /.profile, /.login, and ./cshrc files. ASET also checks whether the directory specified in the PATH variable should not be writable. The UMASK variable is also checked to ensure that no file that can be freely read or written to by all the users is created. Any security weaknesses found during these checks are reported to the administrator.

The eeprom Task

This task involves setting the eeprom parameter based on security level. If security level is medium, the parameter is set to command. It is set to full if the security level is high. A warning is generated if the parameter is not configured correctly.

The firewall Task

ASET provides security for firewalls configured on a network. The main task is to disable IP forwarding and to display routing information. Firewall provides security for both information coming into the network and information going out of the network.

ASET Environment File (asetenv)

As mentioned earlier, the ASET environment file is available in the /user/asset directory and is used by ASET for specifying the default working directory. The file consists of
two parts. The first part is called the *User Configurable Parameters*. This part contains certain environment variables that administrators can use for customizing ASET to perform
in a predefined manner. The other part is known as *ASET Internal Environment Variables*.
This part contains certain environment variables that pertain to the internal working of a
computer. These variables should not be modified.

The asetenv file also contains information regarding the list of directories whose environment variables need to be checked for security loopholes. The directories are placed at
one of the three security levels: low, medium, and high. All information stored in the
directories is checked regularly, and discrepancies, if found, are brought to the notice of
the administrators. Not all the files are checked; only the files listed in the directory list
and passed as a parameter to the ASET command are checked.

The asetenv file contains an environment variable named YPCHECK, which is a Boolean
parameter. This variable determines that the computer should check for security weaknesses both on system tables and on their equivalent NIS+ tables. This option is enabled
if the value is true and disabled if the value is false. Another variable, UID_ALIASES,
stores information about aliases for each user ID. In normal circumstances, ASET warns
the administrator if multiple user accounts are found sharing the same user ID. However,
in the case of alias files, users are allowed to share the same user ID and no warning is
generated.

You now know how to secure files and information stored on the computer by using NIS+
and ASET. I'll now discuss the Solaris Fingerprint Database and how to use it to check
for the authenticity of files and other stored information.

Solaris Fingerprint Database

In a networked environment, it is very difficult to determine that a user has modified any
of the system files and or startup scripts. Many tools are available that attempt to detect
modifications by checking the current copy of the file with an original copy. The original
copy is created and saved when the system is installed for the first time. *Solaris Fingerprint
Database* (sfpDB) is one such service that administrators can use to authenticate the
integrity of stored system files and scripts. The service checks for the authenticity of all
files stored in the /bin/su directory, Solaris patches, and any other products. The files
stored with the service should be updated to reflect any change whenever a software patch
is applied or a new application is installed. The files stored with the service forms the baseline on which all future checks are performed. The sfpDB provides an excellent mechanism to determine whether system binaries have been replaced by Trojans or other
malicious software.

How the Fingerprint Database Works

The sfpDB uses an MD5 hash encryption algorithm to compare digitally signed fingerprints with the original copies of the files stored with the service. This information is available over the network, so the verification can be performed online. After the check has been completed, you can determine whether the files have been tampered with. When any changes are made to the file, the original MD5 digital fingerprint is lost.

The database stores different types of information in the digital fingerprint. It stores information about the versions of packages, the path where they are stored, the name of products, and other information related to the product. You can have the same file used for different products as a product can have many versions.

The Solaris Fingerprint Database provides a complete list of digital fingerprints for all files available on a computer. Because the files need to be kept up-to-date, the database is updated regularly.

Generating a Fingerprint

As mentioned earlier, MD5 encryption is used for creating fingerprint signatures. Following is an example of how to create a fingerprint:

```
# /opt/md5/md5 -sparc /user/bin/su
MD5 (/usr/bin/su) = gj6dy63f5fkj6ga2krs9n2hjk48nbdyitnm3e68f43fj7
```

Similarly, you can create multiple MD5 entries. You can use the find() command to create an MD5 signature for files that have been modified recently. You can also create MD5 digital fingerprints for all the files stored in a particular directory.

Summary

In this chapter, you learned about the various network security tools available in Solaris. You learned about NIS+ and how it differs from NIS+, although both share similar names. You also learned how to setup NIS+ master servers and NIS+ clients. Then, you learned about LDAP and how you can migrate from NIS+ to LDAP. Next, you learned about ASET and discussed its features. Finally, you learne about the Solaris Fingerprint Database and how you can use the utility to authenticate the integrity of stored system files and scripts.

Check Your Understanding

Multiple Choice Questions

1. Which of the following services runs on the NIS master server and performs the task of replicating NIS maps to the slave servers?

   a. YPXFRD

   b. YP

   c. YPBIND

2. Which of the following daemons provide NIS+ client computer access to NIS maps?

   a. YPXFRD

   b. YP

   c. YPBIND

3. Which of the following statements are true?

   Statement A: NIS maintains information in multicolumn tables.

   Statement B: The YP server daemon runs on all the slave servers and services all NIS client requests.

   a. Both A and B are correct.

   b. A is correct while B is incorrect.

   c. A is incorrect while B is correct.

   d. Both are incorrect.

4. Which of the following are valid differences between NIS+ and NIS? (Select all that apply.)

   a. Commands and names used in NIS are not case-sensitive, whereas the ones in NIS+ are case-sensitive.

   b. In NIS, the client queries are bound to one server, whereas in NIS+, any server can handle client queries.

   c. NIS+ follows a hierarchical domain model, whereas NIS+ follows a flat model.

   d. There are a maximum of 1,024 bytes in an NIS record, but there is no such restriction for NIS+ records.

5. Which of the following statements are true? (Select all that apply.)

   a. NIS uses incremental updating to synchronize records between the master server and the slave servers.

   b. NIS+ uses incremental updating to synchronize records between the master server and the slave servers.

    c. Both NIS+ and NIS provide facility for authorization, authentication, and RPC.

    d. The facility for authorization, authentication, and RPC is only available in NIS+.

6. Which object available in NIS+ is used for storing information about the user accounts and administrative groups available in NIS+?

    a. Directory object

    b. Table object

    c. Group object

    d. Link object

7. Which object available in NIS+ is similar to NIS+ maps and is used for storing network information?

    a. Directory object

    b. Table object

    c. Group object

    d. Link object

8. Which of the following statements are true?

    Statement A: In NIS+, each subdomain has its own master server and domain servers.

    Statement B: It is advisable to have at least one replication server in a domain.

    a. Both A and B are correct.

    b. A is correct while B is incorrect.

    c. A is incorrect while B is correct.

    d. Both are incorrect.

9. Which task in ASET is executed only once?

    a. `cklist`

    b. `usrgrp`

    c. `tune`

    d. `sysconf`

10. Which script is used for creating root domains in NIS+?

    a. `nisserver`

    b. `nispopulate`

    c. `ninsd`

    d. `ninscat`

11. From the list of tables given below, identify all the valid NIS+ tables.

    a. `auto_master`

    b. `auto_slave`

    c. `auto_home`

    d. `protocols`

    e. `bootparams`

    f. `users`

    g. netmasks

Short Questions

1. What is a directory service?
2. Define LDIF and discuss what is it used for? .

Answers

Multiple Choice Answers

1. **a.** The `YPXFRD` service runs on the master server and replicates the NIS maps to the slave servers.

2. **c.** The `YPBIND` daemon is used to allow an NIS client computer to access NIS maps.

3. **c.** In NIS, all information is stored in the form of a two-dimensional table. In NIS+, all the information is stored in the form of a multicolumn table. The YP server daemon runs on all the slave servers and is responsible for processing all NIS client requests and queries.

4. **b, c, d.** In NIS, the commands and the names are case-sensitive. In NIS+, the commands and the names are not case-sensitive. In NIS, clients are directly bound to a specific server. Therefore, when the client queries for certain information, the query is directed to a predefined server. However, in NIS+, the client query can be serviced by any of the available NIS+ servers. This is because all the servers have the same updated NIS+ maps. NIS supported the concept of flat namespaces. This means that only one domain was available in NIS that could be accessed by the host or the client. In contrast, NIS+ supports hierarchical domains. The hierarchical structure of the NIS+ namespace can be based on the logical hierarchy implemented in the organization. This helps in providing meaningful names and administration of the network. You can also create separate domains for each level or division of the organization. There can be a

maximum of only 1,024 bytes in an NIS record. In contrast, there is no such restriction in the case of NIS+ records.

5. **b, d.** In NIS, any change made to the NIS maps means that the master server has to resend all the NIS maps to each of the slave servers. In NIS+, the master server only needs to update the changes made to NIS+ maps stored on the master server to the copies stored on the slave servers, which is called incremental updation. This leads to a more efficient and faster replication. The master server can easily synchronize its information with the information available on the slave servers. NIS+ performs the tasks of a naming service and provides information about RPC. It stores information about RPC program names in the /etc directory. This service was previously not available in NIS.

6. **c.** The group object stores information about the administrative user groups available in NIS+. These administrative groups are assigned the right to manage and modify the namespace based on the rights of every user.

7. **b.** The table objects are similar to the NIS+ maps and store network information. The tables can contain either an entry object or the value zero. The value zero indicates that the object is empty. By default, the table contains 17 objects and is administered using the `nist blodm` command and the `nisdetect` command. Each entry object creates a new record in the table.

8. **a.** In addition to the root server, there can be multiple master servers and slave servers. Each subdomain will have its own master server and slave servers. Although the presence of a replication server is optional, it is advisable to have at least one replication server. This ensures that the replication server can act as a backup if the master server is down.

9. **c.** The `tune` task is performed once at the time of installation. The task involves adding restrictions or tightening permissions regarding system files. After installation, all the system files and directories have limited security settings on file permissions to facilitate sharing of information.

10. **a.** The `nisserver` script is used to create the root domain.

11. **a, c, d, e, g.** From the given list, the valid tables that are available in NIS+ are `auto_master`, `auto_home`, `protocols`, `bootparams`, and `netmasks`.

Short Answers

1. A directory service is a database whose primary objective is to provide information rather than to write the information. A directory is not used for performing complicated transactions and does not provide the facility to rollback incomplete or unsuccessful transactions. A directory performs updates by implementing either all the changes or none at all. Directories provide faster search and lookup procedures because of their simple structure. The directories replicate information on multiple servers to ensure easy availability and reliability of information, which also ensures faster lookup of specific information. Although

there might be a slight time lag between replication on each of the servers, ultimately all the servers will contain the same information.

2. LDAP Data Interchange Format (LDIF) is in ASCII format and is used for transferring directory information between two LDAP directory servers or between a client and a server. It can also be used for working with command-line utilities on the LDAP server. An LDAP file contains information that is stored in a hierarchical order of entries.

Chapter 5

*Implementing
System Security*

In this chapter, you'll learn how to implement security on a Solaris computer. You'll also learn how to identify the system settings and make modifications to the settings based on your system requirements. In addition, you will learn more about auditing. Chapter 1, "Security: An Overview," introduced you to auditing. This chapter will elaborate on concepts related to auditing. In Chapter 1, you learned that all auditing information is stored in log files. Log files are created when errors are raised or when certain information, which is critical to the functioning of the operating system, needs to be stored safely. Log files are also created for auditing user and application activities. You may wonder why administrators do not perform auditing in a systematic manner when logging is such a critical activity. Not all administrators are equally experienced. Some administrators may not be able to implement effective auditing, while some may not be able to analyze the logs properly at regular intervals to retrieve the relevant information. You need to analyze log files at regular intervals to ensure that intrusions or errors are detected and preventive measures are implemented in time.

Solaris records all information related to security or events that may cause security threats in system logs. To modify these logs in future, you need to fully understand how these logs are created.

System Identification

When hackers try to gain access to your computer, they want to know the system configuration setting of your computer. This is the information that uniquely identifies your computer on the network. However, not all hackers entertain this concept. Some amateur hackers attempt to search for any system on the network that has an open or unsecured port. They use this unsecured port to gain access to the computer. Some of the utilities that may expose unsecured ports are Telnet, File Transfer Protocol (FTP), and applications running on Web servers. Hackers can also use port sniffers for detecting unsecured ports, but this is not a very common occurrence. Most system administrators make sure that all ports exposed to external users are adequately secured. In most cases, professional hackers gain access to a computer based on the system configuration settings of the computer. For example, the data packets that enter or leave a network may contain information about the operating system from which the data packets originated, the address of the source computer, and the information about firewalls such as (routers) through which the data packets passed.

Addressing the security issues of all servers individually is tedious and time-consuming. Therefore, it is preferable to automate the process of securing servers. For this purpose, Solaris provides a tool called *JumpStart*. This tool was introduced in Solaris 2.1 and is used for automatically installing Solaris with the required security settings. JumpStart provides a common baseline security setting for all servers. The following section focuses on this tool.

Using JumpStart

As mentioned earlier, the JumpStart toolkit provides all servers a common baseline security setting by installing a group of servers with the same security settings. You can also use the JumpStart environment to help apply the latest updates to the environment. The JumpStart environment does so by re-building the entire system from scratch with new updates, or by installing the new software directly onto the system. Another important advantage is the simplification of system reconstruction due to major hardware failures and replacements. A JumpStart client computer boots from the network, and the client then broadcasts a request on the network to search for the JumpStart server. The server responds to the request after confirming that it has the appropriate permissions for installing and configuring Solaris on the client computers. However, to start client installation, you first require a running JumpStart server. The following section focuses on how you can install and configure a JumpStart server.

Installing a JumpStart Server

To begin the installation of a JumpStart server, you first need to create a /jumpstart directory and copy the Solaris image file to a /jumpstart/OS directory. The name of the directory should be based on the version of the Solaris that is being used. You can create multiple directories if you want to maintain copies of the updates and new releases of Solaris. Then you execute the setup_install_server command, which is available on the Solaris CD. The syntax of the command is as follows:

```
# ./setup_install_server /jumpstart/OS/Solaris_9.0_06-02
```

In the preceding code, the . (dot) symbol used in the path refers to the current folder on the first Solaris CD. After the first CD has been installed, you need to repeat the process by using the second CD. In case of the second CD, you need to use the following command:

```
# ./add_to_install_server /jumpstart/OS/Solaris_9.0_06-02
```

The add_to_install_server command is available in the current folder of the second Solaris CD. The rest of the process is automated, and the JumpStart server is installed. After the server has been installed, you need to configure the server for processing the client requests. For this purpose, you need to add the following entry in the /etc/dfs/dfstab file:

```
share -F nfs -0 ro -d "JumpStart Directory" /jumpstart
```

Next, you need to provide access rights to all the clients that try to access the server by using the following command:

```
# shareall
```

Now that you have installed the JumpStart server, you can continue with installing the JumpStart client computers.

Installing JumpStart Clients

Before a client can be installed using information stored on the JumpStart server, the IP address of the client computer needs to be registered on the server. This information can be provided either by using NIS or NIS+ or by adding an entry for each client in the /etc/hosts and the /etc/ethers files. When the add_install_client command is executed on the client computer, it creates an entry for the JumpStart server in the /etc/bootparams file stored on the client computer. The following entry is added to the /etc/ethers file:

```
6:0:62:75:d6:6f solclient01
```

The following line is added to the /etc/hosts file. You need to add a separate entry for each client that requires access to the JumpStart server.

```
190:160:165:107 solclient01
```

Now you need to execute the following command for registering the JumpStart client on the JumpStart server.

```
# pwd /jumpstart/OS/ Solaris_9.0_06-02/Solaris/Tools
# ./add_install_clinet -c solserver:/jumpstart \-p solserver:
/jumpstart solclient01 sun4m
```

The add_install_client command automatically starts any service that is required for the installation and configuration of the JumpStart client computer. The service can even exist on the JumpStart server. However, for the server to be able to install all the required services, you need to create a rule file containing these specifications.

Creating a rule File

The rule file is a simple text file that contains information regarding how Solaris needs to be installed on client computers and what services need to be installed on the client computer. This file must be located in the JumpStart directory of the JumpStart server. You can create different rules for creating different types of client computers. Following is a sample entry in a rule file.

```
hostname www - Profiles/inet.profile -
```

A typical `rule` entry contains five fields, `rule_keyword`, `rule_value`, `begin`, `profile`, and `finish`. The `rule_keyword` field, the `rule_value` field, and the `profile` field are essential, while the other two fields are optional. A brief explanation of the fields is given below:

◆ **`rule_keyword`.** This field is used for specifying a system attribute that needs to be searched on the client computer. For example, in the preceding code, the attribute `hostname` will be searched. The toolkit contains a sample `rules.SAMPLE` file, which uses a keyword any to match all client systems.

◆ **`rule_value`.** This is used for specifying a value that needs to be searched. This information corresponds to the attribute defined in the `rule_keyword` field. The field will contain the name of the client computer that is added to the JumpStart server. In the sample `rules.SAMPLE` file mentioned above uses a hyphen (-) to correspond with keyword any.

◆ **`profile`.** This is a reference to a different file that is used for storing information about the Solaris operating system. This field contains information about the system configuration settings that need to be applied to the client computer. This configuration information may contain information like Solaris OE cluster specifics— whether the JumpStart will be an initial installation or upgrade, or the layout of Disks `rules.SAMPLE` file uses a hyphen in this field to see that the JumpStart server performs a default configuration.

◆ **`finish`.** This is used to contain a reference to an executable Bourne shell script. This shell script is run immediately after the client installation is completed. The toolkit uses a script named `Driver script` that references other scripts available in the toolkit to implement the system settings. The `nomatch.beg` script is called by `rules.SAMPLE` file to display JumpStart client information.

 NOTE

You may have noticed that only four of the five fields have been explained in the preceding list. This is because the JumpStart toolkit uses these four field rules during installation.

If you need additional information regarding how to configure the JumpStart toolkit, you can refer to the documentation available at the Sun site http://www.sun.com/documentation/. Other tools are available in Solaris that are used for system identification. For example, the `ifconfig` command is used for assigning address to network interfaces while the `host id` command is used for displaying the host ID information. Some of these tools are discussed in the following section.

Using Other System Identification Utilities

The ifconfig command is primarily used for assigning addresses to network interfaces. The utility also provides certain parameters that can be used for configuring network interfaces. You can use the utility for assigning the network address during or after installation, for specifying the address, or for changing it. You can also execute the command without any parameter for displaying the network address of a network interface. Two versions of ifconfig are available on a computer. These versions are stored in the /sbin directory and the /user/sbin directory. The primary difference between the two versions is the way in which the names are checked. In the case of the /sbin/ifconfig command, the sequence in which the names are searched is fixed at the time of system booting, while in the case of the /user/sbin/ifconfig command, the sequence of names can be changed using the /etc/nsswitch switch.

Following is a list of some options that can be used with the ifconfig command:

- ◆ **arp**. This is used for enabling *Address Resolution Protocol (ARP)*. This protocol is used for providing a link between link-level addresses and network-level addresses used on a computer. You can disable the use of this protocol by using the -arp option.

- ◆ **addif**. This is used for creating a logical interface on a specified network interface.

- ◆ **auto-dhcp**. This is used for configuring an interface to be automatically assigned an IP address from a DHCP server.

- ◆ **wait**. This is used for pausing the command execution for a specific period or until a specific task is completed. In case no wait period has been provided and the application has not finished executing, ifconfig will wait for 30 seconds.

- ◆ **drop**. This is used to remove a specific network interface from DHCP control.

- ◆ **ping**. This is used to check whether a network interface is working and whether it has been assigned an IP address by a DHCP server. There are certain options that can be used with the ping command for gathering information about machines on the network. Some of these options are extend, inform, release, start, and status.

The host id command is used to display the host ID information about the current computer in a hexadecimal format. Every computer has a unique host ID, which is displayed using this command.

The arp command is used for displaying and modifying information about the Internet addresses used by ARP. The Internet-to-Ethernet address translations are available in the form of tables, which can only be referenced using the arp command. If you do not specify a parameter with the command, the ARP entry for the current system is displayed. You can specify the hostname by either using the assigned name, IP address, or the Internet name. The Internet name always follows the dot notation. Following is a list of the options that can be used with the arp command:

◆ **a.** This is used for displaying all the ARP entries that exist in the current table.

◆ **d.** This is used for deleting a specific ARP entry and can only be accessed by the **superuser** account.

◆ **f.** This is used for reading a file whose name is passed as parameter and creates corresponding entries in the ARP table.

◆ **s.** This is used for creating an ARP entry for a specified host computer and uses the specified Ethernet address.

Another method of ensuring system security is implementing auditing on the computer. Auditing helps you keep track of the activities that occur on a computer. In addition, it helps you detect traces of intrusion. This concept will be discussed at great length in the next section.

Enabling Logging

You can use the default logging mechanism available in Solaris or any third-party logging mechanisms for enabling users to log on to your computer. Some of these applications only need to be enabled once, while others need to be manually started every time the computer restarts. Other applications have to be run periodically so that information can be retrieved in the log files and analyzed. You can also set different levels of security in these log files so that while some log files generate alerts for all events, others raise alerts only at specific events. Instead of storing information in the default location, you can assign certain files or directories where this information is stored. Make sure that you have adequate disk space to store the files and that the log information conforms to the security policies implemented on your computer.

It is also important to ensure the security of the logged information and protect it from unauthorized access and from being modified by unauthorized users. Only the root or selective users and services should have the right to read from or write to the log files. You must also ensure the physical security of the log files so that an unauthorized user cannot access the old log files or make modifications to the files. Following are some of the measures that you can implement to make sure that only authorized users are able to access the log files.

◆ **Encrypt log files.** Ensure that all the log files are encrypted before storage so that intruders are not able to read the log files even if they get physical access to the server.

◆ **Maintain log files on a separate server.** It is preferable to maintain a separate log server that is dedicated to storing log files. The log server should be placed in a separate physical location that cannot be easily accessed from the network.

◆ **Change log attributes.** It is possible for you to change the file attributes of log files so that information can only be added or appended to the log files but cannot be modified or deleted.

◆ **Archive log files.** It is preferable to archive log files in certain media that can only be written to once. For example, you can store the log files on CD-ROMs or tape drives that can only be written to once; information stored on these media cannot be easily erased or modified.

It is preferable to store the log files on the local computer, because it is not easy to secure all local computers from intruders. You can also store the log files on external storage media that can be written to once. Although this task involves additional effort and a constant supply of media, it is the most secure method. You can also store the information on a remote server. Make sure that the server is kept in close proximity to the clients that generate the log files. It is a recommended practice to connect the clients and the server using single point-to-point cables. This ensures that hackers cannot get access to the information that is transmitted between the computers. If it is necessary to keep the log server at a distant location, you need to reduce the number of network connections and routers that the information has to pass through. Each network point and each router is a potential security threat and point of intrusion. You can also encrypt the data as it is generated before being stored on the server.

Solaris provides many logging mechanisms for generating the log files and storing the information. I'll now consider the system logs generated in Solaris in detail.

Defining a System Log

A system administrator's job involves managing and monitoring system resources. Administrators have numerous tools for ensuring the security of a computer. System administrators can use log files created on a computer as one of the fundamental but effective security tools. These log files are also known as *system logs*. A system log stores information about certain events or activities that have occurred on the computer. Sometimes these events are caused because of errors that occur on the system. These events are grouped into severity levels based on the type of the error. The events are recorded in the log files based on the type of log file and the conditions set by an administrator for the file. A system log file typically stores information about the event along with the timestamp and other information specific to the message. You can use the system log files to trace the cause of problems and the source of errors. These logs also contain information about the damages caused to the system because of errors raised by certain services. One of the utilities that an administrator uses to ease the job of maintaining logs is the syslog utility.

Using syslog

As mentioned earlier, Solaris uses the syslog utility for logging errors and other pieces of information. The utility is easy to configure and supported in almost all the versions of Solaris. The same logging mechanism was also available in UNIX. The utility executes a daemon known as syslogd. The daemon starts when the system boots into the multiuse mode and continues to run until the system is powered down. You can use the `syslog` utility to implement logging on both the local computer and remote servers. The `syslog` utility contains the following files and functions:

◆ `logger`. This is a UNIX command and adds single-line entries to log files. You can specify multiple arguments with the command, and each command creates a separate entry when it is executed. If no parameter is specified, then the standard input is directly entered into the log file. You can use the `-f` option to specify an existing file as the source of information.

◆ `/etc/syslog.conf`. This file provides information about what entries should be logged in the file. It also contains information about where specific entries should be logged.

◆ `syslog()`. This is an Application Program Interface (API) that is accessed by multiple files.

◆ `syslogd`. This is a system daemon that is used to receive and route system log events received from the `syslogd()` API and the `logger` command. The file examines the messages received by the system and directs them to the correct user or log file. The final destination of a message is based on the priority of the message and the service from which it is derived. The daemon creates an entry in the `/etc/syslog.conf` file. Each entry stores information about when the entry was created and the priority of the message. The priority information is stored in the form of a number contained within two angle brackets (`<>`). The priority information is an ASCII integer value encoded using eight bits. The first three bits provide information about the severity level of the message, and the last five bits provide information about the message facility. Therefore, you can have eight possible severity levels and 32 possible facilities. In the upcoming sections, you'll learn about message facilities and severity levels.

Creating Messages in syslog

All messages in `syslog` are created as plaintext and stored in an ASCII format. These messages are then displayed in a simple format to users. You need to be clear about the difference between logged messages and `syslog` messages. Simple logged messages are immediately entered into the log files or are directly displayed to users. In contrast, `syslog` messages are directly sent to the `syslog` utility for processing. The template for the message format is stored in the file `syslog.h` located in the `/user/include` directory. This file contains information about the priority level of the message and the facilities that generate this message.

A typical `syslog` message contains the following components:

◆ Priority information about the message

◆ Timestamp containing information about when the error occurred and when the message was created

◆ Actual text providing a description of the error

After a message is raised, the `syslogd` daemon sends the logged message directly to users, log files, or the console. The `syslog` utility contains a library of functions that are used for process these messages.

Facilities Available in syslog

Facilities in Solaris can be considered as service areas for which error messages are generated. All services available in Solaris can be classified under one of the following facilities or service areas. Table 5-1 lists all the facilities available in Solaris.

Table 5-1 Facilities Available in *syslog*

Facility	Description
LOG_USER	This is the default facility available on the system. This stores errors that are unsystematically generated by user processes. It is used to store information that cannot be classified under any other category.
LOG_MAIL	This is used to store errors generated by the mail system.
LOG_KERN	This is used to store errors that are specific to the kernel and cannot be raised by a user process.
LOG_LOCAL0-7	This is reserved for storing messages raised by eight categories that are classified locally by the system. It contains messages raised from LOG_LOCAL0 to 7.
LOG_DAEMON	This is used to store errors raised by system daemons, such as `ftpd`, `routed`, `smtp`, and `rsh`.
LOG_AUTH	This is used to store errors raised by the authorization programs available on a computer, for example, `su`, `getty`, and `login`.
LOG_LPR	This is used to store error information generated by the printer.
LOG_NEWS	This is used to store error information generated by the UseNet News system.
LOG_CRON	This is used to store error information generated by `cron` and `at`.
LOG_UUCP	This is used to store error information generated by the UUCP system.
LOG_MARK	This is used to store error information generated by syslog and contains records of the time when the entries were created.

In addition to facilities, certain severity levels are available in Solaris. All error messages generated by the system are categorized under one of these severity levels. You'll now learn about these severity levels in detail.

Severity Levels in System Logs

Certain severity levels are associated with the syslog utility. Following is a list of the severity levels and their description:

◆ LOG_ERR. This severity level covers all other system errors.

◆ LOG_NOTICE. This severity level raises warnings about errors that are not critical.

◆ LOG_DEBUG. This severity level raises messages that contain debugging information.

◆ LOG_INFO. This severity level raises messages that provide information about the working of a computer.

◆ LOG_WARNING. This severity level raises warnings about errors.

◆ LOG_EMERG. This is the most critical severity level and can cause the system to shut down without warning.

◆ LOG_CRIT. This severity level provides advance warning about imminent hardware or software failures.

◆ LOG_ALERT. This severity level generates information about system events that require immediate attention.

Now that you know about the services that raise errors and the severity levels of the messages, you can focus on how to configure syslog to handle these error messages and alerts.

Configuring syslog

The task of configuring syslog involves retrieving error messages raised by different applications. These error messages can be either stored in log files on the local computer or at a central computer. The error messages can also be directly sent to the users currently logged on to the computer. If the messages are stored at a central computer, the computer should be dedicated for only storing syslog information. The syslog information is stored in the /etc/syslog.conf file. Figure 5-1 shows a typical syslog.conf file.

As shown in the preceding figure, the file contains information about where the error logs must be sent and the corresponding actions that need to be performed. The information is divided into two parts. The first part is called selector, and the second part is known as action. A tab character separates both the pieces of information. The selector part contains the facility and severity level grouped together. You can create a separate entry for

```
Text Editor - syslog.conf
 File  Edit  Format  Options                                                                Help

#ident  "@(#)syslog.conf    1.5    98/12/14 SMI"  /* SunOS 5.0 */
#
# Copyright (c) 1991-1998 by Sun Microsystems, Inc.
# All rights reserved.
#
# syslog configuration file.
#
# This file is processed by m4 so be careful to quote (`') names
# that match m4 reserved words.  Also, within ifdef's, arguments
# containing commas must be quoted.
#
*.err;kern.notice;auth.notice                 /dev/sysmsg
*.err;kern.debug;daemon.notice;mail.crit      /var/adm/messages

*.alert;kern.err;daemon.err                    operator
*.alert                                        root

*.emerg                                        *

# if a non-loghost machine chooses to have authentication messages
# sent to the loghost machine, un-comment out the following line:
#auth.notice                   ifdef(`LOGHOST', /var/log/authlog, @loghost)

mail.debug                    ifdef(`LOGHOST', /var/log/syslog, @loghost)

#
# non-loghost machines will use the following lines to cause "user"
# log messages to be logged locally.
#
ifdef(`LOGHOST', ,
user.err                                       /dev/sysmsg
user.err                                       /var/adm/messages
user.alert                                     `root, operator'
user.emerg                                     *
)
```

FIGURE 5-1 *A sample* `syslog.conf` *file*

each pair of facility and severity levels. A few sample entries are `facility.level`, `mail.debug`, or `auth.notice`. There can be different valid combinations created using each facility and severity level. The `action` part stores the name, path information, and `userid` of the system.

CAUTION

It is important to remember that both the parts of an entry, `selector` and `action`, must be separated by a tab and not by spaces.

The first part of the file contains certain commented information that needs to be followed if you make some changes to the file or add new entries manually to the file. The next line of code specifies the action that needs to be performed if an `err` message is raised by all the facilities and a `notice` error is received from the `kern` and `auth` facilities. This information is sent to the device `/dev/console`. The entry appears as shown in Figure 5-2. The next entry directs the following messages to the `/var/adm/message` file. These facilities and severity levels that raise the messages are:

◆ The `err` messages for all facilities
◆ The `debug` message returned by the `kern` facility
◆ The `notice` messages raised by the `daemon facilities`
◆ The `crit` from the `mail` facility

```
#ident  "@(#)syslog.conf      1.5      98/12/14 SMI"   /* SunOS 5.0 */
#
# Copyright (c) 1991-1998 by Sun Microsystems, Inc.
# All rights reserved.
#
# syslog configuration file.
#
# This file is processed by m4 so be careful to quote (`') names
# that match m4 reserved words.  Also, within ifdef's, arguments
# containing commas must be quoted.
#
*.err;kern.notice;auth.notice               /dev/sysmsg
*.err;kern.debug;daemon.notice;mail.crit    /var/adm/messages
```

FIGURE 5-2 *Entry on how the* `err` *messages are handled*

The next entry provides information about how `alert` messages should be handled. The user `operator` processes the `alert` messages raised by all the facilities and the `err` messages raised by the `kern` and `daemon` facilities. The next entry sends all the `alert` messages raised to the `root` account for processing. These entries appear as shown in Figure 5-3.

```
#ident  "@(#)syslog.conf      1.5      98/12/14 SMI"   /* SunOS 5.0 */
#
# Copyright (c) 1991-1998 by Sun Microsystems, Inc.
# All rights reserved.
#
# syslog configuration file.
#
# This file is processed by m4 so be careful to quote (`') names
# that match m4 reserved words.  Also, within ifdef's, arguments
# containing commas must be quoted.
#
*.err;kern.notice;auth.notice               /dev/sysmsg
*.err;kern.debug;daemon.notice;mail.crit    /var/adm/messages

*.alert;kern.err;daemon.err                 operator
*.alert                                     root
```

FIGURE 5-3 *Entry on how the* `alert` *messages are handled*

The next entry in the file collects all the `err` messages raised by the facilities and sends them to all the users logged on to the local computer. Next, all the `debug` messages raised by the `mail` facility are sent to the `/var/log/syslog` file. If the name of the local computer is `loghost`, then the information is sent to it. Otherwise, the NIS server or the DNS server resolves the computer name. The `loghost` computer name is specified by default as the name of the local host, and the entry is created in the `/etc/hosts` file. You can change this entry to the name of the computer you want to log on to. You only need to use the `event.lognost` syntax, which is available in the `/etc/syslog.conf` file for creating this entry. A sample entry appears as shown in Figure 5-4.

```
#ident  "@(#)syslog.conf      1.5     98/12/14 SMI"   /* SunOS 5.0 */
#
# Copyright (c) 1991-1998 by Sun Microsystems, Inc.
# All rights reserved.
#
# syslog configuration file.
#
# This file is processed by m4 so be careful to quote (`') names
# that match m4 reserved words.  Also, within ifdef's, arguments
# containing commas must be quoted.
#
*.err;kern.notice;auth.notice                    /dev/sysmsg
*.err;kern.debug;daemon.notice;mail.crit         /var/adm/messages

*.alert;kern.err;daemon.err                      operator
*.alert                                          root

*.emerg                                          *

# if a non-loghost machine chooses to have authentication messages
# sent to the loghost machine, un-comment out the following line:
#auth.notice                     ifdef(`LOGHOST', /var/log/authlog, @loghost)

mail.debug                       ifdef(`LOGHOST', /var/log/syslog, @loghost)
```

FIGURE 5-4 *An entry when the* err *messages should be handled by the local computer*

The final entry in the file sends all the messages raised by the user facility to the console. It also sends the information to the user's root operator and the /var/adm/messages file. The information is sent to the root operator only if the name of the local computer is loghost. The final entry appears as shown in Figure 5-5.

```
mail.debug                       ifdef(`LOGHOST', /var/log/syslog, @loghost)

#
# non-loghost machines will use the following lines to cause "user"
# log messages to be logged locally.
#
ifdef(`LOGHOST', ,
user.err                                /dev/sysmsg
user.err                                /var/adm/messages
user.alert                              `root, operator'
user.emerg                              *
)
```

FIGURE 5-5 *Entry on how the* user *facility handles messages*

When the Solaris operating system boots, the syslogd process runs in the user name-space. The syslogd process is one of the first processes to be started. This ensures that services that are started after the syslogd process can use the log files already created by the syslogd process. The /etc/syslog.conf file provides the initial information for the syslogd process to function. You can also configure the syslogd process to search the configuration file by sending the SIGHUP signal to the file. You can send this signal by using the kill -1 syslogd_pid command.

Debugging syslog

The syslog utility has a built-in debugging facility that administrators can use to check the flow of information. The process of debugging syslog involves two steps. These steps are:

◆ At system startup, all the information stored in the `syslog.conf` file appears in a two-dimensional format.

◆ After the **syslog** utility is configured, all the messages are displayed and information about how these messages will be processed is recorded.

The following steps need to be performed for starting debugging in `syslog`.

1. Use the `kill -15 222` command to kill the `syslogd` process. The output appears as shown in Figure 5-6.

FIGURE 5-6 *Using the* `kill` *command to stop the* `syslogd` *utility*

2. At the command prompt, type the `/usr/sbin/syslogd -d` command to restart `syslogd`. The utility is started in the debug mode, and the output appears as shown in Figure 5-7.

```
# kill -15 222
Apr 24 15:39:52 solaris1 syslogd: going down on signal 15
# /usr/sbin/syslogd -d
main(1): Started at time Wed Apr 24 15:42:27 2002
getnets(1): found 1 addresses, they are: 0.0.0.0.2.2
amiloghost(1): testing 127.0.0.1.2.2
conf_init(1): I am loghost
```

FIGURE 5-7 *Restarting the* `syslogd` *utility*

As shown in the preceding figure, the utility displays the address of the computer and the computer name. The next section contains information that has been retrieved from the `syslog.conf` file. The information is displayed using the `cfline` command. This section appears as shown in Figure 5-8.

```
# kill -15 222
Apr 24 15:39:52 solaris1 syslogd: going down on signal 15
# /usr/sbin/syslogd -d
main(1): Started at time Wed Apr 24 15:42:27 2002
getnets(1): found 1 addresses, they are: 0.0.0.0.2.2
amiloghost(1): testing 127.0.0.1.2.2
conf_init(1): I am loghost
cfline(1): (*.err;kern.notice;auth.notice                    /dev/sysmsg)
cfline(1): (*.err;kern.debug;daemon.notice;mail.crit    /var/adm/messages)
cfline(1): (*.alert;kern.err;daemon.err                operator)
cfline(1): (*.alert                                          root)
cfline(1): (*.emerg                                           *)
cfline(1): (mail.debug                    /var/log/syslog)
open_door(1): creating door: DoorFd=8
```

FIGURE 5-8 *Using the* cfline *command to display information from the* syslog.conf *file*

The current version of the syslogd file appears as shown in Figure 5-9. The figure also displays the matrix of all messages raised and processed by the system. The various facilities are displayed in the columns and each row signifies a user or a file that processes the message.

```
  syslogd: version 1.89
  Started: Wed Apr 24 15:42:27 2002
Input message count: system 0, network 0
# Outputs: 6

------------------- priority = [file, facility] -------------------

0 0 0 0 0 0 0 0 0 0 1 1 1 1 1 1 1 1 1 1
0 1 2 3 4 5 6 7 8 9 0 1 2 3 4 5 6 7 8 9
-------------------------------------------------
5 3 3 3 5 3 3 3 3 3 3 3 3 3 3 3 3 3 3 3 CONSOLE: /dev/sysmsg
7 3 2 5 3 3 3 3 3 3 3 3 3 3 3 3 3 3 3 3 FILE: /var/adm/messages
3 1 1 3 1 1 1 1 1 1 1 1 1 1 1 1 1 1 1 1 USERS: operator
1 1 1 1 1 1 1 1 1 1 1 1 1 1 1 1 1 1 1 1 USERS: root
0 0 0 0 0 0 0 0 0 0 0 0 0 0 0 0 0 0 0 0 WALL:
X X 7 X X X X X X X X X X X X X X X X X FILE: /var/log/syslog
```

FIGURE 5-9 *Severity levels and version information*

The columns that appear are as follows:

◆ kern

◆ user

◆ mail

◆ daemon

◆ auth

◆ security

◆ mark

◆ syslog

◆ lpr

◆ news

◆ uucp

◆ cron

◆ local0-7

Each value in the matrix signifies a severity level. The numbers correspond to the following levels:

◆ panic   0

◆ emerg   0

◆ alert   1

◆ crit   2

◆ err   3

◆ error   3

◆ warning   4

◆ warn   4

◆ notice   5

◆ info   6

◆ debug   7

◆ none   16

Figure 5-10 displays severity levels and services as they appear in the syslog.config file.

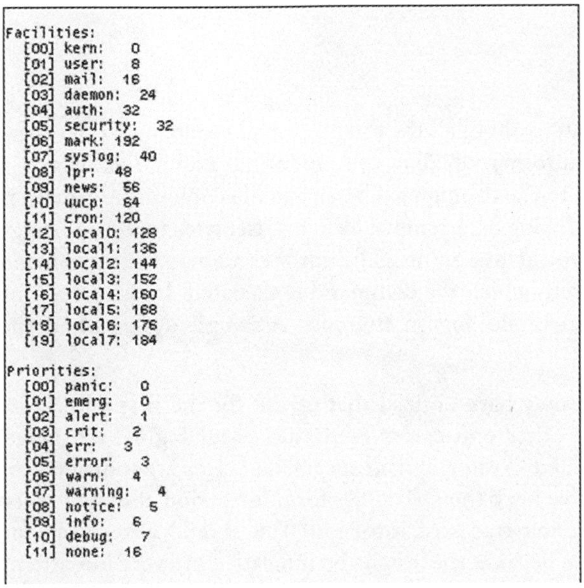

```
Facilities:
  [00] kern:    0
  [01] user:    8
  [02] mail:    16
  [03] daemon:  24
  [04] auth:    32
  [05] security:  32
  [06] mark: 192
  [07] syslog:  40
  [08] lpr:   48
  [09] news:   56
  [10] uucp:   64
  [11] cron:  120
  [12] local0: 128
  [13] local1: 136
  [14] local2: 144
  [15] local3: 152
  [16] local4: 160
  [17] local5: 168
  [18] local6: 176
  [19] local7: 184

Priorities:
  [00] panic:   0
  [01] emerg:   0
  [02] alert:   1
  [03] crit:    2
  [04] err:     3
  [05] error:   3
  [06] warn:    4
  [07] warning:   4
  [08] notice:    5
  [09] info:    6
  [10] debug:   7
  [11] none:   16
```

FIGURE 5-10 *The severity levels and facilities information*

The information also appears in a tabulated form. A separate entry is created for each file and each user. Each entry displays the total number of errors in the file.

3. You can test the syslog facility either by waiting for an event or by deliberately causing an event to occur. In both the cases, an entry is added to the appropriate log file. You can use the logger to cause an event to occur and to create a corresponding entry in the system log file.

4. You can end the syslog testing process by pressing Ctrl+C. syslog comes out of the debug mode and displays information as shown in Figure 5-11.

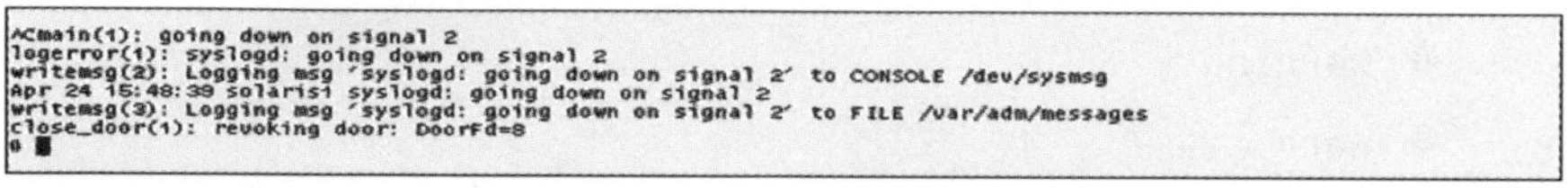

```
^Cmain(1): going down on signal 2
logerror(1): syslogd: going down on signal 2
writemsg(2): Logging msg 'syslogd: going down on signal 2' to CONSOLE /dev/sysmsg
Apr 24 15:48:39 solaris1 syslogd: going down on signal 2
writemsg(3): Logging msg 'syslogd: going down on signal 2' to FILE /var/adm/messages
close_door(1): revoking door: DoorFd=8
#
```

FIGURE 5-11 *The information displayed when the* syslog *utility is stopped*

5. You can then restart the syslogd utility in the normal mode by typing the command /usr/sbin/syslog.

You can also store information about the users who tried to log on to the network. The sulog file contains information about both successful and unsuccessful logon attempts. The following section will discuss this file in detail.

Using the sulog File

The sulog file stores information about all the attempts made to logon to the network by using the su command. This information allows you to monitor all individuals or services attempting to gain root access to the computer. The sulog file contains information about both successful and unsuccessful log on attempts. When a user tries to log on using the su command, an entry is added to the sulog file. The entry contains information about the date, the time, and the port from which the command is executed. It also stores information about successful and unsuccessful log on attempts. A sample sulog file is shown in Figure 5-12.

In the preceding log file, you may have noticed that except for the first entry, where the user uucp was unknown, all other entries represent successful logins. All failed login entries are indicated by a minus (-) sign, and all successful logins are indicated by a plus (+) sign. You need to regularly check the sulog file for information about all failed login attempts. This helps in detecting traces of intrusion. You should also check for login attempts during unusual hours because this might be indicative of intrusion attempts.

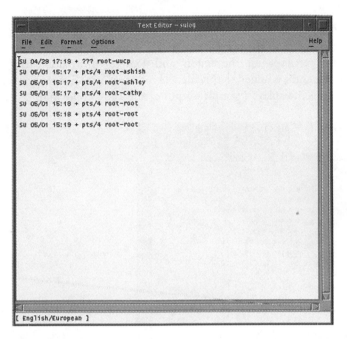

FIGURE 5-12 *A sample* sulog *file*

Using the loginlog File

The loginlog log file records information about all the unsuccessful login attempts made by users. If the number of successive incorrect login attempts exceeds five, an entry is added to the /var/adm/loginlog file. The user root and the group sys own the file. Only root has read and write permissions for the file.

Using the Volume Manager Log File

The volume manager information is stored in the /var/adm/vold.log file. The file stores information about when a user accessed the CD-ROM and disk drives on the computer. The log contains the userID and the time when the resource was accessed.

Using the Install Log File

The install log is found in the /var/sadm/system/logs/install_log file and contains information that was generated when Solaris was installed on the computer. All setup information gathered at the time of installation is logged in the log file. This contains information about the number of partitions created, the type of formatting performed, the software modules installed, and the active partition.

Using the Last Log File

You can use the last command to retrieve a list of all the users who last logged on to the system. The command retrieves all the logon and logout information from the /var/adm/wtmpx file. An entry is added to this file when a user logs off from and logs on to the computer. Figure 5-13 displays a sample output of the last command.

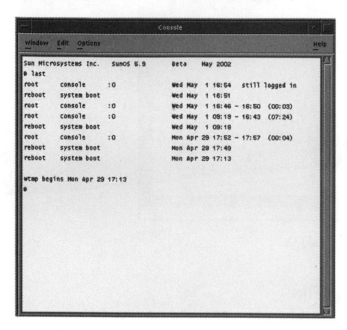

FIGURE 5-13 *A sample output of the* last *command displaying logged user information*

In case you use the last command along with a username as an argument, then the system shows the information of all previous logins of the username. For example the following code shows entries of all previous login details of the user user1.

```
# last user1
user1      pts/5      212.1.1.8       Sun Jul 28 12:19    still logged in
user1      pts/5      212.1.1.8       Sat Jul 27 15:32 - 12:19   (20:47)
user1      pts/6      212.1.1.54      Sat Jul 27 09:15    still logged in
user1      pts/6      212.1.1.8       Fri Jul 26 10:49 - 09:15   (22:26)
user1      pts/6      200.1.2.16      Thu Jul 25 18:40 - 18:49   (00:09)

wtmp begins Tue Jun 18 10:48
```

You can also store information about any changes made in the system configuration. This information is stored in the sysidtool log file.

Using the sysidtool Log File

The sysidtool log file is stored in the /var/sadm/system/logs directory. The file is created at the time of installation, and it automatically runs when a new component is installed or when the sys-unconfig utility is used to uninstall an application. You can use this file to keep track of changes made to the computer by the installation and uninstallation of components.

The logging of information or errors raised by services running on the system is an important part of an administrator's responsibility. However, you need to remember that uncontrolled or unstructured logging leads to large log files that cannot be analyzed easily. Therefore, you need to restrict auditing to events that are necessary for ensuring the security of your computer. By default, Solaris creates numerous log files to keep track of changes that occur on the system. Over a period of time these log files occupy precious disk space, which also effects system performance. Even some of the applications, such as su, which run automatically, create log files for the applications.

Many commands are available in Solaris that you can use to identify the amount of disk space utilized by log files. One method is typing the command du /var/adm at the command prompt. The command lists all the log files created under the /var/adm directory and their size, as shown in Figure 5-14. You need to periodically keep track of the size of the log files and delete the log files at regular intervals. Most errors are logged in the /var/adm/messages file; you need to keep a regular check on this file to ensure that it

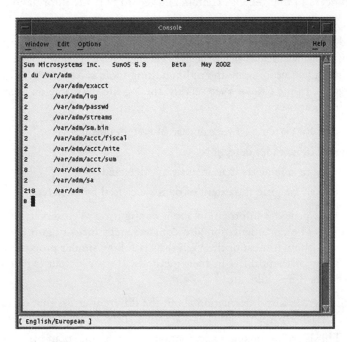

FIGURE 5-14 *Sample output of the* du /var/adm *command displaying the log files and the size of the subdirectories*

does not become very big. You can also use this file to identify any critical errors that might have occurred on the computer.

The unit of measurement used while mentioning the directory size is the block size of the operating system (OS). Therefore, in the first entry 2 /var/adm/exact, the 2 mentioned as the subdirectory size implies that the /var/adm/exacct subdirectory is equal to two times the size of OS block. Many tools are available in the market that assist you in obtaining the relevant information from the log files. The next section will focus on how you can enable auditing on Web servers.

Enabling Logging on to Web Servers

It is important to log events that occur on the Web servers to make sure that adequate security measures have been implemented and to detect intrusion. You can enable default event logging mechanisms, which are available with the Web server software, during installation. However, the default measures are often inadequate and you need to install other tools based on the security requirements of your organization. The default logging mechanisms do not provide information about the server's performance or about programs that attempt to retrieve information about the server. You need to list all the logs that are available on the server and their purpose. After you have understood each log, you can customize the auditing process so that the logs contain and record only the information that you need.

You may have realized by now that logs provide an excellent mechanism for detecting and recording information about suspicious behavior over the network. However, for implementing effective auditing, you need to use the right auditing tools and implement auditing for the relevant events. In the case of Web servers, the log files available on them are needed for the following purposes:

◆ Provide assistance for system recovery in case of system crash or error

◆ Provide assistance in intruder detection

◆ Provide facility for raising alerts if an intrusion is detected

◆ Provide assistance in gauging the extent of damage caused by intruders

Most Web server software provides information about configuring Web servers in their respective documentation. The documentation also contains steps for configuring auditing on the Web servers. Although most of the Web servers follow similar procedures for configuring auditing, many of them differ in their methods. Primarily, four log files are maintained on Web servers. These files are:

◆ **Error log**. This log contains information about the different errors that occur on the Web server. Each error is recorded as a separate entry.

◆ **Referrer log**. This is an optional log and contains information about users or services that access the network by using the HTTP protocol. It also contains the link that a user may have followed for accessing files or resources available on the network.

◆ **Transfer log**. This log contains information regarding the transfer of information that occurs on the network. This information is stored in different formats and a separate entry is created for each transaction.

◆ **Agent log**. This is also an optional log and contains information about the client software that is assigned the right to access resources and information from the network.

The Transfer log stores information in different formats. The following are the formats in which information is stored in the Transfer log.

◆ **Combined Log Format**. The log contains certain fields that store information about the transaction and the information available in the Agent and the Referer logs. An advantage of keeping all the information together is easy accessibility and speed. The fields that the log contains are listed below:

  ◆ Name of the remote host

  ◆ Identity of the remote host

  ◆ Authentication information about the user available in Basic Authentication Scheme

  ◆ Date of the transaction

  ◆ The URL that requested access to the resources or information available on the network

  ◆ Status of the request

  ◆ Amount of information transferred

◆ **Common Log Format**. Information stored in this format contains all the fields mentioned in the previous point.

◆ **Extended Log Format**. This format is used for storing information about all types of information that should be stored in the log files. Information regarding what needs to be stored and the version number of the log file is stored in the first two lines in the log file. These lines contain information about the date and time when modifications were made to the file, the primary IP address of the Web server, and the time taken to transmit the information. Information about the amount of information transferred and the HTTP version is also stored.

◆ **Other log formats**. There are other types of file formats that are specific to certain Web server software. For example, information can be stored in databases or text files where each entry is separated by a delimiter.

As mentioned earlier, the type and amount of information that is logged depends on the types of applications and programs that run on the Web server and that affect the performance of the Web server. In the case of user-created applications, you need to devise a logging plan based on the information available about the Web server hosting the program because the logging mechanism is not necessarily defined. You need to be careful about what information is being logged because this information is stored on the Web server and is appended in the systems log file. Therefore, if you do not restrict auditing only to the critical events, the log file might overflow and the computer might not have enough space to store the log file.

Following are certain steps that you can implement for enabling logging on to Web servers.

◆ You can use the Remote User Identity information. This information is provided in RFC 1413.

◆ You can use the Combined Log Format in cases where the Referer log or Agent log is not available.

◆ You can store information in the Transfer log by either using the Combined Log Format or manually converting the information to be stored into the standard format.

◆ You can use software that provides administrative access control for the log files during the startup of the program. These software can also be used for controlling access to the log files and preventing accidental erasure of system critical information. You can enable or disable these programs based on your network requirement.

◆ You can create and use separate log files for different virtual hosts. These hosts can then be used as a single Web server.

Many tools are available in the market that provide support for analyzing Transfer logs. The formats that are commonly used by these tools are the Common Log Format and the Combined Log Format. The tools store information regarding the IP address used on the network and the ports that provide access to the network. The Error logs store most of the general errors that occur on the network. However, they do not store any information about programs that might have tried to retrieve information for the Web server or access certain databases on the network.

Using Logcheck

Logcheck is a software program that can be configured to run periodically and inspect system log files for any intrusion attempt or security violation. The program helps identify security weaknesses by analyzing the rights assigned to files. For example, you might install and configure an effective Intrusion Detection System (IDS) on the network. You might also configure an effective firewall that inspects every data packet that enters or leaves the network. However, if the rights assigned to the log files are incorrect or if you do not periodically check the system logs, auditing becomes ineffective. An intruder might gain access to the network and you may not know about it because you did not check the audit files. Most auditing programs have provisions to take regular backups of the files. They also ensure that no user except the `root` user account has the `write` permissions for the log files. When a hacker gains access to the network, the hacker first ensures that no traces of the intrusions are registered in the audit logs. The hacker also deletes all the relevant entries from the log files. You can prevent this by implementing log file monitoring and raising an alarm if any users, except the `root`, tries to modify the log file.

Logcheck maintains a checkpoint called `logtail` that keeps track of the last position up to which the log file was read. All new searches are performed from this location. The software has a simple source code and can be easily implemented. The tasks of auditing the computer and logging any critical errors or dangers are essential for effectively detecting any intrusion on the network. Although Solaris has its default utility `syslog` for detecting intrusion, the utility logs all events that occur on the network. This is irrespective of whether these events can be classified as intrusions or errors. Logcheck filters out the routine or harmless network events and only retains information about errors and any other suspicious activities. If any suspicious activity is detected, the network administrator is immediately alerted by e-mail. Logcheck maintains a file containing certain keywords. This file contains information about all known security threats. The log file is compared against the file and information about any suspicious activity is filtered out. Logcheck maintains certain files that it uses to check for intrusion. These files are as follows:

- ◆ `logcheck.violation`. This file contains information about past security violations, and the log files are checked against these patterns. For example the file can contain negative words such as `denied and refused`. The file can also contain positive words such as `successful` in the search patterns. Information is stored in these files in the form of keywords. Alerts are raised if any matching keyword is found. This might also be the case where false alerts are raised. Since the keyword file is modified when a new suspicious activity occurs, an error might be missed once but is bound to be caught during subsequent audits. Therefore, you should add keywords for suspicious activities when they occur and keep the keywords file updated.

- ◆ `logcheck.hacking`. This file contains information about known hacking occurrences. This information is searched for in the log file. You should only include information about known hacking events to prevent raising misleading alerts. This file is only useful if you have accurate information about past hacking attempts. Hacking searches are mostly performed for `sendmail` attacks and Internet Security Scanner attacks.

- ◆ `logcheck.ignore`. This file contains information about intrusion patterns that should be ignored. Therefore, even if a match for the pattern is found during an audit, an alert should not be raised. You can use this file to specify that certain types of errors should be ignored or to prevent against recurring false alerts.

◆ `logcheck.violations.ignore`. This file contains a more descriptive explanation of security violations patterns. The values might not be serious errors but might cause alarm based on how they are worded. For example, the `refused` keyword used with the sendmail messages can be a simple error or a major source of concern. One reason could be that the requested host was not found and, therefore, the mail could not be delivered. It is also possible that you tried connecting to an unsecured or illegal port and the connection was refused. Therefore, you have to decide which entries should be included in the file. However, you need to add a few critical entries to the file so that any serious security lapses are not overlooked. The file mostly contains entries related to the sendmail.

CAUTION

It is important to note that the `logcheck.violations.ignore` file should never be left blank. An empty file implies that all errors need to be ignored.

◆ `logcheck.sh`. This file is the primary script for the logcheck utility. It is used for processing and analyzing log files. All the relevant records are filtered out using the `grep` command. You can configure the utility to execute periodically using the `cron` command and send the result to `sysadmin`.

◆ `logcheck`. This file is used to determine the point to which the logs have been checked. This ensures that the same content in the log files is not checked twice. After a log has been reviewed, a file named `xxx.offset` is created, where `xxx` is the name of the log file. This file contains the flag `logtail` and identifies the point up to which the log was last checked. If this file is deleted, the flag is destroyed and the logs are checked again from the beginning. The logcheck utility maintains a counter to keep track of the size of the log files. If the file size changes, the counter is reset and the log is analyzed again. Logcheck tracks the size and inode of log files to enable it to tell when a log file has been accessed. If the inode of the log changes, or the file size is smaller than the last run, logtail will reset the counter and parse the entire file.

All scripts related to the logcheck utility are stored in the `/usr/local/etc` directory. After configuring all the log files and scripts, you need to ensure that the utility runs after specific time intervals. You can use the `cron` command to perform this action and make the required entry in the `/etc/crontab` file.

Summary

In this chapter, you learned about system identification, auditing, and system log files. You learned about the JumpStart toolkit and how to use it to automatically install multiple computers by using the same security settings. Next you learned what a system log is and how you can use it. You also learned how to create messages in syslog. In addition, you learned about the facilities available in syslog and the severity levels of messages: the way in which the system handles errors or raises alerts depends on the severity level of the error raised. You then learned about the various elements of the syslog file stored on your computer and how to debug syslog and the log files available with it. Next you learned how to enable logging on to Web servers. Finally, you learned about the logcheck tool.

Check Your Understanding

Multiple Choice Questions

1. Which options can you use with logger commands to specify that an existing file will provide the logged information for analysis?

   a. -i

   b. -f

   c. -t

   d. -p

2. Which facility available in syslog is used for sharing error information generated by syslog and contains a timestamp of when the entries were created?

   a. LOG_USER

   b. LOG_DAEMON

   c. LOG_KERN

   d. LOG_MARK

3. In the following security levels available in syslog, which is the most critical?

   a. LOG_ERR

   b. LOG_EMERG

   c. LOG_DEBUG

   d. LOG_ALERT

4. Identify the two parts in which information stored in the syslog.conf file is divided.

   a. section

    b. `action`

    c. `selector`

    d. `execute`

5. Which log file stores information about all the login attempts made on the network using the su command?

    a. `sulog`

    b. `loginlog`

    c. `last log`

    d. `install log`

Short Questions

1. You are using a Solaris utility for configuring auditing on your computer. However, no entries are being recorded in the log files. How can you solve this problem?

2. Why are rules essential for creating an effective JumpStart environment?

Answers

Multiple Choice Answers

1. b. The `-f` option is used along with the logger command to specify that an existing file will provide the logged information for analysis. The `-i` option is used for logging the process ID of the logger process. The `-t` option is used for specifying a tag for each line in the log file, while the `-p` option is used for specifying a priority level for the message.

2. d. The `LOG_MARK` facility stores error information generated by `syslog` and contains records of the time when the entries were created.

3. b. The `LOG_EMERG` severity level is the most critical security level and can cause the system to shut down without warning.

4. b, c. The information stored in the `syslog.conf` file is divided into two parts. The first part is called `selector`, and the second part is known as `action`. A tab character separates both the pieces of information. The `selector` part contains the facility and severity level grouped together. You can create a separate entry for each pair of facility and severity levels. There can be different valid combinations created using each facility and severity level. The `action` part stores the name, path information, and userID of the system.

5. **a.** The `sulog` file stores information about all the attempts made to logon to the network by using the `su` command. It contains information about both successful and unsuccessful attempts.

Short Answers

1. You need to check whether an entry for the auditing program exists in the `syslog.conf` file. As the default logging facility is local, you need to send a `SIGHUP` signal to the `syslogd` daemon running on your computer so that the `conf` file is read again. Since `syslogd` does not create the log files, you need to check whether any of the log files need to be created manually.

2. The `rules` files are an important part of JumpStart because they help to decide how JumpStart clients will be configured. The rules are stored in simple text files and provide information about how Solaris will be installed and what security settings will be configured on the client computer. You can create different rules for installing client computers with different security settings. You can also add general instructions by using the `any` argument in the `rules` file. This argument is used if a client computer does not match with any of the previously set rules.

Chapter 6

As a network administrator, you already are conversant with the file system available in Solaris. However, to refresh your knowledge, this chapter will briefly discuss the Solaris file system. A *file system* can be defined as a data structure that is used for organizing individual files in a structured manner. This chapter discusses the hierarchical file system available in Solaris. A *hierarchical file system* is a method that is used for logically organizing files on a computer in a hierarchy. The file system follows a class structure while storing information on the disk. While searching for any information, the search is performed from the top of the structure to the bottom. Most of the operating systems follow their own unique hierarchical structure for storing files. This chapter also briefly discusses some of the key concepts related to file and directory security in Solaris. It also explains the security measures that are available for securing the file structure in Solaris. Before discussing security, I will first discuss some of the basic concepts related to file systems and the Solaris file system in particular.

The Solaris File System

A file system, also referred to as a data structure, is used for storing and administrating files stored on the computer. These files can be either system-related files or application files. You can also use the file system to manage data stored in the files and to perform administrative tasks on the files. Administering files and directories involves assigning access rights and permissions for them. You can assign different rights to different users. A user may have the right only to read a file, both to read and write to a file, or to execute a file.

Many of the security and rights-related problems occur on the network because either the file system has not been properly configured or file and directory access rights have not been properly assigned. I will now discuss the file and directory permissions available in the Solaris file system and how they can be used for implementing security.

Solaris stores files and directories in a hierarchical structure. You can picture this as either an inverted tree or a pyramid. Each object in the pyramid has certain subobjects connected to it. Each row of objects forms a different level in the hierarchy. Information is arranged in such a way that you can systematically store and find data in the files. By default, each user in Solaris 9 is provided only one home directory. Users can create their own subdirectories under their home directory. Figure 6-1 displays a sample directory structure available in Solaris.

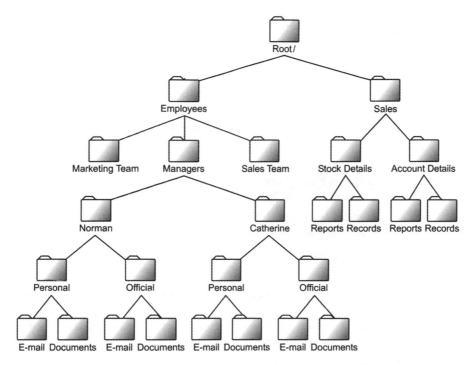

FIGURE 6-1 *A sample directory structure*

As shown in the preceding figure, each user has two subdirectories, `personal` and `official`, under their respective home directory. These directories also contain subdirectories named `e-mail` and `documents`. Users can further expand the tree based on their respective requirements. In Solaris, the top-most node is called the `root` (/). All directories are created under this `root` node, and all files are saved in their respective directories. A file is a group of bytes stored together that provides information about a common topic. Each file is assigned a unique name and is saved as a single document. You only need to ensure that the name of file remains unique in the directory in which it is stored. You can have files having similar names in several directories. A file cannot contain another file, therefore, the branch of a tree ends with a file. A directory is a folder that contains another directory or files and is used to store files of various applications or on many subjects in separate locations. This not only helps to effectively organize and store data but also provides faster search facility. If you need to access a file related to a specific topic, you only need to search in a specific directory instead of on the entire disk. Following are the main types of file system available in Solaris:

◆ **Disk-Based File System.** Following are some examples of disk-based file systems available in Solaris:

The **Unix file system (UFS)** is primarily based on the BSD Fast file system and is considered as the default disk-based file system for systems running Solaris 2.5 and above.

The **PC file system (PCFS)** exists in the memory and maintains a list of active processes running on the system. You need to use the `ps` command to view the information stored on this file system.

The **High Sierra file system (HSFS)** is the first CD-ROM file system available in Solaris. It is currently a read only file system and follows the ISO-9660 standard.

◆ **Network Based File System.** Network file system is the default network-based file system available in Solaris.

The **Network file system (NFS)** provide the facility for accessing files over the network, such as over LAN or WAN.

◆ **Virtual File System.** The virtual file systems exist in the memory and the most commonly used virtual file system is the Temporary file system.

The **Temporary file system (TMPFS)** is also known as the *swap space* or `/tmp` directory and (as the name suggests) is not permanent. Therefore, the files and information stored on the file system are either deleted when the file system is unmounted or when the system shuts down or reboots.

In the next section, I will discuss about the file and directory permissions that you can use for implementing security of information on the above mentioned file systems.

File and Directory Permissions

In Solaris, there are three kinds of users who can be assigned rights to access files and directories. These users are:

◆ **Owner of the file.** File or directory owners are normally the users who have created the file or directory. These users have full access to the file or directory and can assign access rights to other users. However, the ability to assign rights is restricted to only the files and directories created by the user.

◆ **Group to which the owner belongs**. Every user on the local computer or on the network belongs to a specific group. This information is stored along with the `userID` for the local computer or with the NIS password for the network.

◆ **Others or everyone**. This user group contains user accounts other than the owner.

You can assign separate access rights for the owner, group, and everyone. However, before assigning any rights, you first need to identify the rights that you can assign to the different user groups.

Types of Permissions

There are three kinds of access permissions that you can assign to a file or directory: read, write, and execute. Solaris stores information about each right in the form of bits. Therefore, there is a read bit, a write bit, and an execution bit. In the case of directories, since an execution bit cannot be set, you have a search bit. A bit can have only a value of 0 or 1. Therefore, if the value is 1, the bit is set to on, otherwise, the bit is set to off. If the bit is set to off, the user is denied access to the file or directory. Table 6-1 lists all the permissions that can be assigned to a user.

Table 6-1 Rights Assigned to a User

Right	Type	Description
Read	File	Specifies that users have the right to read the content of a specific file.
Read	Directory	Specifies that users have the right to list the content of a specific directory, but not to open the file.
Write	File	Specifies that users have the right to modify the contents of a specific file. Although users can delete the content of the file, they cannot move the file to another location. This right to move files can only be assigned at the directory level.
Write	Directory	Specifies that users have the right to add, delete, or move files between directories. This right does not depend on whether the user has rights to modify the files or not.
Execute	File	Specifies that users have the right to execute files.
Execute	Directory	Specifies that users have the right to open the files listed in the directory. The users also have the right to move the files to any other directory in the parent directory by using the cd command.

You can use these rights to allow or restrict users to list files in directories or to open files. You can also use restrictive rights to curtail rights of specific users. For example, you can provide users with rights to view the content of a directory but not to open files. Alternatively, you can provide users the right to read the files but not to make any modifications. You can also hide files from unauthorized users.

There are other kinds of permissions that you can set for files, as follows:

◆ **Using SetUID for files**. This flag is set only if the file is a runnable or an executable program. If the SetUID bit is set for a particular file, then the process that runs the file takes on the privileges of the owner of the file, rather than the user who executed the process. For example, the passwd file can only be accessed by the root account. If an administrator needs to access the file from a user's login, normally the administrator would need to log off and then log on again using the root account. However, if the SetUID flag is set, then the administrator does not need to log off but can directly run the file with administrative privileges.

◆ **Using SetUID for directory**. In case of directories, the SetUID flag has a different meaning. When SetUID permission is applied to a directory, the files created in the directory belong to the owner of the directory, and not to the user who creates the file or files. Any user with write permissions may create a file there, but the file owner would be the directory owner. The root user and the owner can set the SetUID permissions on an executable file using the chmod command and the octal value 4000. For example:

```
# chmod 4555 <file_to_execute>
```

◆ **Using SetGID for file**. This flag provides a functionality that is similar to the functionality provided by the SetUID flag. This flag is used for changing the group ID of the user currently running the program to another group ID. The running process takes on the privileges of the group to which the file belongs. In this way, a user belonging to one group can be provided with the same rights and access permissions assigned to users of another group.

◆ **Using SetGID for directory**. This flag is used for assigning a default group ID to files created in a directory. All newly created files in the directory inherit the group ID of the directory instead of the group ID of command or process that created the file. For example, if the group owner of the sales directory is managers, then all new files in the directory are assigned the managers group ID instead of the group ID of the user creating the file. If this bit is not set, the default group ID of the process is retained. The root user and the owner can set SetGID permissions on an executable file using the chmod command and the octal value 2000. For example:

```
# chmod 2555 <executable_file>
```

◆ **Using sticky bit for file**. Although setting this bit currently has no significance, in earlier versions of Solaris and UNIX, setting this bit caused a snapshot of this program to be retained in the computer's memory. Therefore, when the program is recalled, it provides faster access to the program.

◆ **Using sticky bit for directory**. If a directory has the sticky bit set, only the owner of the file, the owner of the directory, or root, can delete a file in the directory. Thus, the sticky bit protects the files within the directory. It is hence used for public directories. This flag is commonly set only for the /tmp and the

/var/tmp directories. This is because these directories require public access and this flag restricts users from manipulating files belonging to other users.

Figure 6-2 shows how you can share the right to use SetUID with another user.

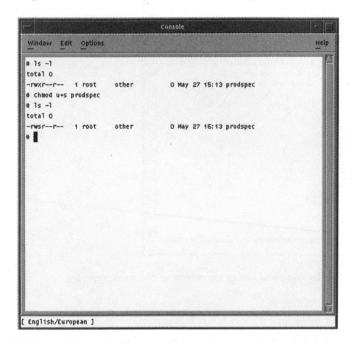

FIGURE 6-2 *Changing the file permissions symbolically to use* SetUID

As shown in the preceding figure, the right s is visible in place of the execute permission of the file owner. This indicates that the SetUID right is assigned to the owner of the file.

Now that you know about the various permissions that you can set for files and directories, I will discuss how you can view the current rights assigned to specific files or to the contents of a directory. The next section covers these topics in detail.

Viewing Permissions

The ls command is used for viewing the permissions of individual files in a directory or the permissions for the entire directory. There are many options available with the ls command. The most important from a security point of view is the -l switch. The option -l stands for *long listing* and displays the complete details about files and directories. Figure 6-3 displays the output of an ls command.

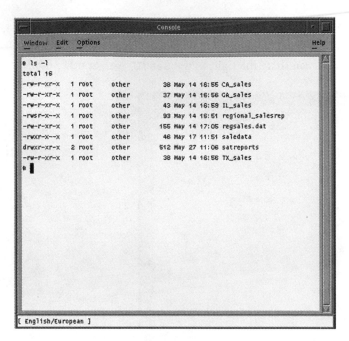

FIGURE 6-3 *Output of an* ls *command listing the content of the directory*

As shown in the preceding figure, all entries corresponding to directories start with d and the rest of the entries are files. The rwx and - characters indicate rights assigned to individual users, groups, and others. You might notice that the right entries appear in three sets. The first set corresponds to owner's rights, the second set to group rights, and the third set for all other users. If any right is either revoked or not provided, it is replaced by a hyphen (-).

You can also see the rights assigned to an individual file. To view information about a single file, you can use the command ls -l <file name>. You can also view information about a directory without viewing information about the files it contains. You can use the command ls -ld to view this information.

You can also change the rights currently assigned to files to restrict or provide access to the current user or to an entire group. The most commonly used command for this purpose is the chmod command. Let's look at the command in detail.

Using the chmod Command for Assigning Permissions

The chmod command is used for changing the access permission modes of certain files and directories. The mode indicates the users who are authorized to read, modify, and execute the files. You can use the command to change the access permissions for the owner of the file (u), the group to which the user belongs (g), and to everyone else (o). You can also change the access permissions for all users by using the a switch.

You use the chmod= command to assign permissions to various groups. The chmod+ command is used for adding permissions or specifying multiple permissions, while the chmod- command is used for removing permissions. Following is the syntax of the command:

```
chmod [who] + [permissions]
```

In the preceding code, who refers to the user groups to whom the rights need to be assigned or denied, while the permission option refers to the actual rights. For example, Norman is the new vice president of the marketing department. He wants access to a program, regional_salesrep, which provides a summary of all the regionwide sales of all products. The regionwide sales information is stored in the regsales.dat file. As shown in Figure 6-4, only the owner of the file has access to the files.

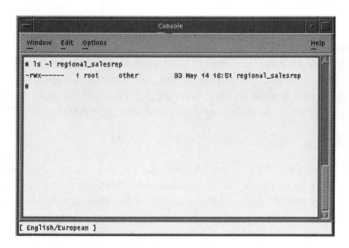

FIGURE 6-4 *Rights assigned to the sales report application and associated file*

As a network administrator, you provide this access by issuing the following command:

```
chmod go+rx regional_salesrep
```

The preceding statement changes Norman's rights as shown in Figure 6-5.

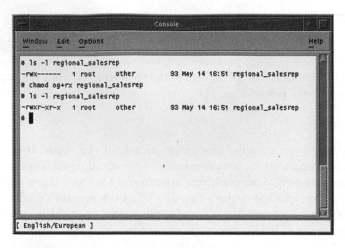

FIGURE 6-5 *Norman's changed rights*

As shown in the preceding code, Norman's rights have changed, providing him with the right to execute the program. However, this causes another problem. When Norman tries to execute the application, an error message is generated because the rights for the `regsales.dat` `file` have not been changed. Since the rights to access the dat files cannot be provided to everyone, a feasible solution is to provide Norman the right to access the program as an administrator. The following code provides this permission:

```
chmod u+s regional_salesrep
```

The previous code provides the owner of the file with the right to allow other users to access the program with the same rights that the owner has. Therefore, Norman can now execute the program with the rights assigned to the owner of the program. When he tries to execute the `regional_salesrep` program, his user ID briefly changes to the file owner's user ID, and the program can access the `regsales.dat` file.

You can also use the `chmod` command to modify the access permissions for all files stored within a specific directory. You use the `-R` switch with the `chmod` command to make this change. The `-R` option is used to apply any command recursively to all files directly inside the directory as well as to files inside the subdirectories of this directory. The use of the command is shown in Figure 6-6.

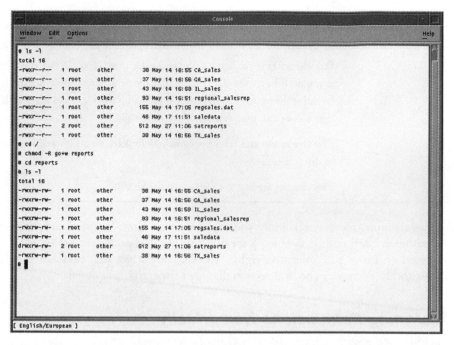

FIGURE 6-6 *Changing the access rights of file stored in the* reports *directory*

As shown in the preceding figure, before the execution of the command, only the owner of the directory had the write rights for the files. After the execution of the command, all the files stored in the directory are writable by the group and others. Table 6-2 lists the various permissions available with the chmod command.

Table 6-2 Permissions Used with the chmod Command

Permission	Description
r	Provides read permission to a file owner, group, or everyone.
w	Provides write permission to a file owner, group, or everyone.
x	Provides execute permission to a file owner, group, or everyone.
X	Provides search or execute permission to a directory owner, group, or everyone. You can also use this option for setting the execute permission for a file, provided, one or more executable bit has been set for the current mode.

continues

Table 6-2 (*continued*)

Permission	Description
l	Provides locking facility for files and directories. You can use this option is you need to ensure that a particular file or directory should remain locked while another application is accessing the file. Locking implies that no one can read from or write to the file.
s	Provides setuid and setgid permissions for executing files and searching in directories.
t	Provides the facility to specify a sticky bit value.

Besides assigning rights symbolically, you can also assign rights by specifying their associated number. Each right is assigned a specific number, and each user is assigned a number based on his or her cumulative rights. You can similarly assign cumulative rights to groups and to everyone. The next section discusses these rights in detail.

Assigning Permissions Numerically

In addition to assigning permissions in symbolic form, you can also assign the rights by using their equivalent numbers. Besides being easy to use, assigning rights using numbers is important while working with utilities such as umask that involve assigning rights using numbers. Rights can be assigned numerically by using three- or four-digit groups of numbers. There is a separate set of rights for each group of users. Following is the syntax of how to assign rights numerically:

```
chmod <perm num> <file/directory name>
```

In the preceding code, the perm num option is the numeric equivalent of the access rights that are either assigned or removed using the chmod command. The file/directory option is used for specifying the name of the file or directory for which you need to provide or deny access. You can also specify a list of files or directories instead of a single file.

Each permission is assigned a specific number, which can then be used to assign or remove the specific right. The numeric permissions are numbered as follows:

- ◆ 1. Execute
- ◆ 2. Write
- ◆ 4. Read

If you need to assign a user read and write rights but not execute rights, you'll assign the number 6 (2+4), and if all the rights need to be assigned, you'll use the number 7 (1+2+4). In case the value 0 is used, it means that no permission is assigned to the user. Similarly, rights are assigned for groups and other users. You can then use the combination of these rights to set rights for user, group, and others. Since the rights are listed in the sequence owner, group, and others, you also need to assign the rights in the same order. Therefore, the right 400 will provide read access only to the owner while no rights to any other group, whereas the right 754 provides the owner with all the rights, the group with the read and execute rights, and everyone else with only read rights.

Let's take an example. You have a directory called `futuresales`. This directory contains files and applications that can be used by managers for estimating future sales. You need to change the file permission so that only you have the right to read and modify the files and execute the applications. The other managers should have the right to read the files and execute the applications, while everyone else should have the right to read the files. Figure 6-7 shows how to set these rights and the output of the command.

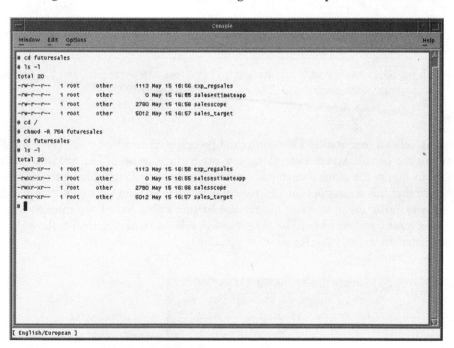

FIGURE 6-7 *Changing the rights of the* `futuresales` *directory*

As shown in Figure 6-7, the owner of the files has all the rights, the group has read and execute permissions, and everyone else has read permission. Another way of assigning rights is by specifying the rights that the file or directory should not have. If this value is set, then all newly created files and directories will have the rights set by you. You can use the `umask` command to set this value. The following section discusses this concept in detail.

Using the umask Command for Creating File Masks

You can use the umask command for specifying the default rights of newly created files and directories. These default rights are assigned by the file system and can be changed by either individual users or processes based on their requirements. The information about the umask value is stored in either the .profile or the .login files. You can create new files using the vi, cp, and touch commands, and the rights assigned to the files are calculated by subtracting the umask value from the default rights value of either 666 or 777. For example, if the current umask value is 0056 and you create a new file named south-sales, the default rights assigned to the file would be 610 (666–056). This means that the owner of the file would have read-write permissions, the group would only have execute permission, and everyone else would have no permission.

 NOTE

As a practice, the default file permissions of text files are set to 666 and the default permissions of directories and executable files are set to 777.

umask follows inheritance. Therefore, child processes created by a main process will also inherit the parent's umask value along with other characteristics. The umask command is used to specify the rights that should not be assigned to a file or folder when it is created. Notice that this is just opposite of what happens when you use the chmod command. The rights are assigned in numeric format and contain rights for all the three user groups, owner, group, and everyone. The default umask value is 0022. Figure 6-8 shows how you can assign an umask value for all subsequent files.

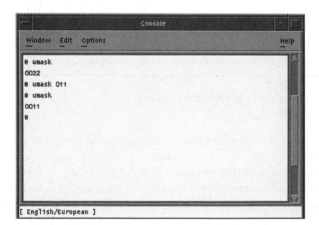

FIGURE 6-8 *Using the* umask *command for changing access permission for newly created files*

After the execution of the preceding code, all files created thereafter would, by default, provide their owners all rights and the group and everybody else with read and write rights.

 NOTE

A recommended practice is that all files created by the root user account should be accessible only to the root. Another solution is that the group should have only read and execute permission while others should not have any permission. Therefore, the umask for the root account can be either 077 or 027.

By now, you have learned how to secure files by assigning appropriate permissions to them. However, sometimes you may need to search for the file before you can view its rights or assign new access permissions. The find command is used for this purpose. The following section discusses the command in detail.

Searching for Files Using the find Command

Sometimes you may need to find certain files containing specific security settings. The find command, which is available in Solaris, provides this functionality. It is a very effective command that you can use to search the entire file system for one or more specific files. You can specify many search criteria with the find command and execute commands on the returned files. You can also use the find command to perform searches in multiple subdirectories. The search criteria could consist of the file names, file size, or the time when the files were created. This utility allows you not only to search for specific files, but also to perform certain actions based on the searched files. You can execute commands such as chmod and rm to perform actions on the searched files.

Following is the syntax of the find command:

```
find <search path> <search type>
[-exec <command name> ] -name <file name>
```

In the preceding code:

- ◆ The <search path> option is the location where you want to perform the search. If you specify a period (.) it implies that the search will be performed only in the current directory, while the (/) symbol implies that the search will begin from the root directory. You can also specify multiple directories to indicate that the search should occur only in the specified directories.
- ◆ The <search type> option implies the type of files that should be returned by the search. You can search for files, directories, and links.

◆ The <command name> option contains the various commands that should be executed for all the returned files or directories. The most commonly used command is the chmod command used for changing the access permission for files or directories.

◆ The <file name> option contains the name of the file that needs to be searched. You can also specify wildcards in the search criteria. The most commonly used wildcard is *.

Table 6-3 lists some examples of how you can use the find command and its output.

Table 6-3 Examples of *find* Command

Command	Description
find / -name Employeedetails - type f -print	This command searches for all files named Employeedetails in the entire file system and displays all the files found on the screen.
find /reports -name "Expen*" -type f -print	This command searches for all files in the reports subdirectory whose name begins with the word Expen and displays all the files found on the screen.
find /reports/eastzone -name "Expen*" -type f	This command searches for all files in the -exec chmod 741 {} \; eastzone subdirectory whose name begins with the word Expen and changes the access permission of the files found to 741.
find southzone northzone -name "Sales*"	This command searches for all files in the -type f -exec chmod 764 {} \; southzone and northzone subdirectories and whose name begins with the word Sales. The access rights of all the found files are changed to 764.

Command	Description
`find / - type f -perm 4000 -print`	This command searches for all files in the entire file system whose access permissions have been changed using the `SetUID` command. A point to be remembered is that the octal value corresponding to `SetUID` is 4000
`find / - type f -perm -g+rw -print`	This command searches for all files in the entire file system where the group account only has the read and write permission.
`find / - type f -perm 2000 -print`	This command searches for all files in the entire file system whose access permissions have been changed using the `SetGID` command. A point to be remembered is tha the octal value corresponding to `SetGID` is 2000.

You can also search for files not accessed in the last 15 days by using the `-atime` option with the `find` command. You use the `-ctime` option to view all files not modified recently and the `-mtime` option to list all files not accessed for a certain time period. For example, if you need to find all files in the reports subdirectory that have not been modified in the last 10 days, you'll use the following code:

```
find /reports -mtime +10 -print
```

You can also use a combination of options to retrieve specific files that fulfill specific criteria. For example, the following command searches for all files that were accessed in the last 24 hours and whose size is more than 8000 bytes. The output of the command appears in Figure 6-9.

FIGURE 6-9 *Output of the* find *command using multiple parameters*

You can also use the -type switch to specify that the find command should only return files or directories. Now that you know about how the file system can be secured by using simple Solaris commands, the next section focuses on some of the file system security tools available in Solaris.

File System Security Tools

You can use many tools available in the market for ensuring security of system files and to implement auditing on the computer. You have already learned about some of these tools in the previous chapters; for example, you learned about the Automated Security Enhancement Tool (ASET). You learned how to use ASET for improving the security on your computer and for checking access permissions of files stored on the computer. The following section discusses some of the other file-system-related security tools available in Solaris.

tiger

The tiger utility was developed at the A&M University in Texas. Although it was originally developed for securing UNIX computers, over the years it has been used for securing computers running other operating systems, such as Solaris. The utility regularly checks the computer for security problems and warns the administrator when such a problem is detected. The utility can be downloaded from the Web location **ftp://coast.cs. purdue.edu/pub/tools/unix/tiger/TAMU/***. You also need to download the latest version of the digital signature that is appropriate for the operating system running on your server. The signatures are available at the FTP site **ftp://coast.cs.purdue.edu/pub/tools/unix/ tiger/TAMU/tiger-sigs/***. The site also provides a script `installlsigs` in the `utils` subdirectory that you can use for installing the updated signature. There are fairly complete signature files for various releases of SunOS available in the `tiger-sigs/os-dist` directory. You can use these signatures if you want to thoroughly scan your system for altered binaries.

The most critical file in the utility is the `tigerrc` file that is used for configuring the TAMU host and for determining what should or should not be checked. A recommended practice is to maintain a copy of the original and use the file after making modifications based on the security requirements of your organization. If you require a complete evaluation of your computer, you can use the `tigerrc-all` file. You should run the utility on a regular basis, preferably once a day on the servers. The check at the workstation level can be performed based on the level of security required.

The utility contains scripts that check for embedded pathnames, while other scripts are used for gathering file names that in turn are used for checking embedded pathnames. The script that is used for checking these embedded pathnames is the `check_embedded` script. This file checks the provided file names and determines who their owners are and what their access permissions are. The current version of `tiger` provides support for MD5 encryption. The utility also provides another file called `tigercron` that can be used to configure the computer to run the utility at regular intervals to identify any security problems and to report to the administrator about any weaknesses found. The utility also ensures that all deleted files are checked before being actually deleted from the computer. This ensures protection against accidental deletion of system files.

Tripwire

Tripwire is another utility provided by Purdue University. It is used as a file system auditing tool and is used to detect intrusions on computers running UNIX or Solaris. The utility contains a configuration file that stores information about which files need to be checked for intrusion. The result is compared against a checklist of the files that gets created when the computer was first installed. This checklist forms a baseline and determines the expected status of the system files. All differences between the expected status and the current status of files are immediately reported to the system administrator. The administrator then determines if the changes are as expected or signs of intrusion. Based on the result of the check, administrators can take appropriate preventive actions. Tripwire uses digital hashing algorithms such as MD5 to create file signatures that are impossible to forge. The slightest change made to a file results in the hash being changed.

COPS

Computer Oracle and Password System (COPS) was developed at Purdue University and consists of a collection of tools that can be used to secure the computer. The utility provides an advance warning to system administrators, programmers, operators, or anyone responsible for ensuring security. It performs a service similar to the `tiger` utility and provides warnings about security weaknesses of a computer. COPS scans the local host for common configuration problems and security vulnerabilities. The utility primarily consists of three components:

◆ A set of programs that automate the process of performing security checks

◆ A detailed documentation that describes how the COPS utility needs to be installed and configured

◆ A list of possible additions to the utility in the future as well as a reference about other utilities that a system administrator can use for ensuring security

COPS provides many types of programs that aim to solve some of the common security problems that occur on the local computer or on the network. Some of these problem areas are listed below.

◆ File, directory, and device access permissions

◆ Weak or blank passwords

◆ Files and applications stored in the `/etc/rc*` directory and `cron` files

◆ `SetUID` files that have write permission

◆ Users' home directory and startup files that are writable by everyone

◆ Anonymous FTP access and access by unauthorized users

◆ Sendmail and TFTP

◆ Format and security of password and group files

You can use some of the file tools that are available in COPS for solving the previously mentioned problems, as follows:

◆ `root.chk`. Checks whether the root login files are writable by everyone and also checks the value of the `umask` and `hosts.equiv` options for the root login.

◆ `user.chk, home.chk`. Scans all files stored in the users' home directories that provide write permission for everyone.

◆ `suid.chk`. Searches all newly created `SetUID` files.

◆ `dev.chk`. Ensures the security of devices that store data on the disk. The file checks all the system device directories and searches for any weakness that can be manipulated by hackers.

◆ `file.check, dir.check`. Searches for all files and directories that have write permission for everyone.

When the utility detects a problem, it sends an alert to the system administrator. However, the utility cannot be used to correct the problem; it becomes the system administrator's responsibility to correct it. The biggest advantage in using COPS is that you do not need to use an administrative account to run the program. The only case when you need to run the program using the root account is while checking for SetUID files. COPS is a simple utility that is used for determining any simple security-related weakness that may have been caused by operator error or any system administration related problem. The utility cannot be used to detect any program that can cause security problems or bugs that may exist in programs currently running on the computer.

COPS can easily be configured on your computer. You first need to download the program from the FTP location **ftp://coast.cs.putdue.edu/pub/tools/unix/cops**. As mentioned earlier, detailed instructions about installing and configuring COPS is also available at the site. After you have installed the utility, you can start running COPS by typing the command cops at the console. The utility executes certain programs that check the computer for security weaknesses and reports the result to the system administrator. The COPS utility should be run regularly both on the servers and on workstations. You should execute the program on the server every day, whereas you can execute it once a week on the workstations. It is important to frequently run the utility on the server because hackers leave traces of their intrusion in SetUID files stored on the computer. You can configure COPS to be executed regularly by using the cron or the at commands.

You can also configure COPS to keep logs of every security check instead of mailing the information to the system administrator. You need to set the MAIL=NO option in the configuration file of the COPS utility to instruct the utility to add a record in a log file every time a check is performed. The log file contains a timestamp of each check and also contains information about the time and the computer on which the log was created. COPS maintains a file named warnings that contains records of all the warnings generated on the computer, a brief description about what each warning means, and a suggested solution.

It is a recommended practice that you keep all the access rights related to the directory that stores the file associated with COPS to yourself. This restriction is important because although COPS is just a tool for detecting security problems, hackers can use the information stored by the utility to hack into a computer.

You can maintain multiple copies of COPS in case you administer a network containing different architectures.

lsof

The lsof or the *List of Open Files* utility is used for listing all the files currently open on the computer. The processes running on the Solaris system use this utility for listing the processes that invoke the files. The latest version of the lsof utility is version 4. This version has been tested on various flavors of UNIX, such as Linux 2.1, FreeBSD 5, and all versions of Solaris from version 6 on.

You can download the utility from the Web locations **ftp://vic.cc.purdue.edu/pub/tools/ unix/lsof.tar.gz** or **ftp://vic.cc.purdue.edu/pub/tools/unix/lsof.tar.z**. The site also contains revisions or updates of the utility. Some of the current updates provide support for FreeBSD 4.5 and 5, provide facility for compiling OpenBSD and NetBSD lsof in case the system source is not available, and offer support for Solaris 9.

The general procedure for using the utility is to download the source code from the site and to compile it on your own system to create the binary file. The binary files for certain versions and platforms are already available on the Web site. However, you need to be cautious while using these files instead of generating your own binary files. You need to remember that the hardware and software configuration of the system on which the binary file was created may be different from your own system. Lsof uses the `setuid` and `setguid` commands that transfer the rights on your system to other users. Since these rights are critical for the security of your system, you need to be sure that the files have not been tampered with and will not weaken the security settings on your computer. There are also many options that can be used with the lsof utility. The use of these options depends on the system on which the binary files are generated. It is important to ensure that the binary file that you download is compatible with your current system. Therefore, before you download these precreated binary files, you need to thoroughly understand the information provided in the README file. You also need to determine whether the system settings of the computer on which the binary was created matches the configuration of your system. The best option is to retrieve the source code and create the binary file on your own computer.

Security and authenticity of the downloaded files are ensured by the use of MD5 and PGP certificates. All downloaded files on the site are encrypted using MD5 encryption, and all lsof source tar files that have an `asc` extension are certified using PGP certificates.

By now, you should be clear about the various file permissions that can be assigned to users. Until now, you have learned how to assign rights at the user level. Solaris provides Access Control Lists (ACLs) that can be used to assign rights globally. The next section discusses this concept in detail.

Using Access Control Lists (ACLs)

ACLs are one of the most beneficial features of Solaris. The ability to assign rights to individual users may have its advantages, but in the case of large networks, it becomes a cumbersome exercise. Previously, administrators used multiple user accounts, groups, and `SetUID` files for solving the problem of managing a large number of user accounts. Although these measures solved the problem for some time, they also led to security related problems. Users required root level access for these programs to work effectively, which added to the complexity of assigning rights. ACLs allow you to manage access to the file system in a more structured manner. The best feature about ACLs is that they are easy to use. They can be used both by system administrators and by ordinary users for globally assigning rights for files and directories. While traditional UNIX file systems allowed you to define rights for only three classes of users, namely the owner, group, and others, ACLs allow you to assign rights for specific users and groups in addition to these categories.

For example, if the owner of the file, Ashley, has assigned read rights to the manager group, but needs Cathy to have write access as well, he can assign different rights to Cathy particularly. This was not possible in the traditional UNIX file system.

Solaris provides two utilities, named `getfacl` and `setfacl`, for retrieving and assigning information about ACLs from files and directories. The `getfacl` utility takes file names as parameters, retrieves the ACLs associated with the file, and stores them in text format. Similarly, the `setfacl` utility takes rights as parameters and assigns the rights to the files specified as parameters. Following is the syntax of the `setfacl` command:

```
# setfacl -s user::perms,group::perms,other:perms,mask:perms,
acl_entry_list filename
```

In the preceding code, the `-s` option is used for specifying ACL for the file names specified along with the command. The command changes the access permissions for the user, group, and everyone else. The `user::perms` specifies access permissions for the file owner, the `group::perms` provides access permissions for groups, and the `other::perms` option specifies the access permission for everyone else. The `mask` option, when used with the `setfacl` command, provides a mask or default access permission for all newly created files. You can also store all the ACL entries in a specific directory and provide the path to the directory in the `acl_entry_list` option. The final access rights assigned to the files are a combination of both the mask values and the ACL entries. The final option is the name of the files whose permissions need to be changed.

The `-m` option is used with the `setfacl` command to modify the ACL for files and directories. If the `-m` option is used to specify access permissions for an existing file, the current access permissions for the file are automatically replaced. On the other hand, if the file doesn't exist, then a new entry is created for the file. For example:

```
setfacl -m u:cathy:rx- statreport
```

In the preceding code, the rights for the user `cathy` is changed to read and execute for the file `statreport`. Similarly, the `-d` option is used with the `setfacl` command to delete an ACL entry. You can provide the username or the UID of the user to delete the entry. In the following code, the ACL entry for `cathy` is removed from the file `statreport`.

```
setfacl -d u:cathy statreport
```

You might notice that in the preceding code, rights are not assigned while deleting an ACL entry.

Figure 6-10 displays the output of the `getfacl` command for the `reports` subdirectory.

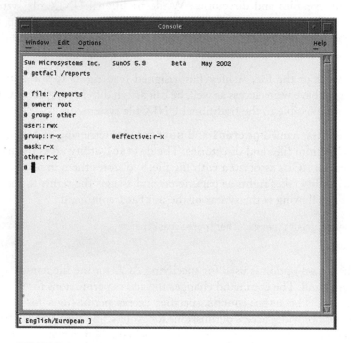

FIGURE 6-10 *Output of the* `getfacl` *command for the* `reports` *subdirectory*

You can create ACLs for existing files and newly created files. The default ACL is used for creating a set of default rights that are immediately assigned to files when they are created. However, you need to remember that default ACLs can only be created for directories and not for individual files. Therefore, when a new file is created in the directory it automatically inherits all the rights assigned to the directory using the default ACL.

As a network administrator, you may need to create hundreds of user accounts. It would be a very tedious process if you needed to individually set rights for the home directory of each user. However, Solaris provides the `-f` switch along with the `setfacl` command for copying an existing set of ACL rights to another directory. Therefore, you can retrieve the rights currently assigned to a particular directory using the `getfacl` command and use the `setfacl` command to set the ACL rights for a new directory. Figure 6-11 illustrates this concept.

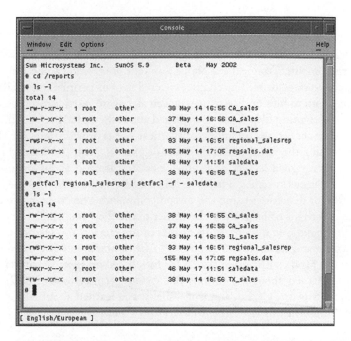

FIGURE 6-11 *Using the* `setfacl` *command to copy the access rights of one file to another*

As shown in the preceding figure, the ACL rights of the `regional_salesrep` file are retrieved using the `getfacl` command, and the `setfacl` command is used to set the same ACL rights for the `saledata` file. You can similarly assign the ACL of one directory to another. Another option that is commonly used with `setfacl` is the `-r` option. Following is the usage of this option:

```
# setfacl -r
```

This option recalculates the permission for ACL mask entry. The permissions specified in the ACL mask entry are ignored and replaced by maximum permissions necessary to grant access to all additional user, file group owner, and additional group entries in ACL.

ACLs are useful in cases where the system administration tasks need to be delegated to other users. For example, typically only the administrator can perform the administration of the `passwd` file. Consider that this task needs to be delegated to another nonroot user. This would mean assigning the user root level access, which can cause security issues. A more feasible solution is to create ACLs for the `/etc/passwd` file, which allows the user the right to access the file and make changes.

ACLs provide a more flexible and structured method for assigning rights to users and groups. They are very useful and effective in situations where you do not want to assign rights to individual users and groups. You only need to create a single ACL for a directory and provide users access by using the ACL.

Summary

In this chapter, you learned about the file system available in Solaris and how to secure files stored on a Solaris computer. You learned about different users who can be assigned rights for accessing files and directories. The chapter covered various permissions available in Solaris that you can assign to files or directories, as well as how to restrict specific users from reading, writing, or executing files. Then you learned about the SetUID, SetGID, and sticky bit flags that you can set for files and directories; these rights provide users the ability to execute programs using the rights of another user or process. Next you learned how to view the current rights assigned to files and directories. You learned about the use of the ls command and its various switches. Then you learned how you can change the permissions assigned to files or directories using the chmod command. The chapter also discussed how you can assign rights collectively to the owner of the file, group, and everyone, and how you can assign numeric equivalent rights to files or directories. You learned about the use of the umask command and how you can use it to set rights for newly created files and directories. Using the find command to search for files based on specific criteria was also covered. Then you learned about the various file system security tools available in Solaris, including tiger, tripwire, COPS, and lsof. Finally, you learned about ACLs and how you can easily and uniformly assign rights to users and groups.

Check Your Understanding

Multiple Choice Questions

1. Which of the following statements are true?

   Statement A: In Solaris, by default, all newly created files are set as executable.

   Statement B: The umask command not only sets file permissions for newly created files, but also changes the file permissions of existing files.

   a. Both A and B are correct.

   b. A is correct while B is incorrect.

   c. A is incorrect while B is correct.

   d. Both are incorrect.

2. The umask value is 016. What will be the access permission for a newly created directory in Solaris?

   a. rwxrw---x

   b. rw-rw-r--

   c. rw-r-----

   d. rwxrwx--x

3. The umask value is 022. What will be the access permission for newly created files in Solaris?

   a. rw-rw-rw-

   b. rw-rw-r--

   c. rw-r--r--

   d. rw-rw----

4. What is the umask value that you need to set for a root account so that only the root user has write permission for all newly created files? The group and everyone else should have only read permissions.

   a. 166

   b. 022

   c. 044

   d. 066

5. You want to change the access rights to a file called target sales so that only the file owner has all the rights while the group and everyone else has only read permission. Which of the following commands will you use?

   a. chmod 644 targetsales

   b. chmod 622 targetsales

   c. chmod 744 targetsales

   d. chmod 722 targetsales

6. You need to search for all files stored in the Sales subdirectory, which is created under the root directory, on the computer and whose names start with the word sale. After the files are found, you need to change their access permissions so that only the file owner has execute permission, the group has read/write permission, and everyone else has read permission. Assume that you are currently in the root directory. Which of the following commands will you use?

   a. find . -name "sale*" -t f -exec chmod 764 {} \;

   b. find /Sales -name "sale*" -t f -exec chmod 764 {} \;

   c. find . -name "sale" -t f -exec chmod 764 {} \;

   d. find /Sales -name "sale*" -t d -exec chmod 764 {} \;

7. Which of the following commands is used for searching all SetUID files stored on the computer?

   a. find / -type f -perm 2000 -print

   b. find / -type f -perm 400 -print

   c. find / -type f -perm 4000 -print

   d. find / -type f -perm SetUID -print

8. Which of the following commands is used for searching all files stored on the computer that have not been accessed in the last six days?

 a. `find / -ctime +6 -print`

 b. `find / -mtime -6 -print`

 c. `find / -mtime +6 -print`

 d. `find / -atime +6 -print`

9. Which of the following commands is used for searching all files stored on the computer and that have been accessed in the last 24 hours?

 a. `find . -atime -1 -print`

 b. `find . -mtime +1 -print`

 c. `find . -mtime -1 -print`

 d. `find . -atime +1 -print`

10. Which script is used in the `tiger` utility to check for embedded file names?

 a. `tiger`

 b. `tigerrc`

 c. `check_embeded`

 d. `tigercron`

11. Which script is available in the `tiger` utility and can be used for scheduling the utility to run periodically?

 a. `tiger`

 b. `tigerrc`

 c. `check_embeded`

 d. `tigercron`

12. Which file available in COPS is used to search for all newly created `SetUID` files?

 a. `suid.chk`

 b. `user.chk`

 c. `root.chk`

 d. `file.chk`

Short Questions

1. How can you ensure the security of system files immediately after installation? How can you ensure the security of the root account?

2. What change should you implement in the file access permissions of the /etc directory to ensure that it is secure from hackers? What is the file access permission that should be implemented on the /etc/utmp subdirectory?

Answers

Multiple Choice Answers

1. **d**. In Solaris, by default, newly created files only have read and write permission and cannot be set as executable. The umask command does not affect the file permissions of existing files. It is only used for setting the default permission for newly created files.

2. **a**. The default permission of the newly created directory would be rwxrw---x. The default permissions of directories are set to 777. Therefore, the directory owner would have full permission (7-0), the group would have read/write permission (7-1), and everyone else would only have execute permission (7-6).

3. **c**. The default permission of the newly created files would be rw-r--r--. The default permissions of files are set to 666. Therefore, the file owner would have read/write permission (6-0), whereas the group and everyone else would have only read permission (6-2).

4. **b**. The default permissions of files are set to 666. Therefore, the correct umask value is 022. The owner would have read-write permissions (6-0), whereas the group and everyone else would have only read permissions (6-2).

5. **a**. The chmod 644 targetsales command is used for setting the file permission so that the file owner has all the permissions (1+2+4=6) while the group and everyone else only has read permission (4).

6. **b**. The command find /Sales -name "sale*" -t f -exec chmod 764 {} \; is used for searching for all files stored in the Sales subdirectory and whose name begin with sales*.

7. **c**. The command find / -type f -perm 4000 -print is used to search for all SetUID files stored on the computer.

8. **d**. The find / -atime +6 -print command is used to search for all files stored on the computer that have not been accessed in the last six days.

9. **c**. The find . -mtime -1 -print command is used to search for all files stored on the local machine and that have been accessed in the last 24 hours. The -symbol is used to indicate that the search is for less than one day.

10. **c**. The check_embedded script that is available in the tiger utility is used for checking embedded pathnames. Other scripts provide these pathnames to the

check_embedded script. The script checks the file for their owners and their access permissions.

11. **d**. The tigercron file is available in the tiger utility and is used for configuring the computer to run the utility at regular intervals, to identify any security problems, and to report to the administrator about any weakness found. The utility also ensures that all deleted files are checked before being actually deleted from the computer. This ensures protection against accidental deletion of system files.

12. **a**. The suid.chk file is used for searching all newly created SetUID files.

Short Answers

1. You can use the fix-modes script that is available by default in all Solaris versions to assign appropriate file access permissions to system files. The script modifies the file access permissions, available by default in Solaris, making access to system files stricter. It also makes it difficult for non-root users to access the system files and modify the files. You can secure the root account by changing its default umask value to either 077 or 027. This ensures that even if a user is able to get access to the root account, he or she will still be unable to get complete access to the computer.

2. You need to ensure that all files in the /etc directory should not provide group write access. You can change or remove the group write permission by using the chmod -R g-w /etc command. You need to ensure that the file access permission for the /etc/utmp directory is maintained at 644. This means that the file owner has read/write permission while the group and everyone else has only read permission. You could also use the sticky bit for the subdirectory.

Chapter 7

**Securing Users
and Applications**

In this chapter, you'll learn to secure user accounts and applications in Solaris. You'll learn about the different types of attacks that can occur on the network and some preventive measures you can implement to secure the network. You'll also learn how to create user accounts on a Solaris computer and ensure their security. This chapter also covers the various tools available in Solaris for ensuring security. Let's begin by understanding the different types of attacks that can exist on the network.

Types of Attacks

The introduction of the Internet in our lives has brought with it both advantages and disadvantages. One of the most critical disadvantages is the risk of network attacks. Although there are different types of networks, the types of attacks they face remain the same. Networks are prone to attacks because they transmit different types of information between clients and servers. Therefore, a recommended practice is to deploy multiple levels of security in a network. If one level of security fails, another level can detect the intrusion. Most networks are configured in such a way that each security level is configured to protect the network against a specific type of network attack. All levels when combined together provide a complete solution to all network security issues. Any change on a computer that is not made by authorized users or services can be classified as a network attack.

A computer processing information slowly, especially while connected to other networks or to the Internet, is a symptom of a network attack in progress. Generally, a network attack is not directed toward a single individual. In case of a network attack, unsecured computers are used for gaining access to the network.

In most of the UNIX and Solaris computers, password authentication forms the frontline defense against unauthorized users. However, hackers can overcome these security measures by utilizing some of the common weaknesses of the system. Most users prefer to use their names, date of birth, or common dictionary words as their passwords. Some users even prefer to leave their passwords blank. These passwords are considered weak because experienced hackers can easily decipher them. If hackers are able to access the password file, they can copy the file to their computer and decrypt the passwords using a variety of decryption programs. Even a single decrypted password can provide hackers access to the network or computer. Most password decryption programs run dictionary searches on the password files and systematically check each password for a match of common dictionary words.

Common types of network attacks are listed as follows:

- **IP spoofing**. An IP address defines the identity of a computer on the network. Each computer's IP address is unique. Therefore, you can equate an IP address to the name of a computer on the network. If a hacker is able to obtain access to the IP address of a valid computer on the network, the address can be used to impersonate the computer. This is known as *IP spoofing*. In IP spoofing, when a client attempts to communicate with a server, it establishes a TCP connection with the server. The connection involves an exchange of messages between the client and the server. The client sends a message to the server and the server acknowledges the message by replying with another message. The client then responds to the server's message, completing the connection. In this process, both the client and the server are authenticated. After the connection is established, the server and the client can exchange information. The danger appears when the server sends an acknowledgement and it is intercepted during transit by a hacker. Since the client has not yet received the message, the process of authentication cannot be considered complete. This state is known as *half-open connections*. Hackers can use such half-open connections to hack current sessions. A hacker can use the address to create data packets that can be used to gather confidential information from the network. These data packets travel the network unchecked because they contain a valid IP address of the network. A hacker can also reroute, modify, or delete data packets originally addressed to an authenticated computer. Information can also be used to perform other types of attacks on the network.

- **Network sniffing**. If data packets are transmitted over the network as plaintext or in unencrypted format, hackers can easily gain access and modify information. Hackers can use programs called network sniffers to intercept and read the unencrypted information. Most of the time, only the first few bytes of all communications are captured. These data bytes normally contain the usernames, passwords and other critical information about the user. Encrypting all transmitted information using cryptographic techniques is the only solution to the problem. In addition, segmenting your network by using switches, bridges, and routers helps check this menace. Sniffers can only sniff the data on the particular segment to which they are attached.

- **Service-layer attack**. In this kind of attack, hackers target individual services running on a computer. Hackers search for known weaknesses of the services and exploit them to gain access to your computers. For example, the `sendmail` service is one of the most common example of weak services. Hackers can use this service to gain access to the servers. They can use the `telnet` utility to retrieve the information about the version of `sendmail` running on the computer. They can then use the known weaknesses of the utility to exploit the system. Another possible weak service is the FTP daemon that can be used to retrieve configuration files from the source computer. The Trivial File Transfer Protocol (TFTP) can be used to retrieve password information from the

/etc/password directory. The weak point of this service is that no authentication is required to run the service. Some of the transmission protocols used on the Internet also have their weak points. For example, because the UDP services are stateless, there is no feedback regarding whether the data packets sent to a recipient reach safely or not. If the HTTP protocol is incorrectly configured on the Web servers, hackers can gain access to a file stored on the server or the network. Hackers can also get access to the password or any configuration information stored on the host computer. Other targets that are vulnerable to hacker attacks are computers that are inadequately secured or running too many services. If proper patches are not applied to the servers or if the security of unused user accounts is not ensured, hackers can use them for intrusion. In addition, if many services are running on a single server, it will not only increase the load on the server but also cause you to neglect the security critical services. Hackers can use this service for DoS attacks.

◆ **Password attacks**. Most operating systems use password authentication, in one form or the other, for implementing network security. A password-based authentication mechanism requires both a valid login and the corresponding password for authenticating a user on the network. Before the use of password-based authentication mechanism, user information was transmitted along with the data packets without being encrypted. Hackers could easily gain access to the unencrypted user information and use it for impersonating the valid user or computer. For example, if a hacker is able to gain access to the login information of the root user account, the hacker will also get the associated rights. For example, hackers can use Trojan Horses to search for and detect passwords of valid users. A Trojan horse is a type of malicious program that hides in a simple and appealing program but infects just like a virus. Some people use the terms Trojan horses and viruses interchangeably, while both of them are different. A virus is a program that spreads by infecting other programs that exist on the host computer. While, a Trojan horse is a program that acts similar to a virus but hides inside a simple program that is visually appealing, for example a game or an animation program. In Windows, most these virus spread in the form of executable programs containing the file extensions vbs, exe, bat, and, com.

◆ **Denial-of-Service (DoS)**. A DoS attack is planned explicitly for rendering a computer of a network incapable of providing service to valid users. The most common targets are connectivity and bandwidth. Hackers flood the network with unnecessary data packets, causing network traffic to slow down or even stop. Valid users are then unable to access important services. In the case of connectivity attacks, hackers can flood a server with a large number of connection requests. These requests consume all the server resources, and the server is unable to service connection requests by valid users. In TCP Service Queues, hackers can flood a host computer with manipulated data packets. The purpose of these data packets is to ensure that all the services are busy responding to these fictitious requests and do not have time to respond to requests made by authentic users. Smurf attacks are another form of DoS attacks. In case of smurf attacks, the Internet Control Message Protocol (ICMP) is used for disrupting network traffic. The protocol is used to check for connectivity with a host computer by sending continuous echo requests. If an answer is received, then the server is functioning properly. The command that is used for this purpose is the ping command. A hacker can use this command to continuously ping to a server or a group of servers, using a false IP address. When the servers reply to the service request, the computer whose IP address is used for the request is flooded by the responses and stops functioning. For example, hackers could use smurf attacks, which is a type of brute for attack, to gain entry to the network. They do so by overwhelming the network with data packets. As the network is unable to bear the burden of the data packets, it becomes very slow or stops functioning.

◆ **Secret key attacks**. In encryption, information transmitted over the network is encrypted using a secret key. If a hacker gains access to the key, the hacker can use it to decrypt all information. In addition, any information that is passed on the network and is encrypted using the compromised secret key can be easily read and modified by the hacker.

◆ **TCP hijacking**. In the case of TCP hijacking, hackers continuously monitor the network for unsecured data packets. If such a data packet is detected, hackers can retrieve confidential information from the data packet and manipulate the data for their purpose. They can also use the IP address stored in the data packet to impersonate a valid user.

◆ **Man-in-the-middle**. In this attack, hackers can position themselves between two authenticated users. The hackers can then monitor, intercept, and manipulate data packets transmitted between the two users without either of the users knowing the difference. Hackers can also impersonate either the sender or the receiver and access all information. For example, a hacker modifies the data packets originating from one user and replaces the owner's IP address with the hacker's own IP address. When the data packets reach the recipient, the recipient assumes the hacker to be a valid sender and continues future transactions with the hacker. Moreover, if the hacker sends the manipulated data back to the original sender, the sender will assume the hacker to be a valid recipient. In this way, hackers can send false or manipulated information to both the sender and the receiver.

You can implement different measures on your computer to secure it against malicious attacks. The next section discusses these measures in detail.

Handling Malicious Attacks

A number of practices are recommended for improving the security of information on the network and for handling malicious network attacks. Following are some of the commonly implemented security practices that are recommended for information security:

◆ A recommended practice is to use passwords that are easy to use, are sufficiently long, and include both alphabetic and numeric characters. This makes sure that the password is not only difficult to read but also difficult to decrypt.

◆ Another recommended practice is to use special characters in the passwords. This ensures that only the valid user remembers the original password. In case you suspect that a hacker has gained access to the password file, you must immediately change all the passwords on the computer.

◆ In general, you should periodically change the password on the computer. This ensures that hackers never know when the passwords might be changed the next time.

◆ You should also secure all accounts currently not being used by either deleting them or by disabling the accounts. Some of the system-created accounts provide their own passwords at the time of creation. These passwords should be immediately changed to protect them from hackers. Sometimes the passwords of system accounts are automatically changed after the application of service patches. To prevent this, you need to regularly check the system accounts after applying patches and change the password, if required.

◆ Another recommended security practice is not to reuse the same password for multiple accounts. If the password is deciphered at one location, all the locations where the password is used are automatically left unsecured.

◆ A recommended practice is to use technologies, such as SSL or Kerberos, to secure passwords as they are being transmitted over the network and across different platforms.

 NOTE

You'll learn more about Kerberos in Chapter 8, "Implementing Kerberos in Solaris."

◆ For services such as sendmail, users can use the telnet utility to retrieve the current version of sendmail implemented on the computer. Users can then apply the security patches pertaining to the version. In addition, there are certain tools shipped with the current version of sendmail that can be used to secure the utility. For example, the smrsh or *sendmail restricted shell* can be used to manage mail received by the computer and prevent unauthorized commands to be executed on the computer. You can also use the `mail.local` file to control the way in which the `/bin/mail` application is used by the computer to handle mail. Always run the latest version of `sendmail` along with the appropriate service pack. This ensures that all mail sent and received on your computer is secured.

 NOTE

You'll learn more about the sendmail service in Chapter 10, "Securing Web and E-Mail Services."

◆ FTP service is another service for which you need to ensure that the latest version is installed. You need to ensure that the proper security precautions have been taken and that only authorized users have access to the service. A recommended practice is to create a separate group for accessing the FTP services. You can then assign appropriate access permissions to the group and only add users who require access to the FTP service. When discussing securing FTP connections between firewalls it is also important to consider the difference between *active* and *passive FTP*. Simply defined, FTP is a service that transmits data across the network using two specific ports called data port and command port. Mostly, these ports are configured on port 21 of the source and destination machines. The problem arises when the data port cannot be configured on port 21 as the port might already be in use. This is where the difference between active and passive FTP arises. In case of active FTP, the client connects to command port on the FTP server using a port selected at random. The server then establishes connection with the client using the client port information received by the FTP server. The disadvantage of this type of connection is that the FTP client doesn't actually connect to the FTP server. The client only passes the information about the port on which it wants to establish connection and the server has the responsibility of establishing the connection at the specified port number. However, in case of passive FTP, the client not only initiates the connection with the server, but also resolves all issues relating to the transfer of data between the FTP server and client.

◆ You also need to ensure the security of the network components. Most vendors provide the components with only the basic security measures implemented for the configuration files. For example, the `/etc/hosts.equiv` file supplied by vendors contains a plus (+) sign before all entries. This indicates that the computer where this file is implemented trusts all other computers on the network. You also need to make sure that all other `.rhosts` files on the computer are not writable by everyone else.

The security of all system files and directories, such as the root directory and all files stored in the /etc directory and subdirectories, needs to be ensured. You also need to make sure that all files have appropriate access permissions and file ownership. Installing the latest service patches is essential for ensuring the security of the computer. Most service patches update the file and provide solutions to known bugs on the system. Finally, you need to check that all services running on your computer that access external computers, such as the FTP and the Web services, are properly secured. All network traffic sent and received from the external sources should be properly checked and authenticated.

Managing User Accounts

In Chapter 3, "System Startup and Data Access Security" you learned about the Role-Based Access Control (RBAC) model available in Solaris. You can use this model to assign rights to specific roles and assign users to these roles. This ensures that you do not need to assign all the rights to a single user.

One of the tasks involved in administering a Solaris computer is creating and administering user accounts. A standard user account contains the following pieces of information:

◆ **Login name**. This is the name assigned to the user on the network. This name is unique to each user and identifies the presence of the user on the network. All audit logs store user information based on the login name. Another point to remember is that the login name or the user name must be unique within your organization. This is true even if the organizational network contains multiple domains. A typical user name must contain two to eight characters, which should be alphanumeric for better security. Alphanumeric passwords are difficult to crack as compared to plain alphabets because of the larger range of possible combinations. However, the first character should always be an alpha character and at least one character in the user name should be in lowercase.

CAUTION

Each new login name must be distinct from any mail aliases known either to the system, NIS or NIS+ domain. In the case where you do not ensure the uniqueness of the login name, the mails would be delivered to the alias instead of being sent to the actual user.

◆ **Password**. This is used for ensuring the security of a user's login on the network and is stored in an encrypted form. As mentioned earlier, all logs store user information based on the login name. Therefore, if hackers are able to decrypt the password, they can log on assuming the identity of the user and perform malicious tasks. Only after the correct login name and password have been provided should a user be allowed access to the computer. Ideally a password should be a combination of six to eight alpha, numeric, or special characters. Security should also be considered while setting passwords. Users who don't change their passwords regularly pose a major risk to network security. This is because passwords are susceptible to hacking attempts by hackers who want to gain access to the login information of valid users. This is especially true in case of remote users who logon from a remote location. In case the authentication information transmitted by the remote machine is not in an encrypted format, hackers can easily gain access to the information. This is why the concept of *password ageing* was introduced. This forces all network users to change their passwords after a specific interval of time. Only an administrator or a superuser has the right to set the maximum and the minimum time period for which a password can remain valid. Solaris provides the use of the `password` command along with the `-x` and `-y` options for configuring the password settings. The `-x` option is used for setting the maximum time period and `-y` option is used for setting the minimum time period for which the password can be active.

◆ **UID**. A *user identification number* or UID as it is commonly called is linked with each user's name and is used to uniquely identify the user on the network. The UID information is used to identify the user with the system on which the user attempts to login. The system then uses the UID to provide the user with the rights to access the resources for which the user has the rights. In case a user has accounts on multiple systems, it is a recommended practice to use the same user name and UID. This helps while moving files between different systems since the owner of the file remains the same. Typically, a UID should be a whole number, which should range between 0 and 2147483647. There are certain UID's that are considered as reserved and generally should not be used. These UID's, which typically range between 0 and 99, are generally used for system accounts. However, in exceptional circumstances you could assign a UID from this range to a user account but these accounts should not be regular users. Typically, UID 0 is assigned to the root account and UID 1 is assigned to the daemon.

◆ **Path to home directory**. This section stores the path to a user's home directory. Every user is allocated a separate home directory where the user can store all personal files and create subdirectories. After the user logs on to the computer, the current directory is the user's home directory. For example the home directory for a user named `user1` can be `/export/home/user1`. The folder `user1` is created under the `home` folder in the `exports` sub folder under the root.

◆ **Initialization files**. This section contains shell scripts that determine a user's working environment and provide other information regarding which services are available to users when they log on. For example, the `.login`, `.cshrs`, `.profile` files in user's home directory store and provide information about the user.

After a user account is created, every user needs to be assigned to a specific group. A *group* can be defined as a set of users who have similar rights and share files and other system resources. A group determines the level of user rights and permissions. It determines which resources a user can access and which resources a user cannot access. Each group has a name, and a *group identification number* (GID) by which the system identifies the group. There are basically two types of groups to which a user can be assigned - *primary group* and *secondary group*. It is compulsory to assign a user to a primary group, however it is optional to assign a user to the secondary group. The operating system assigns a user's primary group details to files created by the user.

Creating User Accounts Manually

Although Solaris provides certain tools that automate the task of creating user accounts, it is always good to understand how user accounts are actually created. The task of creating a typical user account involves the following activities:

◆ Add an entry for the user in the /etc/passwd file.

◆ Add an entry in the /etc/shadow file in case the user account requires a shadow password.

◆ Assign an appropriate password for the user account and set the appropriate policies.

◆ Add the user to the appropriate group by adding an entry in the /etc/group file.

◆ Assign a home directory for the user and change the access rights for the directory so that only the user has the appropriate rights for the home directory.

◆ Assign appropriate rights to initialize files after copying them to the user's home directory.

 CAUTION

The passwd file should not be manipulated manually unless an experienced network administrator who has knowledge about the task does it. If this file is corrupted, all users will be denied access to the computer and the operating system would need to be reinstalled. Therefore, it is recommended to regularly back up the passwd file along with other system files and to keep the passwd file updated.

◆ After adding the required entries in the /etc/passwd and the /etc/shadow files, you need to edit the /etc/group file. When creating a new user, the useradd command can be used with the -g option to assign a group to the user. Following is the syntax of the useradd command:

```
useradd [ -u uid ][ -g gid ][ -G gid [,gid,.. ]][ -d dir ][ -m ][ -s
shell ][ -c comment ] loginname
```

In the preceding code:

-u uid – Sets the unique UID for the new user.

-g group – Assigns a predefined group's ID or name to the user.

-G group – Defines the new user's secondary group memberships.

-d dir – Defines the full pathname for the user's home directory.

-m – Creates the new home directory if it does not already exist.

-s shell – Defines the full pathname for the shell program to be used as the user's login shell. By default /bin/sh is assigned to a user.

-c comment –Used to specify the user's full name and location.

-o – Allows a UID to be duplicated.

-e expire – Assigns an expiration date on the user account. The date is assigned in the mm/dd/yy format and specifies the date on which a user can no longer log in and access the account. After the specified date the account is locked.

-f inactive – Sets the number of inactive days allowed on a user account. If the account is not logged into during the specified number of days it is locked.

-k skel_dir – Specifies an alternative directory location containing customized initialization files to be copied into the user's home directory. The default directory location is /etc/skel.

◆ After assigning a group to the user, the next task is to create the user's home directory. You can use the mkdir command to create this directory. You must also ensure that you use a consistent name for creating the user's home directory. This name should match the name that you specified in the /etc/passwd file while creating the user account. By default, all newly created directories belong to the root account.

◆ Finally, you can use the chmod and the chown commands to change the file access permissions for the directory.

All initialization and startup files for users are stored in their respective home folders. These files, also known as dot files because of their extension, are used for configuring a user's environment and startup settings.

Although it is possible to create user accounts manually, Solaris offers a number of utilities for creating and administering these accounts. In Solaris, one of the utilities commonly used for managing a user account is the admintool utility. This utility helps to create user accounts in a simple manner after prompting for certain essential information. The following section focuses on the admintool in detail.

Using the admintool for Managing User Accounts

Solaris provides the admintool for administering network user accounts. The admintool is a graphical tool that is used for administering both local computers and distributed networks. It is also used for configuring printers, ports, and software and for local account management in the CDE. The right to use the tool is restricted to the sysadmin group and everyone else has only read permission. The members of the sysadmin tool use the utility for manipulating system files.

The admintool utility can be used to perform the following tasks:

◆ **Modifying user accounts**. The admintool utility can be used for modifying existing user accounts based on the username or user IDs (UIDs). You must remember that the UID of two user accounts cannot be same. In case the UID of two user accounts are similar, you need to delete one account and re-create it using a different UID. It is not possible to modify the UID of an existing user account. However, if two user accounts have the same username, you can use the admintool utility to modify the name of one of the user accounts. You can also use the utility to modify user group information. You can either assign a secondary group to a user or directly modify the user's group information. You can also change the password, login shell, and comments information.

◆ **Deleting user accounts**. You can use the admintool utility for deleting user accounts that are no longer required. The admintool deletes not only the user account information, but also the corresponding information in the passwd and group files. The user home directory can also be deleted with the account, if required.

◆ **Customizing initialization files**. You can use the admintool for storing the user initialization files in the user's home directory. However, you cannot use the utility for creating the initialization files. The template initialization files are available in separate directories called skeleton directories, which are located in /etc/skel. These initialization files must be customized for each user.

◆ **Disabling user accounts**. You can use the admintool for deleting existing user accounts or for disabling them for a certain period. You can disable a user account either by locking the password for the account or by specifying an invalid password. This ensures that the user can no longer use the login for logging on to the computer. You can also disable an account by setting an expiry date for the password.

◆ **Managing passwords**. You can also use the admintool for either specifying a password for a user account or for specifying that the user should specify a password the first time the user logs on to the computer.

The next section discusses the steps that you need to perform for creating a user account by using the `admintool` utility.

Adding Users by Using the admintool Utility

Perform the following steps to add a new user account by using the `admintool` utility:

1. At the command prompt, type `admintool &`. The Admintool:Users window appears as shown in Figure 7-1. If another option is selected, you might need to select the Users option under the Browse menu to view the Admintool:Users window.

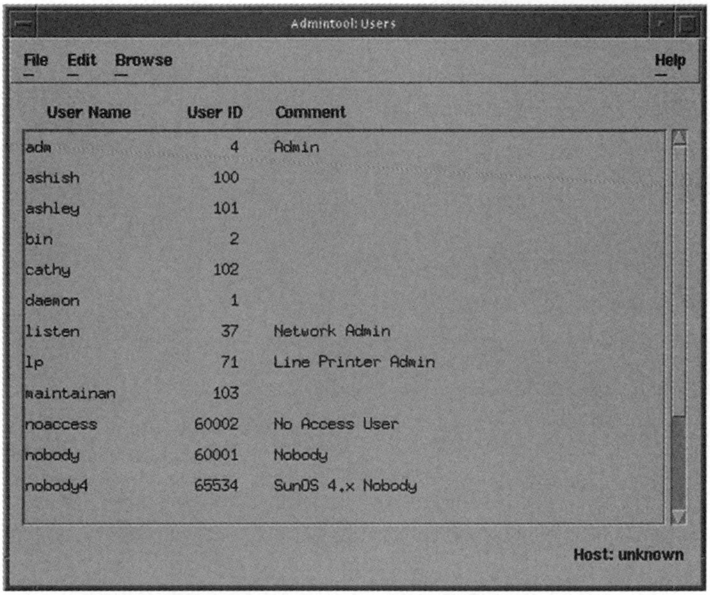
Admintool: Users
File Edit Browse
Help
User Name User ID Comment
adm 4 Admin
ashish 100
ashley 101
bin 2
cathy 102
daemon 1
listen 37 Network Admin
lp 71 Line Printer Admin
maintainan 103
noaccess 60002 No Access User
nobody 60001 Nobody
nobody4 65534 SunOS 4.x Nobody
Host: unknown

FIGURE 7-1 *The* `Admintool:Users` *window*

2. From the `Edit` menu, choose `Add`. The `Admintool:Add User` window appears as shown in Figure 7-2.

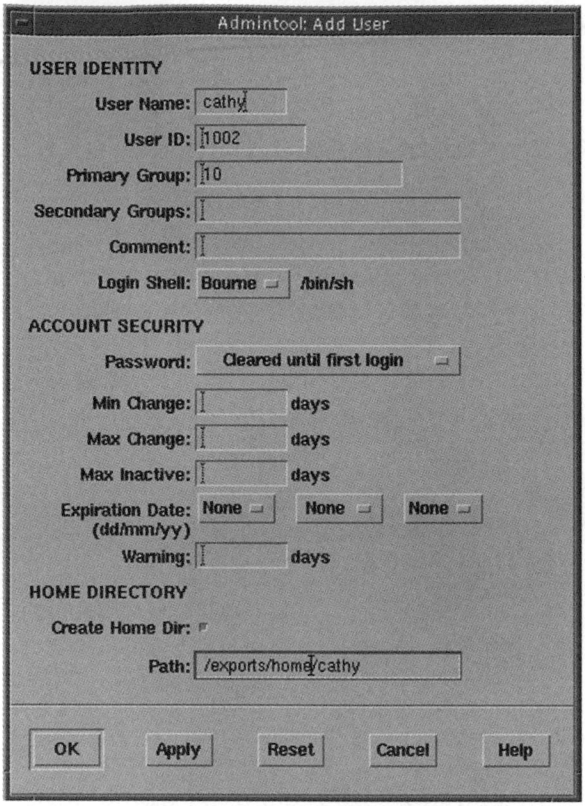

FIGURE 7-2 *The* Admintool:Add User *window*

3. Enter the user information in the Admintool:Add User window. The user's home directory should be created in the /exports/home subdirectory.

4. Click OK to submit the user information and create the new user account. The new user is added to the list of available users in the Users window.

You can also create a new group for grouping all users with requirements for similar access permissions.

Adding Groups by Using the admintool Utility

Perform the following steps to add a new group by using the admintool utility:

1. Ensure that the admintool is currently running, otherwise, at the command prompt, type admintool &.

2. From the Browse menu, choose Groups. The Admintool:Groups window appears as shown in Figure 7-3.

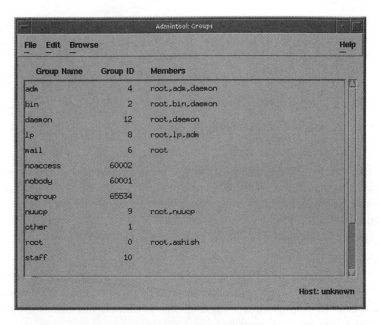

FIGURE 7-3 *The* Admintool:Groups *window list the groups already registered on the computer.*

3. From the Edit menu, choose Add. The Admintool:Add Group window appears, as shown in Figure 7-4. Enter details about the group in this window.

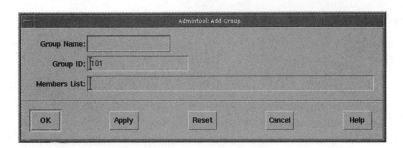

FIGURE 7-4 *The* Admintool:Add Group *window*

4. In the Group Name box, enter the name for the group.

5. In the Group ID box, enter a unique group ID for the group.

6. You can also assign users to the group by typing the username in the Members List box. This is an optional field because you can also assign user to the group at a later stage.

7. Click OK to add the group to the list of currently available groups in the Admintool:Add Group window.

Next, you need to share the user's home directory. It is important to restrict the access permission for the home directory to an appropriate user. This ensures that only the authorized user can access information stored in the home directory.

Sharing a User's Home Directory

Perform the following steps to share a user's home directory:

1. Log on as a superuser on the computer containing the home directory.
2. Ensure that the mountd daemon is running. This information is stored in the /usr/lib/nfs/mountd line returned by the ps -ef command. If the daemon is not running, you can start it by using the /etc/init.d/nfs.server start command.
3. Use the share command to list all the file systems shared on the computer.
4. Verify that the file system on which the user home directory is created is shared. Otherwise, add the line share -F nfs /<file system> to the /etc/dfs/dfstab file where <file system> is the file system that you want to share. Execute the command shareall -F nfs to execute the share commands stored in the /etc/dfs/dfstab file.
5. Verify that the user's home directory is shared by using the share command.

Next, you'll learn how to modify the details of an existing user account.

Modifying a User Account

Perform the following steps to modify the details of an existing user account by using the admintool utility:

1. Ensure that the admintool is currently running, otherwise, at the command prompt, type admintool &.
2. From the Browse menu, click Users.
3. From the Users window, select the user account whose details you want to modify.
4. From the Edit menu, choose Modify. The Admintool: Modify User window appears as shown in Figure 7-5.
5. Now you can modify whichever information you want. You can also modify the user settings.
6. Click OK to submit the changes and modify the user account.

In the next section, you'll learn how to change the settings of a user password.

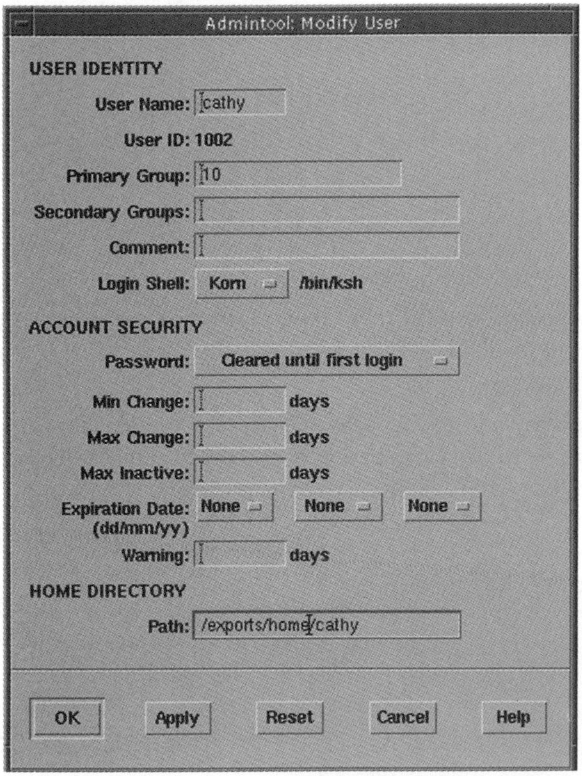

FIGURE 7-5 *Using the* Admintool: Modify User *window for modifying user details*

Changing a User's Password Settings

Perform the following steps to change the password of an existing user account by using the admintool utility:

1. Ensure that the admintool is currently running, otherwise, at the command prompt, type admintool &.

2. From the Browse menu, click Users.

3. From the Users window, select the user account whose details you want to modify.

4. From the Edit menu, choose Modify. The Admintool: Modify User window appears. You need to make modifications to the user's password settings as shown in Figure 7-6.

5. From the Password menu, choose Normal Password. When you select the option, the Set User Password dialog box appears. You can assign a password for the user account using this dialog box. You will need to enter the password twice. The password is entered once in the Enter Password field and the second time in the Verify Password field. Click OK to submit the password.

CAUTION

You cannot assign a NULL password to a user account.

6. In the `Min Change` box, enter 7. This field provides the minimum time that should lapse before the password can be changed. Therefore, a user needs to wait for a minimum of seven days before changing the password.

7. In the `Max Change` box, enter 30. This field provides the maximum time that should lapse after which the password must be changed. Therefore, a user needs to change the password every month.

8. In the `Max Inactive` box, enter 60. This field provides the maximum time for which the account can remain inactive before being locked. Therefore, the current user account can remain inactive for a maximum of 60 days.

```
                    Admintool: Modify User

USER IDENTITY
              User Name: │cathy
                User ID: 1002
          Primary Group: │10
       Secondary Groups: │
                Comment: │
            Login Shell:  Korn  ▭  /bin/ksh

ACCOUNT SECURITY
               Password:    Normal Password...    ▭
             Min Change: │7     │ days
             Max Change: │30    │ days
           Max Inactive: │60    │ days
        Expiration Date:  16  ▭   Aug  ▭   2002 ▭
            (dd/mm/yy)
                Warning: │15    │ days

HOME DIRECTORY
                   Path: │/exports/host/cathy        │

        OK       Apply      Reset      Cancel      Help
```

FIGURE 7-6 *Using the* `Admintool: Modify User` *window for changing the user's password settings*

9. Change the value of the Expiration Date field. This field is used for setting the expiration date for a user account. This process is generally followed for temporary user accounts.

10. In the Warning box, enter 15. This field provides the information about the number of days that must be remaining for the password to expire before the warning message is flashed.

11. Click OK to submit the changes and modify the user details.

Disabling a User Account

Perform the following steps to disable an existing user account by using the admintool utility:

1. Ensure that the admintool is currently running, otherwise, at the command prompt, type admintool &.

2. From the Browse menu, click Users.

3. From the Users window, select the user account that you want to disable.

4. From the Edit menu, choose Modify. The Modify Users window is displayed containing the user's details.

5. From the Password menu, choose Account is locked.

6. Click OK to disable the account. You can attempt to log on using the disabled account to verify that the account has been disabled.

Deleting a User Account

Perform the following steps to delete an existing user account by using the admintool utility:

1. Ensure that the admintool is currently running, otherwise, at the command prompt, type admintool &.

2. From the Browse menu, click Users.

3. From the Users window, select the user account that you want to delete.

4. From the Edit menu, choose Delete. The Admintool: Warning dialog box appears asking you to confirm the deletion, as shown in Figure 7-7. You can also delete the user's home directory and the files.

5. Click the Delete button in the Admintool: Warning dialog box to delete the user account or the Cancel button to cancel the deletion.

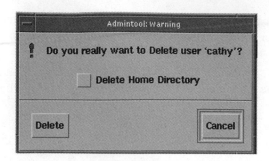

FIGURE 7-7 *The* Admintool:Warning *dialog box appears and requires you to confirm the deletion.*

Deleting a Group

Perform the following steps to delete an existing group by using the admintool utility:

1. Ensure that the admintool is currently running, otherwise, at the command prompt, type admintool &.
2. From the Browse menu, click Groups.
3. From the Groups window, select the group that you want to delete.
4. From the Edit menu, choose Delete. The Admintool: Warning dialog box appears asking you to confirm the deletion.
5. Click Delete to delete the group entry or Cancel to cancel the deletion.

In the next section, I'll explain the difference between authentication and authorization.

Authentication and Authorization

Authentication is the process of establishing the identity of users by using UIDs and passwords. You can validate the UID and password by using a cryptographic algorithm. You should know the authentication mechanism used and the data exchange process between the client and server. This is important for ensuring the security of information that is exchanged between the two computers. Each authentication mechanism has its own weaknesses that need to be secured before information can be safely transmitted over the network.

Authorization is the process of identifying how users are provided the rights to access the files and directories. You must periodically review these rights to ensure that only authorized people have access to resources. The allocation of rights depends on the requirement and designation of the user in the organization.

Following is an example of improper authorization and improper assignment of rights by the administrator on the server. David, a new trainee, has been employed by Soft Commerce to enter a backlog of ledger entries on a server. For evaluating a few entries, he copies certain programs on root directory of the server. When David tries to execute the programs, he finds that he cannot execute the programs since he doesn't have the appropriate access permissions. David happened to know the root password, so he uses the root access to change permissions for all files on the server using the chmod command. He specifies that all the files available on the server should be readable and writable by everyone. After entering all data, David decides to delete the files he had earlier copied. However, along with his files, he also deletes the passwd file available in the /etc directory. This situation could have been avoided if the administrator had restricted the right to delete system files to the root user account and placed David in a group with rights only to enter data on the server.

David could have also prevented the mishap from occurring by using the setuid command. He could use the command to modify the execute properties of program(s), so that he gets administrative access to them. Once he has done this he can execute those programs with administrative privileges, even when having logged on with his own user id.

Secured Shell (SSH)

Secured shell (SSH) is a utility that allows a user to securely log on to another computer or network. You can also use the utility to execute commands on the remote computer and transfer files securely over the network. It provides a secure means of transferring information because of its effective authentication and encryption mechanism. It is primarily used as a replacement for the previously used unsecured programs, such as rsh, rlogin, and rpc. These commands were vulnerable to hacking attempts; any hacker who gained root access to a computer could use these commands to gain access to other resources available on the network.

SSH encrypts information by using various encryption techniques available, such as Triple DES, IDEA, and Blowfish. It also uses the RDA and DSA cipher mechanisms for providing authentication facilities.

SSH provides security against the following types of attacks:

◆ **DNS spoofing**. In this type of attack, hackers add some fictitious DNS entries that can be later used to gain access to the network. The process of DNS spoofing involves replacing the existing IP address mapped to a DNS name with another IP address. Hackers perform this type of attack by corrupting the DNS database on the target computer so that they can easily map the computer names (which are easily readable since the DNS database is corrupted) to their corresponding IP addresses. Therefore, when a client requests a connection using a machine's DNS name, the request is redirected to the machine designated by the hackers. Hackers can then use this method to obtain the login information of valid users. The hacker's machine can also pass false information to the client machines. This type of attack is also known as a *Man-in-the-middle attack*. SSH provides security against this type of attacks by providing the use of the `slogin` command, which is more secure as compared to the commonly used `rlogin` command. This is because the `slogin` command encrypts the entire session including the authentication information passed between computers. In case a hacker manages to gain access to the network, the maximum damage that the hacker can perform is to force SSH to disconnect. Hackers cannot gain access to any information because all information is encrypted.

◆ **IP spoofing**. In IP spoofing, hackers manipulate the address of data packets so that they appear to originate from a trusted host computer. SSH provides security against hackers on the local network who might try to impersonate authentic routers on the local network. SSH provides protection by using a strong authentication method.

◆ **Password hacking**. Here, hackers attempt to gain access to a password being transmitted over the network. SSH provides security against this type of attack by encrypting all confidential information, such as passwords and user information, before it is transmitted over the network.

◆ **Data manipulation**. In this type of attack, hackers attempt to manipulate data as it is transmitted over the network. They might gain access to an intermediate host computer and manipulate the data as it passes through the host computer. The SSH packets appear to be random without a key to decrypt them. Thus, manipulation is not possible.

◆ **Weaknesses in X server**. Hackers can take advantage of the inherent weaknesses of the X server by manipulating the X server authentication process and spoofing the connection to the X server. SSH provides security while forwarding of random TCP connections and for securing X connections .

SSH provides adequate security against hackers who might gain access to the computers on the network. These hackers might be able to stop SSH, but they cannot use the utility to gain access to confidential information being passed over the network. However, SSH is only effective when all network traffic is properly encrypted. If encryption is not used, then SSH becomes ineffective.

SSH provides the facility for establishing a secured communication between two unsecured computers that do not have a trust relationship between them over an unsecured network, for example, the Internet. The computer that needs to connect to the other computer specifies the other computer's name as the host name. The user account is then authenticated on the host computer. Many methods can be used for authenticating the UID. The client computer or the computer from which the user attempts to try connecting could be listed in the host computer's `/etc/shosts.equiv` or `/etc/hosts.equiv` files. The user account should also exist both on the host computer as well as on the client computer. If both these conditions are met, the user is authenticated on the host computer. Another way for the user to be authenticated is for an entry for the client computer and the user account to exist in the `.rhosts` or `.shosts` file stored on the host computer. However, both of these methods are generally not used by themselves because of their unse-cured nature and the risk of hackers modifying the files.

A more common approach for authenticating remote users on the host computer is using both of the previously mentioned methods along with a RSA-based host authentication mechanism. In this case, after the user account has been authenticated and an entry for the client computer is found in either of the previously mentioned files, the client's host key is also authenticated. Only after the key has been authenticated is the user allowed access to the remote computer.

Another method in SSH can be used for authenticating users on the host computer. This method is completely RSA-based authentication and uses the public and private key cryptography for ensuring encryption of information being passed over the network. Every user on the client computer creates a unique public and private key pair for themselves. The public key is stored with the servers or computer and the private key is available with the user. Information about all public keys that can be used on a computer are stored in the $HOME/.ssh/authorized_keys file. When a remote user attempts to connect to a host computer, SSH prompts the host computer for the required public key. The host computer searches for the public key in the list of valid public keys stored on the computer. If the key is found, the host computer generates a random number and encrypts it using the public key. The encrypted number is known as a *challenge* and is sent to the user. The user then decrypts the number using the private key. This ensures that the user has the correct private key and is an authentic user. This is also a secure method because none of the keys are transmitted. Therefore, there is no risk of hackers getting access to either the public or the private key.

The use of RSA protocol for encryption is an inherent feature of SSH, so the protocol does not need to be invoked explicitly. The user creates the RSA key pair by using the ssh-keygen command and stores the public key in the .ssh/identity. pub file and the private key in the .ssh/identity file. Both of these files exist in the user's home directory. The public key is then copied to the home directory of the user created on the host computer.

SSH uses yet another method for authenticating users on the host computer. This authentication method uses TIS authentication servers to validate user identity. SSH uses the TIS authsrv command to authenticate user login information with the information already stored in the TIS database. However, it is not always true that user information is used for authenticating users on the host computers. Sometimes the serial number of authentication devices are also stored in the TIS database and compared later for authenticating users. This is common in cases where the user logs on to the remote host computer by using smart cards or other external authentication mechanisms. The information regarding users and their corresponding information, stored in the TIS database, is stored in the /etc/sshd_tis.map file, which exists on the host computer. In case the username or the file does not exist, the host computer assumes that the username and the name in the TIS database are the same.

When SSH uses any of the previously mentioned methods for authenticating users, the users are not prompted to supply their password. However, in case all these authentication methods fail, SSH prompts users to provide their password while being authenticated. This information is then sent to the host computer in an encrypted form. If the user's credentials are accepted or found to be valid, the appropriate command is executed or the user is provided a normal login on the host computer.

The syntax of executing SSH is as follows:

```
# ssh -keygen
```

ssh-keygen is a tool that is used for generating and administering authentication keys for the SSH utility. Any user who needs to create a pair of public and private keys for RSA authentication can use this tool to create the keys. The tool can also be used by administrators for creating host keys for the SSH secure server.

 NOTE

In case of host authentication, the remote host required access to the public key of local host. A copy of the public key of local host is stored in $HOME/.ssh/known_hosts on the remote host.

Table 7-1 lists various options available with the SSH command and their descriptions.

Table 7-1 Options Available with the SSH command

Option	Description
-a	Disables the forwarding mechanism of the authentication agent. You can also deny access to a specific computer. This prevents the specified computers from being able to connect to the host computer.
-c	Specifies the encryption mechanism to be used for encrypting the connection between two computers. As mentioned earlier, Triple DES is used for securing information since it is the most secure mechanism among the commonly used encryption mechanisms. Triple DES is used in case IDEA is not supported by either of the two computers. In recent times, the use of blowfish has gained popularity because of its use of 128 bit encryption.

Option	Description
-f	Runs SSH in the background, after a user has been authenticated and a secure connection has been established between two computers. This is mainly applicable in cases where the user wants to handle authentication and data access but also wants the process to run SSH in the background. This option is mainly used to run X11 applications on host computers.
-i <iden_file>	Specifies a file in which the private key is stored. This key is used for RSA authentication. The default location of the private key is the .ssh/identity file and the file is stored in the user's home directory. You can also create separate identity files for different host computers, in case the same client requires access to multiple computers. In this case, you will need to specify multiple -i options, one for each host computer.
-l login_name	Provides the login name of the users who need to log on to the host computer. You can also create a configuration file containing this information, which is customized based on individual host computers.
-p <port_num>	Specifies the port on the host computer that is used by the client computer to establish the connection. This information can differ for every host computer. Therefore, you can create separate configuration files containing the port number of the appropriate host computer.
-q	Establishes the connection between the two computers in silence mode. This means that all error messages and warnings are suppressed and only the most critical error messages are displayed. Critical error messages are those errors in which the connection between two computers cannot continue.
-p	Establishes connection with certain firewalls that refuse connections to the privileged ports. You can specify unprivileged ports with this option. Unprivileged ports are used in cases where .rhost or .rsarhosts authentication is not required.
-v	Runs SSH in verbose mode. This is the opposite of the -q option, because SSH displays all the error and debug messages encountered by the computer while establishing the connection.
-V	Only prints the version number and then exits the connection.

continues

Table 7-1 (continued)

Option	Description
-C	Compresses all information being passed over the network. This option is important in cases where modems are being used or the network connection is very slow. However, if compression is used on a fast network, it will slow down network traffic.
-L port:host:hport	Specifies a port on the local computer whose information is passed to the remote computer. Information about the host name and the port number are specified using the host and hport parameters. In this case, a socket is assigned on the local computer that transmits the client information to the port specified on the host computer. The configuration files can also contain port information, however, only the root account can forward information to the privileged ports.
-R port:host:hport	Specifies the port address of a remote computer. When a user tries to establish a connection from a client computer, information about the port provided on the host computer is also passed. As mentioned previously, a socket connection is established between the two ports and information is transmitted securely using the connection. You can also specify the port information in configuration files. However, only the root account has the right to forward information to the privileged ports.

You can use a combination of the options mentioned in the preceding table to establish connection between the client computer and the host computer. You can use numerous tools available in Solaris for ensuring the security of user accounts and applications installed on a Solaris computer. The following section discusses some of the commonly available tools in Solaris.

Tools for Controlling Access

At present, the world has become an integrated network of information systems, where the need for ensuring the security, confidentiality, and availability of information is of prime importance. Along with the numerous advantages provided by interoperability, there is also the risk of hackers gaining access to the data stored on the network. Each network or computer that connects to another network provides the possibility of another security loophole that hackers might use to gain access to confidential information. The following sections discuss some of the tools that can be used on Solaris computers for securing user accounts and applications.

TCP Wrappers

A TCP wrapper is a simple tool available on Solaris and UNIX computers that can be used for monitoring network traffic, controlling access of remote users, detecting intrusions, and filter connections to network services. It provides services similar to the ones provided by firewalls. A developer named Wietse Venema developed the first version of a TCP wrapper. It was developed to track a Dutch hacker who had caused a lot of damage on a UNIX server. The hacker logged on to the computer and ran the rm -rf / command. This command, when executed by a user with sufficiently high access rights such as the root account, can cause the deletion of system critical files. The hacker used to use the finger utility to discover the details of users who were currently logged on to the server. The hacker then analyzed the information, identified the users that were idle, and impersonated the user accounts to create havoc on the computer. The wrapper performed the simple task of recording the name of the remote host whenever the connection was established.

You might already know about the Transmission Control Protocol/Internet Protocol (TCP/IP), which is a suite of protocols used for communication over the Internet. The TCP wrapper forms a type of firewall between the host computer and remote computers trying to establish connections with the host computer. The wrapper decides whether certain services should be allowed to run on the server or not. The administrator configures the instructions about which services should be allowed and which should not be allowed to run on the host computer based on the requirements of the clients and the security issues in question. The wrapper, therefore, serves as an interface between the TCP/IP protocol suit and the services running on the host computer. The TCP wrapper is triggered whenever a client requests for a specific network service. When the connection is established, the wrapper checks for the security of the connection. After the wrapper has determined that the connection is secure, the requested program is run and the wrapper waits for the next request. TCP wrappers work on the simple mechanism of moving the network service being requested by the TCP daemon to another file until the client is authenticated. The wrapper works without remote user's knowledge and is application independent. This means that the same wrapper can be used to secure multiple applications. When the wrapper is executed, it first searches for the client computer's address in its list of valid IP addresses. The wrapper then accesses the host.allow file to search for all services allowed for the specified computer. The file contains rules for users, host computers, networks, and for specific services that are allowed to access resources on the server. If an entry is found that allows the user to access the service, the control is transferred to the appropriate process. Following are some of the common features of TCP wrappers:

◆ Do not need to make modifications to existing programs.

◆ Are used for monitoring network traffic and managing access to important network services, such as finger, ftp, telnet, rsh, rlogin, and systat.

◆ Provide facility for logging access information about services and for certain services that are normally not logged.

◆ Pass the connection to the appropriate process after the user has been authenticated and has the appropriate access permission for the requested service.

◆ Provide certain utilities that can be used for predicting the outcome of a certain command execution. These utilities determine if the user should be allowed access to certain services, such as FTP and Telnet.

◆ Can be used for sending information to the client or the user requesting connection to the host computer.

◆ Do not affect the performance of the system or the connection between the clients and the host computer.

TCP wrappers cannot be used on applications that require the service of other protocols besides the TCP/IP protocol. They cannot be used on applications that are continuously running or that require excessive security. Therefore, you cannot consider TCP wrappers as a replacement for conventional security measures, since they are prone to IP spoofing and sniffer attacks. Therefore, TCP wrappers are important for ensuring that limited users are allowed access to the services running on the host computer. They form a security layer required for ensuring the safety of information being transmitted from a server.

rpcbind

You can describe rpcbind as a service that translates RPC program numbers into universal addresses. You must ensure that the Remote Procedure Call (RPC) service is running on the server in order to make RPC calls from the server and rpcbind is the central RPC service agent. You can use the rpcinfo command to list all RPC services currently running on the system. When the service is started, the rpcbind utility is informed about the port number on which future calls will be received. The utility is also informed about the RPC program numbers that would be serviced. Only a superuser can run the utility. When a client tries to make an RPC call, it connects to the rpcbind utility running on the server. The server returns the address of the server that would service the request. Therefore, the rpcbind utility should be the first utility to be started on the server. After the utility is started, it checks the list of computer names against the list of address translations available on the server. If the names and addresses do not match, then the list is considered to be corrupt. In such a case, the rpcbind utility raises an error and terminates execution of the command. Following is the syntax of the rpcbind command:

```
rpcbind [-d] [-w]
```

 NOTE

In case rpcbind is restarted you'll also need to restart all RPC servers.

As shown in the preceding code, the rpcbind utility can be run with either the -d option or the -w option. The -d option runs the utility in debug mode. This means that in case an error is encountered, a warning is generated for recoverable errors while the program terminates in case of irrecoverable errors. The option provides a full listing of all errors encountered while matching the computer name against the address translation table. In case of the -w option, the program writes information about all the currently registered services available on the system before halting execution. The execution is halted in case the server receives the SIGINT or SIGTERM signals. The information is stored in the /tmp/portmap file and the /tmp/rpcbind file. This option allows the rpcbind utility to restart operation from the point where the execution had halted. In this case, the system does not need to restart all the previously working RPC services, since these services were never stopped. You can prevent the system from writing to the previously mentioned files by using the SIGKILL command. However, in such a case, all the services will be restarted. Table 7-2 lists the options available with the rpcbind utility.

Table 7-2 Options Available with *rpcbind* Utility

Option	Description
-d	This option is run in debug mode. In this mode, rpcbind does not work when it starts. The utility will only print additional information during operation and will abort on certain errors. You can also use this option to show the name-to-address translation consistency checks in detail.
-i	This option is used for running the utility in the insecure mode. In this mode, the utility can make calls to SET and UNSET from any host. In secure mode, rpcbind accepts requests only from the loopback interface for ensuring security. This is not true in the insecure mode. This mode is necessary for running applications that were compiled with earlier versions of the rpc library and therefore don't make requests using the loopback interface.
-l	This option is used for turning on the libwrap connection logging.
-s	This option forces rpcbind to change to the user daemon as soon as possible. This makes rpcbind use non-privileged ports for outgoing connections and prevents non-privileged clients from using rpcbind to connect to services from a privileged port.
-L	This option allows the utility to establish a local connection over the loopback interface. If this flag is not specified, local connections are only allowed over a local socket, using /var/run/rpcbind.sock.

Crack

Crack is a freeware software that is available for decrypting standard UNIX passwords, which have been encrypted by using DES encryption. Both system administrators and ordinary users can use the utility for decrypting passwords. The utility uses the password file and source directories as its parameters. It then combines all the information stored in the directories into a single file and sorts all the password information in a sequential order. The utility then creates a list off all the possible passwords based on the information provided in the merged file.

 CAUTION

You cannot use the crack utility as a replacement for a password-checking program because it does not provide any such information. It does not inform the administrator in case it finds a weak password or a password that does not conform to the rules of an effective password security plan.

Crack performs multiple checks on the consolidated list of passwords. Each round of check is based on a specific rule and the list of decrypted passwords. The user who is running the program specifies this rule. The rules are provided in the gecos.rules and the dicts.rules file and are specified in a simple format. Each line in the file provides a separate rule and a hash (#) character is used to specify blank lines or comments. As mentioned previously, there are two different types of files for storing information. The gecos.rules file, which is stored in the scripts directory, contains rules retrieved from the entries created from the password files. This file contains all the usernames and every possible combination of those names generated by the computer. After the passwords have been checked against the rules stored in the gecos.rules file, additional checks are done based on the rules specified in the dicts.rules file. Consolidating all dictionaries available on the computer creates the rules for these files. All these dictionaries are stored in the DictSrc directory. You can also use user-defined dictionaries by copying them to the DictSrc directory.

Crack creates a consolidated list of all the user information stored on the computer and sorts them into a specific order. The utility then uses this list to decrypt the password for each user. If a password is decrypted successfully, it is marked by the utility, and all decrypted passwords are stored together in a simple text file along with their encrypted version. This saves time when the crack utility attempts to decrypt passwords in the next instance because it only needs to check if the password has been decrypted earlier. The utility also maintains a list of all the passwords it has not been able to crack and disregards the passwords the next time the utility is executed. In case you need to reset the utility so that it checks the passwords it was unable to decrypt at an earlier occasion, you can use the mrgfbk script that is available in the scripts directory. This script removes all entries of passwords that could not be decrypted. This ensures that the next time the `crack` utility is executed, it will attempt to decrypt all passwords. The syntax of the `crack` password is as follows:

```
crack [options] [bindir] /etc/passwd
```

In the preceding code, `bindir` is the name of the directory where the binary files are stored. This is an optional parameter and is useful in case `crack` has to be used on different types of systems. In case the directory does not exist, it is automatically created after an error is displayed. Table 7-3 lists some of the options available with the `crack` utility and their descriptions.

Table 7-3 Options Available with the *crack* Utility

Option	Description
-f	Executes the utility in the foreground mode. This option is only effective in case of small password files, where the number of possible combinations is small. In foreground mode, a message is displayed for every password analyzed. This option is not available when the utility is executed in the network mode.If messages are raised for each password analyzed on a remote computer, the process will slow down the network traffic.
-v	Displays information about the cracked passwords based on the client computer's requirements. Although this creates a large log file, it is effective if passwords need to be analyzed in detail.
-m	Alerts the users whose passwords are easily decrypted. The benefit of using this option is that you can customize the message that is displayed to the users.
-r <point files>	Used when you are running the utility in recovery mode. This means that the utility periodically saves its state to a predefined file, which can be used in case the utility needs to terminate operation in between checks. As a result, the state of the utility is retained and you can restart the utility from the same location where it had previously stopped.

The `crack` utility is useful in cases where the passwords need to be checked for weaknesses and the user has to be informed of the problem. However, the utility is not a substitute for strong password policies that administrators need to implement on the network and on local computers. Administrators can provide templates to users for creating secure passwords.

PPP Security

Point-to-Point Protocol (PPP) is a procedure for using IP and other network protocols. These protocols are either used on a serial link or over a dial-up connection established by using a modem and telephone lines. You can also use an ISDN link to establish the connection. PPP can be used to connect computers running Solaris to servers providing the PPP service. The service provides access to resources stored on the network on which the server is connected. The PPP server forms a gateway or link for computer, which is not a part of the network. The PPP server can also be used to provide dial-up access to other computers for accessing the resources on the network. You can also set up a PPP connection between two networks that exist either locally or at remote locations.

PPP provides service on a peer-to-peer level and does not differentiate between computers that access the server locally or dial in to the server. It also does not differentiate between computers that dial in and the servers that are dialed into. The computers that dial in are known as *client* computers while the computers that provide the dial-up facility are called *servers*. A computer might be a client in one situation while it might be a server in another situation.

Summary

In this chapter, you learned how to secure user accounts and applications in Solaris. You learned about the different types of attacks that can occur on the network and some preventive measures that you can implement to secure the network. Then you learned about root privileges that can exist on the computer and their security. This chapter also covered various tools available in Solaris for ensuring security. Finally, you learned about certain tools that you could use for providing dial-up connectivity to computers that are not a part of a network.

Check Your Understanding

Multiple Choice Questions

1. From the following list of attacks, identify the attacks against which SSH provides protection. (Select all that apply.)

    a. Different types of virus attacks

    b. Attacks related to hackers adding fictitious DNS entries

    c. Denial of Service attacks

    d. IP spoofing attacks

2. Which SSH option can be used to run the SSH process in the background?

   a. -a

   b. -c

   c. -f

   d. -p

3. Which SSH option can be used to run the SSH process in the silence mode?

   a. -v

   b. -q

   c. -C

   d. -V

4. Which protocol can be used to retrieve password information from the /etc/password directory?

   a. SMTP

   b. HTTP

   c. FTP

   d. TFTP

5. In case of smurf attacks, which protocol is used for disrupting network traffic by checking connectivity with a host computer?

   a. SMTP

   b. ICMP

   c. HTTP

   d. FTP

6. Which manager available in the admintool utility contains information about all the client computers serviced by the utility?

   a. Host manager

   b. Database manager

   c. User accounts manger

   d. Serial port manager

7. Which of the following statements about TCP wrappers are true?

Statement A: TCP wrappers can be used to make modifications to existing programs.

Statement B: TCP wrappers are used for monitoring network traffic and managing access to important network services.

   a. Both A and B are correct.

   b. A is correct while B is incorrect.

    c. A is incorrect while B is correct.

    d. Both are incorrect.

8. Which of the following statements about TCP wrappers are true?

    Statement A: TCP wrappers cannot be used on applications that require the service of other protocols besides the TCP/IP protocol.

    Statement B: TCP wrappers do not affect the performance of the system or the connection between the clients and the host computer.

    a. Both A and B are correct.

    b. A is correct while B is incorrect.

    c. A is incorrect while B is correct.

    d. Both are incorrect.

9. Which options available with the crack utility can be used to alert users whose passwords are easily decrypted?

    a. -f

    b. -v

    c. -m

10. Which of the following statements are true?

    Statement A: PGP is used by SSH for encrypting information transmitted over the network.

    Statement B: SSH provides support for PAM on all versions of Solaris.

    a. Both A and B are correct.

    b. A is correct while B is incorrect.

    c. A is incorrect while B is correct.

    d. Both are incorrect.

Short Questions

1. Explain the difference between authentication and authorization.

2. You want to log on to a server kept in a remote location that is running SSH without being prompted for the password. You also want to specify a specific port on the host server that you want to use. How can you configure the system to provide these options?

3. You are an administrator of a corporate network, which exists in a single geographical location. You have a server providing SSH facility on one of your subnets. The administrator of a branch office wants you to provide connection to another secured subnet that exists on his network. You plan to use dial-up connection to provide this connectivity. How can you configure this connection and what should you use?

Answers

Multiple Choice Answers

1. **b, d**. SSH provides security against IP spoofing attacks and DNS spoofing attacks. In DNS spoofing, hackers add some fictitious DNS entries that can be later used to gain access to the network. In the case of IP spoofing, hackers manipulate the address of data packets to make them appear to originate from a trusted host computer. SSH provides security against hackers on the local network who might try to impersonate authentic routers on the local network. However, SSH cannot be used if hackers use other means in addition to hacking encrypted information for accessing data stored on the network.

2. **c**. The -f option is used for running SSH in the background. After the user has been authenticated and a secure connection has been established between two computers, the SSH service starts running in the background waiting to service future requests. This is mostly applicable in cases where the user wants to handle authentication and data access but at the same time wants SSH to run in the background. The -a option is used for disabling the forwarding mechanism of the authentication agent. You can also use the -a option to deny access to specific computers. The -c option is used for specifying the encryption mechanism to be used for encrypting the connection between two computers. As mentioned in the chapter, Triple DES or blowfish is typically used for securing the information, since they are the most secure mechanisms among the commonly used encryption mechanisms. The -p option is used to establish connection with certain firewalls that refuse connections to the privileged ports. You can specify unprivileged ports with this option. Unprivileged ports are used in cases where .rhost or .rsarhosts authentication is not required.

3. **b**. The -q option is used for establishing connection between two computers in silence mode. This means that all error messages and warnings are suppressed and only the most critical error messages are displayed. Critical error messages are those errors in which the connection between two computers cannot continue. The -v option is used to run SSH in verbose mode. This is the opposite of the -q option, since SSH displays all the error and debug messages encountered by the computer while establishing the connection. The -V option is used to only print the version number and then exit the connection. The -C option is used for compressing all information being passed over the network. This option is important in cases where modems are being used or the network connection is very slow. However, if compression is used on a fast network, it will have the effect of slowing down the network traffic.

4. **d**. The Trivial File Transfer Protocol (TFTP) can be used to retrieve password information from the /etc/password directory. The weak point of this service is that no authentication is required to run the service.

5. **b**. In case of smurf attacks, the Internet Control Message Protocol (ICMP) is used for disrupting the network traffic. The protocol is used to check for the connectivity with a host computer by sending continuous echo requests. If an answer is received, then the server is functioning properly. The command that is used for this purpose is the `ping` command.

6. **a**. The Host manager contains the information about all the client computers serviced by the utility. The clients can be either diskless, standalone, or dataless. In case of diskless clients, the clients depend on the server for all their disk space requirements, while in case of standalone clients, the requirement for the file server is optional. In case of dataless clients, the clients use their local disks for only the purpose of root and swap.

7. **c**. `TCP wrappers` do not need to make modifications to existing programs. The `TCP wrapper` forms a type of firewall between the host computer and remote computers trying to establish connections with the host computer. The wrapper decides whether certain services should be allowed to run on the server or not. `TCP wrappers` are used for monitoring network traffic and managing access to important network services, such as `finger`, `ftp`, `telnet`, `rsh`, `rlogin`, and `systat`.

8. **a**. `TCP wrappers` cannot be used on applications that require the service of other protocols besides the TCP/IP protocol. The wrapper serves as an interface between the TCP/IP protocol suit and the services running on the host computer. `TCP wrappers` do not affect the performance of the system or the connection between the clients and the host computer. The `TCP wrapper` simply moves the network service being requested by the TCP daemon to another file until the client is authenticated.

9. **c**. The `-m` option is used to alert the users whose passwords can be easily decrypted. The benefit of using this option is that you can customize the message, which is displayed to the users.

10. **b**. SSH uses PGP for encryption information transmitted over the network. The support for PAM is only available in Solaris 2.6 and later versions.

Short Answers

1. Authentication is the process of establishing the identity of users by using UIDs and passwords. Authentication gives a user the right to login but it does not automatically assign rights to carry out tasks or to change data. The process of providing users the rights to access resources is called authorization.

2. All users need to be authenticated before they can be allowed to access the SSH server. If you want to configure the server to allow access to the server without being prompted for a password, you need to generate a public and private key pair. These keys are stored in your home directory. You need to copy the public key from your home directory on the local computer to the user directory on the

server. This ensures that you are automatically authenticated when you log on to the server. You need to use the -p option if you want to specify a specific port on the host computer to which you can connect. This information can differ for every host computer that you need to access. You can therefore create a configuration file containing the port number of the host computer.

3. You can establish this connection by using PPP over the SSH connection. You can also implement compression by using the -C option for faster network traffic. However, SSH runs over the TCP connection, and PPP might also transmit data packets simultaneously. This might cause the network traffic to slow down.

Chapter 8

In this chapter, I'll discuss the basics of Kerberos. This chapter discusses Kerberos functions and why you need to ensure security on the Kerberos servers. It also discusses how to install the master Key Distribution Center (KDC) and the slave KDCs and how to ensure their security. You'll learn about authentication and why it is critical that the system clocks on the Kerberos servers should be synchronized with each other. I'll begin with a brief overview of Kerberos.

Overview of Kerberos

In the present networking scenario, the Internet forms an important part of our daily life. Therefore, the reliability of the Internet is of major concern to its users. The Internet is vulnerable to attacks because it provides connectivity throughout the world. Most of the protocols used on the Internet have their own vulnerabilities and most networks regularly face attacks by hackers. Hackers use sniffers and other programs to decrypt the passwords of authentic network users being passed over the Internet. Servers recognize authentic clients only by the user information or by the computer name, therefore, it becomes difficult to recognize hackers when they impersonate these users. You might implement firewalls to restrict access to the network. However, sometimes hackers are authentic users who are a part of the internal network but do not have appropriate rights to access certain information. Firewalls provide a restrictive environment that is not always feasible to follow. Moreover, implementing security against Internet threats involves high costs. One of the more feasible solutions is hardening the operating system running on the Web servers. Hardening involves implementing tighter security measures and applying service packs. You can also implement security measures for securing the protocols used on the network. Kerberos is one such protocol.

Kerberos is a network authentication protocol, which was first developed at the Massachusetts Institute of Technology (MIT). It uses DES for providing authentication facilities to client/server applications. Kerberos is also used for authenticating users trying to log on to a network. In Kerberos, the client is authenticated on the server by first storing the current time as a string. This string is encrypted by using the secret key stored on the client machine. The encrypted string is then sent to the server. The server decrypts the key to authenticate the client and establish connection. All communication and data transmitted between the server and client is encrypted for additional security. Kerberos is available both as a source code and as a separate product from reliable vendors. If developers want to examine the code for establishing its authenticity, they can download the source code. Otherwise, they can buy the final product.

When a user attempts to connect to a server, the login information is first authenticated at the *Key Distribution Center (KDC)*. The KDC issues a ticket, called the *ticket-granting ticket (TGT)*. The KDC then authenticates the user. After the user has been authenticated, the ticket is attached to the authenticated login. This ticket is created based on the timestamp created at the time of login. Each timestamp is unique and cannot be recreated. All tickets are also unique. A ticket is retained until the session is valid and is immediately destroyed when the session ends. Kerberos provides a feasible solution to networking problems faced by administrators. It provides a secure authentication mechanism and support for encrypting information being transmitted over the network. It also provides a layer of security, which is free of all restrictions implemented by firewalls.

Assumptions Under Which Kerberos Works

The security implemented by Kerberos is based on the following assumptions:

◆ Kerberos assumes that users will not make a poor choice when deciding passwords. For example, if a user chooses a password such as `password` or `something`, attacker can intercept a few encrypted messages and use a directory attack to easily obtain the correct password. Hackers can do so by creating different combinations of the password and checking if any one decrypts the message. If the attacker succeeds, he can now impersonate the user to verify any software.

◆ Kerberos assumes that adequate security measures are implemented at the workstations or machines level, and only the network connections are vulnerable to attacks. Thus Kerberos assumes that the attackers cannot position themselves between the user and the client in order to obtain the password.

Understanding the Kerberos Mechanism

Let us take the example of an organization that wants to implement security on the network. You as the network administrator suggest the use of Kerberos for authenticating users on the network. Before you begin implementing Kerberos, you need to understand its functioning. The following section discusses the Kerberos mechanism in detail.

A client requests the KDC to issue a ticket for accessing the *ticket-granting server (TGS)*, as shown in Figure 8-1. The request is accompanied by the user's secret key. The KDC authenticates the client based on the information stored in its database. The database contains a list of all client keys available with the authentication server. The KDC then generates a session key S1 and encrypts it using the secret key of the client. The newly created session key is used for creating a secure session between the client and TGS. The KDC also generates a ticket known as TGT. This ticket is encrypted using the secret key of the TGS. Both the S1 session key and the TGT are then sent to the client.

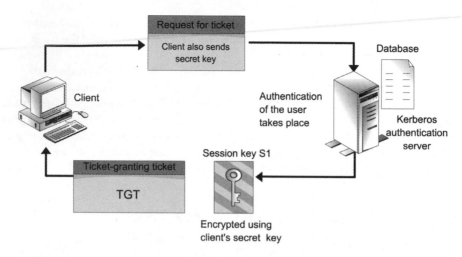

FIGURE 8-1 *Client requesting a ticket from the KDC*

The client computer receives the credentials from the KDC. It then decrypts the credentials and retrieves the newly created session key S1. The client uses this session key to create an authenticator to request access to an application server. The authenticator contains client information, such as the username, IP address, and timestamp when the session was established. The client then sends the authenticator and the TGT to the TGS. The TGS decrypts the authenticator by using the session key S1 stored in the TGT. The TGS authenticates information stored in the authenticator. If the contents are found to be authentic, the TGS creates a new session key S2 and encrypts it using S1. It also creates a granted ticket that contains information regarding the client computer's name, IP address, timestamp, and date when the ticket expires. The ticket also contains the name of the application server to which the client requires access. The TGS sends both the session key and the ticket back to the client after encrypting the ticket with the secret key of the application server. The process is shown in Figure 8-2.

The client decrypts the message and retrieves the new session key S2. The client then creates a new authenticator and encrypts it using the session key S2. The client then sends the encrypted ticket, also known as the *session ticket*, and the authenticator to the application server. The application server recognizes the client to be authentic because the session ticket is encrypted using the secret key of the application server. Hackers cannot easily hack the transaction because it contains the encrypted timestamp. In case the application server needs to authenticate itself back to the client, it creates a message containing the timestamp and encrypts it using the S2 key. As a result, a secure connection is established that the client and the application server can use to communicate securely. The process is shown in Figure 8-3.

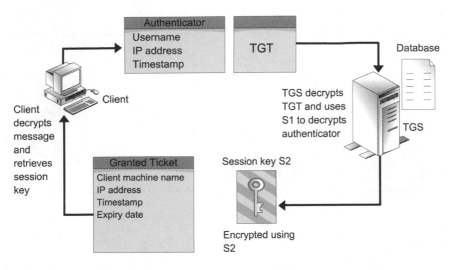

FIGURE 8-2 *Client requesting information from the TGS*

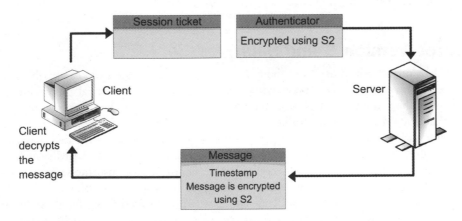

FIGURE 8-3 *Client establishing connection with the application server*

Finally, a secured connection is established between the client and the application server. The client is sure that the message, which it receives, originates from the server and the server is confident that the client, who sends the return message, is authentic. This is because both the messages are encrypted using the S2 key, which is only available with the client and the application server. The process is shown in Figure 8-4.

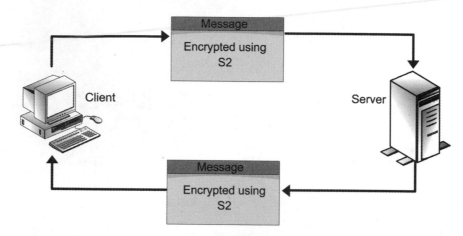

FIGURE 8-4 *Secure transfer of information between the client and server*

Now that you know how Kerberos functions, I'll discuss some of the features available in the latest version of Kerberos. Kerberos Version 5, or Kerberos V5, is supported by Solaris 9. The rest of the chapter discusses Kerberos V5 in detail.

Kerberos Version 5 and Solaris

To deny unauthorized users the ability to access network services, you can disable remote access. However, in present networking scenarios, this is an impractical approach because many of the authenticated users are remote users. Kerberos provides better security and an authentication mechanism. Kerberos V5 is the latest version of Kerberos. It provides a secure authentication environment to ensure the security of service-based applications configured on authentication servers. Kerberos V5 retains the ticket-based system available in the earlier version and uses cryptographic algorithms for ensuring security of transmitted data. It also ensures that access to the server is restricted to authenticate users and provides access to the services available on the server for limited time period. Kerberos V5 replaces the authentication mechanism used in network utilities, such as `ftp`, `rsh`, `telnet`, and `rlogin`.

New Features in Kerberos V5

The earlier version of Kerberos (Kerberos V4) had certain vulnerabilities that left the system susceptible to attacks by hackers. For example, the utility that generated random numbers for creating session keys had some shortcomings that caused the keys to be easily hacked by experienced hackers. The hackers could use the keys to gain access to the services and resources available on the network. Although SUN has provided service packs for solving this problem, you can use Kerberos V5 to avoid these problems altogether. Certain other features available in Kerberos V5 are:

◆ The syslog-based logging was prone to DoS attacks in the earlier version. This problem has been solved in the current version.

◆ There were certain problems associated with `ksu` security, which have been solved in the current version.

◆ Other shortcomings were related to the security of parsing strings. These weaknesses have been solved in the current version.

◆ The current version provides support for CFLAGS by using Makefiles.

◆ The current version raises an error if an empty configuration file is found. In earlier versions, an empty file was created in such circumstances.

◆ Kerberos V5 provides support for `kpasswd`, but it no longer waits indefinitely for an answer when it queries the `changepw` server.

◆ The current version provides a solution to the problem encountered earlier due to the 1.0x.x KDC encrypted timestamp preauth bug.

◆ The current version of Kerberos does not contain the bugs that existed in the entries of the principal conversion table.

◆ Kerberos V5 provides support for TripleDES. However, the support is limited in scope because of numerous compatibility problems.

◆ Kerberos V5 uses the Berkeley DB as the backup database, which provides better and improved performance by KDC.

◆ Kerberos V5 provides support for shared libraries, which are available in a new and better framework. This framework provides easier access and a better facility for sharing libraries.

◆ Kerberos V5 doesn't require separate configuration scripts for every directory. A single script can be used to configure security for all directories.

◆ The current version of KDC provides a solution to the earlier problem encountered in the ASN.1 parser null sequence.

◆ Kerberos tickets can now contain multiple IP addresses and addresses for different types of networking protocols.

Limitations of Kerberos V5

Although Kerberos is widely used, it also has certain limitations. Some of the limitations that existed in Kerberos V4 were solved in Kerberos V5. However, certain limitations and weaknesses continue to exist in Kerberos V5.

◆ **Encryption prefix.** In earlier versions of Solaris, the headers of all data packets were the encryption information. Therefore, hackers could extract the text part of the message without cracking the encryption information. This was discontinued in Kerberos V4, where the header information of all the data packets contained the size of the data packet and a special encryption string. Therefore, if the size of the packet did not match, an administrator knew that the data packet had been hacked.

◆ **Lack of authentication**. No authentication is required when a client requests a ticket from the KDC. Therefore, hackers can retrieve information about user passwords by requesting multiple tickets. A possible solution to this problem can be the use of DH Key exchange.

◆ **Lack of synchronization**. In the case of multiple slave KDCs, there is a lack of synchronization between all the KDCs, leading to an insecure network. A possible solution can be to use the challenge-response protocol while authentication takes place.

◆ **Host-to-host protocol**. Another major limitation in Kerberos until Version 4 was the lack of host-to-host protocol. For example, in Version 4 the user could only be authenticated on the server. This problem has been partially solved in Version 5 by using user-to-user protocol.

◆ **CRC-32 checksum**. Kerberos 5 uses CRC-32 checksum as compared to MD4 that is used in Kerberos 4. The CRC-32 checksum is used for calculating a checksum based on a cyclic redundancy check. The major drawback in CRC-32 checksum is that it cannot avoid collisions of data packets that were possible in MD4. Hackers can use a plaintext attack to create another message that fulfills the requirements set by the checksum. A recommended practice is to use collision-proof checksums in situations where the threats of such attacks exist.

◆ **Between-realm authentication**. The implementation of authentication between realms is possible through forwarding. However, you cannot set priority for authentication between servers.

◆ **Use of timestamp**. The use of timestamp to ensure the authenticity of transmitted data packets continues in Kerberos V5. Timestamps are generally used for authenticating KRB_PRIV and KRB_SAFE messages. This is an insecure authentication method. It is recommended to use a safer method, such as the use of sequence numbers.

 NOTE

Clients use the KRB_PRIV messages to detect hacked or modified messages and to implement confidentiality. Confidentiality is achieved by encrypting all sent messages and by using control information. Clients also use KRB_SAFE messages for detecting hacked messages. KRB_SAFE messages attach collision-proof checksum to all the messages containing user data. The checksum contains an encryption key that is created either by a session key or by subkeys.

After learning about the strengths and weaknesses of the Kerberos mechanism, it is also important to know briefly about the DH authentication mechanism that is used for authentication in Kerberos.

System Authentication and DH Authentication

Kerberos was primarily developed to create a centralized system for authenticating network users. It provides network users the ability to log on to the network after being authenticated. Kerberos solves three purposes, which are as follows:

◆ It provides a central repository for all network passwords and user information.

◆ It provides users with the ability to access all the resources on the network after being authenticated.

◆ It ensures that passwords being transmitted over the network are encrypted so that hackers are unable to intercept them.

Kerberos utilizes the digital ticket technology, so users do not need to specify their passwords repeatedly. After a user has been authenticated, the user is assigned a ticket that can be used for authentication on the network. This avoids the need for transmitting passwords over the network, where there is the perpetual danger of hackers gaining access to the information. Because authentication is simple and a more structured task in Kerberos, it is easier to assign servers to perform all authentication tasks for the network. Besides providing the advantage of a single point of network administration, it provides security for all other client computers on the network.

Kerberos provides a single logon facility for users, where a user only needs to log on once to the network and the authentication continues throughout the session. After a user has been authenticated, if any services running on the network require authentication, the details of the user are automatically sent to the services.

Different types of authentication protocols are used on the network. The Diffie-Hellman (DH) authentication protocol is the protocol that is most commonly used along with Kerberos. The DH authentication protocol was primarily created to provide cryptographically secure authentication.

In DH authentication, the client is identified by using a simple string of characters instead of the integer values specified by the operating system. This character name is known as the network name of the client and is used for referring to the client throughout the network. All client names need to be unique on the network because the client's name is the only way in which a server is able to identify clients. DH authentication is responsible for providing network names for all network users and client computers.

The DH authentication mechanism contains a verifier that is used for validating client details. Generally, this verifier involves a timestamp that is created when the user initiates the session. This value is always unique and can be easily used to ensure that a valid user is trying to gain access to the network. The server decrypts the key to establish its authenticity and the client encrypts the key to ensure that it is secure. The only way a client can secure the key is to encrypt it using the special key, available in the RPC session. This special key is created using DES and is generated by the client. The key is transmitted to the server at the beginning of the RPC session. The key is then encrypted using a public key scheme, which is mostly the DH key exchange. When a server authenticates a client's timestamp, it needs to determine whether the timestamp is for a time period earlier than the timestamp sent by the same client and whether the timestamp has not expired.

At the time of initiating the session, the server validates the timestamp and stores the timestamp in its database. It also stores a *time-to-live (TTL)* value that the client sends and that determines when the timestamp will expire. If either of the authentications fails, the entire session is rejected. If the session is established, the server sends a verifier back to the client. The client uses this verifier to ensure that it has been authenticated and has the rights to access all the services available on the network. The server then sends the timestamp back to the client after deducting one second for the time. This information is encrypted using the session key and is used to authenticate the client on the network.

Configuring Kerberos

Certain tasks are involved in configuring Kerberos. Some of these tasks need to be performed before beginning the installation, while others are performed while installing the master KDC and the slave KDCs. The following sections discuss these tasks in detail and how to implement security on the servers.

The first task you need to perform is to gather certain preinstallation information. This information is essential for configuring the servers to perform their tasks effectively.

Preinstallation Steps

Before you can begin the installation of KDC servers and configure Kerberos on the servers, you need to collect the following information:

◆ **Naming the Kerberos realm**. A realm is logical network, similar to a domain, which defines a group of systems that are under the same master KDC. Kerberos runs in a client-server model, where the KDC acts as the server and authenticates computers, users, and services that exist on the realm. A user's *Kerberos Principal* is the information about the user that appears in the form of <username>@realm name. Although you can assign any number of ASCII values as the name of the Kerberos realm, an accepted practice is to use the domain name as the realm name. Other naming conventions like X.500 and reserved also exist. Although, technically a realm can have any name, interoperability across realm boundaries requires agreement on how realm names are to be assigned and what information do they imply. The only difference between the domain name and the realm name is that the realm name is always capitalized. For example, if the domain name is asc.org, then the Kerberos realm name will be ASC.ORG. In case you need to specify multiple realms for the domain, it is advisable to use descriptive names followed by the domain name. For example, LA.ASC.ORG, TX.ASC.ORG, and NY.ASC.ORG.

You can also configure Kerberos principals that are a part of one realm to authenticate principals that are a part of another realm. This concept is known as *cross-realm authentication*. You need to set up a connection between the two realms and create a cross-realm secret key. This key is then used for authenticating users when users from one realm want to connect to the other realm. Kerberos V5 also supports a variation of cross-realm authentication known as *transitive cross-realm authentication*. In the conventional approach, you set up separate connections between each pair of realms that need to be connected to each other. This leads to a large number of connections being created. In cross-realm authentication, there is a set path through which authentication takes place for all realms. Therefore, you need to move between realms until you reach the realm you require. The basic security risks are that both the realms trust the other realm's KDC not to issue cross-realm tickets to unauthenticated users. A safety feature is that a remote KDC can only issue a ticket for users that exist on its own realm and not to users of any other realm. This ensures that the user is at least an authentic user of the other realm. In addition in Kerberos V5, KDCs of remote realms are not trusted by default. You need to explicitly get into a trust relationship with each realm.

◆ **Mapping hostnames to Kerberos realms**. You can map the hostnames to the Kerberos realms in two ways. You could use the conventional method provided by MIT. In this method, you need to specify a set of rules in the `kerber5.conf` file. This file contains mappings for the entire domain including all subdomains. Although there are separate entries for each host on the network, you can also store exception information in the file. The exception information contains the names of all hosts that are not allowed to access the server. You could also map the hostnames and the Kerberos realms by using another method, which is not commonly used as it involves searching for information in Domain Name Service (DNS) records. If the method is applied on the client machine, adding the prefix `_kerberos` along with the hostname creates the search criterion. In case the record is not found, the search continues to the next level in the hierarchy, which is created by using `_kerberos`, domain name of the host machine, and the parent domain. For example, if the hostname is `SALES.LA.WEST.ASC.ORG`, the following will be the search criteria:

`_kerberos.sales.la.west.asc.org`

`_kerberos.la.west.asc.org`

`_kerberos.west.asc.org`

`_kerberos.asc.org`

`_kerberos`

◆ **Assigning ports for KDC and admin services**. You also need to assign port numbers used by KDC and admin services. By default, KDC uses port 750 and 88 while the admin services uses port 749. In case you want to change these port numbers and assign other ports to either of these services, make changes in the `krb5.conf` and `/etc/services` files. These files are stored on the host computer. If you make any change to the `krb5.conf` file stored on the host computer, you also need to make the corresponding changes to the `kerbs.conf` file stored on client computers.

◆ **Setting up slave KDCs**. Depending on the requirements of your organization, you can also set up slave KDCs on your network. The slave KDCs help the master KDC in ensuring the regular availability of the ticket-granting service. In case the master KDC is not able to provide the service, one of the slave KDCs takes up the task. There is no restriction on the number of slave KDCs you can configure on the network. The proper functioning of Kerberos is dependent on the fact that every client is able to connect to a KDC to request a ticket. Therefore, you need to have at least one KDC as backup, in case the master KDC crashes. In the case of large networks, where it is common that certain sections of the network are sometimes inaccessible to the master KDC, it is recommended that a slave KDC is set up for every such section. The same is applicable if the network stretches across multiple physical locations.

◆ **Specifying hostnames**. According to the guidelines laid down by MIT, the master KDC should use `kerberos` as its DNS hostname and the DNS hostnames of the slave KDCs should be numbered as `kerberos-1`, `kerberos-2`, `kerberos-3`, and so on. As a result, you will only need to change the DNS name of a KDC slave to promote it to the KDC master. You have already read that one of the ways to map the hostnames to the Kerberos realms is to add a new record, known as `SRV`, to the DNS. The record contains information about the hostname and the port number to connect to for accessing the service. Some of the services relating to Kerberos are listed in Table 8-1. It is advisable to use this method in case you need to install a large number of machines, on which it becomes difficult to update Kerberos.

◆ **Replicating the database**. You need to ensure that the information stored in the Kerberos database maintained on the master KDC is regularly replicated on the slave KDCs. The slave servers will not be able to provide authentication services while the database is being replicated; therefore, you need to strike a balance between the time when replication will take place and when the service will be available. In case of large databases or slow network connections, it is recommended to do the replication either in stages or simultaneously. You can divide the slave KDCs in groups, replicate one group, and use the replicated group to replicate other groups. This ensures that the master KDC is not busy and is able to service client requests.

Table 8-1 lists some of the services available in Kerberos.

Table 8-1 Kerberos-Related Services

Service	Description
_kerberos-adm.tcp	This service is configured at port 749 on the master KDC and is used by the kadmin program and other utilities. You need to add an admin_server entry in the krb5.conf file stored on the KDC.
_kpasswd._udp	This service is configured at port 464 on the master KDC. This service is generally used in case users need to change their password.
_kerberos._udp	This service is configured on ports 88 and 750 on each of the KDCs configured on the network. This is the most commonly used entry for establishing connection to KDCs.
_kerberos-master._udp	This service is required only in case a user attempts to log on using an incorrect password from a slave KDC and the KDC is not updated. The password is then checked with the master KDC. If the password is not found, an error is raised.

After you have configured all the required services on the master KDC, you can perform certain configurations in the KDC files. The task of configuring the KDC files involves adding certain entries to the files and ensuring their overall security.

Configuring KDC Files

The KDC configuration information is stored in the /etc/krb5/kdc.conf file. Both KDC and administrative daemons use the configuration information stored in the file for managing KDC performance and for supplying realm specific information. The parameters stored in the kdc.conf file are used to supply information regarding the locations of various files and ports used on the servers. Although most of the information stored in the file is static, certain parameters need to be changed to increase security on the KDC. Table 8-2 lists some of these parameters and their descriptions.

Table 8-2 Adjustable Parameters in the KDC Configuration File

Parameter	Description
max_renewable_life	The maximum time period after which a ticket needs to be renewed. Although the standard duration is seven days, you can renew the ticket by using the

continues

Table 8-2 (*continued*)

Parameter	Description
	kinit-R command. You can also disable the option to renew tickets by specifying zeros in the time value.
max_life	Determines the maximum time for which the ticket is issued before it expires. By default, the value is set to eight hours. In case you want to create tickets more frequently for additional security, you can set a lower time period for the tickets.
kdc_ports	The port that the KDC server monitors for receiving requests. Port 88 is mostly used for Kerberos V5, while port 750 is provided for compatibility with earlier versions.
default_principal_expiration	Stores the time duration for which an entity exists in the realm. This information is specified in the kdc.conf file. It is preferable to use temporary principals. Otherwise, the system will need to keep renewing all the principals as and when they expire. If this information is not defined, the principals do not expire. Although this can cause a security risk, it is acceptable if the administrator keeps removing obsolete and unused principals from the database.
dict_file	Stores the path to the dictionary file. This file contains strings that users cannot use in their passwords. Although it is not defined by default, it is an excellent method for ensuring that users do not specify weak passwords and for preventing hackers from gaining access to the network. KDC only checks the password against the rules specified in the file. Therefore, it is a recommended practice to provide a policy for all the principals in the realm.
supported_enctypes	Specifies the encryption types supported in KDC.

After configuring the KDC files, you need to configure the password policies implemented on the Kerberos servers.

Password Policies in Kerberos

Administrators in Kerberos are also responsible for creating password policies that can be used for setting password guidelines for all principals or for selective ones. A password policy, in general, contains the following restrictions:

◆ **Maximum use of password classes**. Kerberos provides numerous classes that can be used to create passwords. These classes include numbers, letters, and punctuations, and the valid values for these classes are 1, 2, and 3.

◆ **Password length**. The minimum number of characters recommended for a password is eight.

◆ **Password history**. This restriction is on the passwords used by the principal recently and that cannot be reused for a specific time period.

◆ **Minimum password life**. This value specifies the minimum time for which the password should be used before it can be changed. The recommended time period is one hour.

◆ **Maximum password life**. This value specifies the maximum time for which the password can be used before it has to be changed. The recommended time period is 90 days.

All restrictions are grouped together and stored in a policy. You can apply either the same policy to all the principals or separate policies for different principals. Although basic or default values remain the same, you can customize the values for each type of user.

Synchronizing System Clocks

Kerberos ticket authentication depends on timestamps for ensuring authenticity of sessions. Therefore, it is important that the system clock of each server on the network is synchronized. All these servers are supposed to be synchronized within a specified maximum amount of time. By virtue of the feature called *clock skew* Kerberos provides one more security check. If the clock skew is exceeded between any of the participating servers, requests are rejected. The easiest method for synchronizing the clocks is to use the Network Time Protocol (NTP) service. This service is built into the Solaris OE, and Solaris provides software for both the server and the client along with the system software. If the clocks are not synchronized properly, it can lead to denial of service because the server stores the timestamp received from the client down to the last second. If the clock on the server is not synchronized at all, all tickets issued by the server will be invalid and the clients will not be able to access resources even though they are authentic users. The clock synchronization protocol must itself be secured from network attackers.

Now that you know the basics about how to secure Kerberos, I'll discuss how you can set up and configure Kerberos.

Deploying Kerberos

While deploying Kerberos, you need to install a master KDC and slave KDCs. You must also ensure the security of the KDCs. Once a user has been authenticated and given a ticket, the user has access to the network until the session expires. The following section discusses how you can install a master KDC on the network.

Installing a Master KDC

As discussed earlier, the KDC is responsible for issuing Kerberos tickets and storing information about all authenticated clients. This information needs to be regularly replicated on all slave KDCs at regular time intervals. The difference between a master and slave KDC is that a slave KDC can only be used for ticket-granting services, while a master KDC can also be used for the client and database administration. However, as mentioned earlier, it is easy to promote a slave KDC to become a master KDC.

On the master KDC, modify the /etc/krb5/krb5.conf file and the /usr/local/ var/krb5kdc/kdc.conf file to display the realm information and specify the appropriate hostname. You can also provide a path to a log file that will store log information. A sample of the file is shown in Figure 8-5.

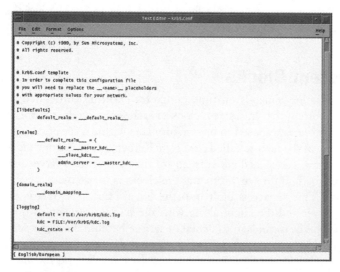

FIGURE 8-5 *The logging section in the /etc/krb5/krb5.conf file*

The next step is to create a database on the master KDC. Kerberos provides the use of the kdb5_util command for creating the database and other configuration files. Administrators also use this command for performing low-level administrative jobs on the Kerberos database. You can use this command to create, destroy, or dump information from ASCII files to the database. This command is also used to create the stash file that stores a local copy of the encryption key. This key is stored in encrypted form in the local hard disk of the master KDC. The file is used to authenticate the local KDC before running the krb5kdc and the kadmind daemons on the server. If the file is not secured properly, hackers can use the file to gain entry to the server. The hackers can then restrict even the administrator from gaining entry to Kerberos database. The security requirements of the stash file dictates that only the root should have the read permission for the file and the file should be stored only on the local hard disk of the server. The file should never be part of a backup unless even the backup data is secured. The kdb5_util command prompts an administrator for the master key of the database before allowing access to the database. The basic functions provided by the kdb5_util command are kdb5_create, kdb5_edit, kdb5_destroy, and kdb5_stash. The following is an example of the kdb5_util create command:

```
# /usr/sbin/kdb5_util create -r KERB1.COM -s
```

After executing the kdb5_util command, the system tries to gain access to the master key, which is important for opening the database. However, execution does not stop if the command does not execute successfully. The command gives an error if the database does not exist or if the stash file is corrupted. A secure master key is one that is easy to remember but difficult to hack. You should not use common words from dictionaries, variations of your username, or simple pieces of text. Secure passwords should contain both alphabet letters and numbers.

When the kdb5_util command is executed, it creates five files in the krb5 subdirectory. These files are the prinicipal.db, principal.ok, principal.kadm5, principal.kadm5.lock, and, k5stash. The information about these files is stored in the kdc.conf file. Figure 8-6 shows a kdc.conf file and the definition of various files. The principal.kadm5 is the Kerberos administrative database file and the principal.kadm5.lock is the administrative database lock file.

 NOTE

The -s option can be used with the kdb5_util command if you do not want to create a stash file.

FIGURE 8-6 *A sample kdc.conf file*

While configuring the master KDC, you need to assign access permissions for the principals. The following section focuses on this topic in detail.

Assigning Access Rights

The next step in configuring the master KDC is to create the Access Control List (ACL) files and store at least one of the administrative principals in each of the ACLs. The administrative principals are assigned in the kdc.conf file, which is also known as the kadm5.acl file. This file stores information about a Kerberos principal and the associated permissions in a tabulated format. Figure 8-7 shows a sample kadm5.acl file. You can also use wildcard characters to assign complete permissions to a principal. Therefore, it is not important to list all the principals in the file. You can assign a generic rule that can be implemented for all principals or specific ones that fulfill specified conditions. However, you must be careful while using wildcard characters because you could assign improper rights to users that can cause security risks. For example, if you want to provide a principal with only read/write permission, you should not assign all permissions to the principal.

FIGURE 8-7 *A sample kadm5.acl file*

Some of the permissions and their associated descriptions are explained in Table 8-3.

Table 8-3 Permissions Assigned to ACLs

Permissions	Descriptions
*	Assigns all permissions to the user
x	Assigns all permissions to the user (similar to *)
c	Allows password modification of principals in the database
C	Restricts password modification of principals in the database
a	Allows addition of principals in the database
A	Restricts addition of principals in the database
d	Allows deletion of principals in the database
D	Restricts deletion of principals in the database
m	Allows modification of principals in the database

continues

Table 8-3 (*continued*)

Permissions	Descriptions
M	Restricts modifications of principals in the database
l	Allows listing of principals in the database
L	Restricts listing of principals in the database
i	Allows queries and searches to the database
I	Restricts queries and searches in the database

After administrators have been added to the ACLs, they need to be added to the Kerberos database. You can use the `kadmin.local` command available on the master KDC server to add an administrator to the database. After the administrator has been added, the Kerberos ticket of the administrator needs to be decrypted. The ticket determines whether or not to provide the administrator access to the database. The `kadmind` key is used for decrypting the ticket and is created using the `kadmin/changepw` and the `kadmin/admin` principals.

 NOTE

The Kerberos database should at least contain one administrative principal. You can only add an administrative principal to the database after it has been added to an ACL.

The `krbrkdc` and the `kamind` commands are used to start the Kerberos daemon on the master KDC. Both the daemons run in the background. You can also configure the daemons to start automatically during startup by adding them to the `/etc/rc` and the `/etc/inittab` files. A prerequisite for adding these entries to the file is that the `stash` file should already exist.

Installing Slave KDCs

After you have installed the master KDC, the next step is to install the slave KDC. As mentioned earlier, every KDC has at least one principal in its database. You can also add additional principals from any other host while the `kadmin` daemon is running.

Although it is not necessary for a master KDC to exist in the Kerberos database, it is beneficial in cases where a user besides the root requires access to the server. You may also require it if you promote a slave KDC to a master KDC.

As mentioned earlier, all KDCs require a special key to decrypt tickets. The optimum situation is one where each key is created on its own local KDC. Otherwise, you need to establish a secure session for transferring the keys from the server on which they are created to the local servers. In this case, the principal should already exist in the Kerberos database.

As all the slave KDCs need to maintain the same information that is available on the master KDC, you need to replicate the databases from the master KDC to the slave KDCs. You can do this by using the kpropd daemon. For replicating the databases, you need to create a file on each of the slave KDCs and name the file /usr/local/var/krb5kdc/ kpropd.acl. This file contains all the principals that will exist in the KDC. Apart from the kpropd.acl file, there are certain other files that also need to be copied from the Master KDC. These file are namely the /etc/krb5/kdc.conf file and the /etc/krb5/ krb5.conf file.

Then, add the following lines in the /etc/inetd.conf file:

```
krb5_prop stream tcp nowait root /usr/local/sbiojnd/kprod kprod
eklogin stream tcp nowait root /user/local/sbind/klogind klogin
```

In the preceding code, the first line is used to start the kpropd database daemon that is responsible for replicating the database, while the second line is used for starting the eklogin daemon. This daemon is used for authenticating users and clients in Kerberos. It is also used for encrypting rlogin on the KDC.

You need to configure replication not only between the master and slave KDC, but also between the slave KDCs that exist on the network. First, replicate the information stored in the database on the master KDC. Then replicate the same database to the slave KDCs. A script that runs in CRON usually performs this replication job. After all databases have been updated, create the stash file and start the krb5kdc daemon. This file is required for authentication of the local KDC during startup. If the file does not exist, type the database master key for the database every time the KDC daemon restarts. Optionally, on the new slave KDC, the master KDC's clock can be synchronized using NTP or another clock synchronization mechanism. After the clients have been configured, you need to start the KDC daemon. The daemon starts automatically if the /etc/rc and the /etc/inittab files have the relevant entries. After the daemon has started running, you need to use the kadmin command to load the required principals into the database. You require a separate principal for the users, hosts, and other services. You can use the kadmin and the ktadmin commands to generate the secret key.

Sun Enterprise Authentication Mechanism (SEAM)

Most firewalls can protect the network from external attacks. However, they are ineffective against internal attacks and hackers. Latest hacking trends indicate that most network attacks come from the local network and most hackers are trusted employees of an organization. *Sun Enterprise Authentication Mechanism (SEAM)* is a client/server architecture that provides an additional layer of security besides the security provided by firewalls. The mechanism provides improved authentication facilities, better data integrity, and single logon facility for ensuring data privacy and integrity. SEAM facilitates for the authentication of both client and server and ensures the authenticity of information being transmitted over the network. Data is encrypted before it is transmitted for additional security. SEAM can also be used to monitor and restrict user access to resources available on the network.

The advantage of using SEAM is that after a user has been authenticated and issued a ticket, the authentication continues for the rest of the session. After a user has been authenticated with SEAM, the user can access any command related to SEAM as well as any available services. SEAM primarily uses Kerberos V5 for authentication and therefore provides interoperability with other operating systems. SEAM can be used on a single domain or across domains.

Following are some of the important characteristics of SEAM:

◆ **Simple to use**. SEAM can be easily administered and managed by using a built-in administrative tool. You can add or remove users in batches. This saves both time and effort and is beneficial for networks that require adding or removing a large number of users over a short duration of time. SEAM also provides single logon facility. This facility is used for user authentication, after which the user has access to all the resources available on the network. However, the user has access to the resources only until the session is active.

◆ **Centralized management and authentication**. SEAM provides a centralized repository of authentication information for all principals available on the enterprise. All records are stored in the KDC, and SEAM uses this information to authenticate all users and services requesting access to the resources available on the network. The authentication requirements of the enterprise are fulfilled from one centralized location. This reduces the cost normally incurred on the administration and implementation of security measures.

◆ **Information security**. SEAM stores information in a distributed architecture and provides reliable and ready access to data. All information stored on the server can be easily replicated to other backup servers. This ensures that in case the server crashes, user accessibility to the service running on the server is never lost. In case the master KDC is completely inaccessible, you can easily promote a slave KDC to master KDC status.

◆ **Key encryption**. SEAM provides additional level of security for information being transmitted over the network. When a client requests the KDC for a ticket for accessing a server, all information being transmitted between the server and the client is encrypted and is not easily accessible.

◆ **Low cost**. SEAM uses the latest security mechanisms that provide easy accessibility and improved features. All these facilities are available at comparatively lower cost than the other third-party utilities. The overhead incurred in maintaining multiple administrators is reduced because all administration is performed from a centralized location,

◆ **Availability of multiple realms**. In case the network is divided into multiple realms, SEAM can be used to work across geographic and network boundaries. A user or computer who is the client of one realm can access the KDC server configured in another realm. SEAM can be used to implement separation of parts of a network from the rest of the network. SEAM can also be used to implement network administration at the local level.

◆ **Improved performance**. SEAM provides faster and more reliable performance as compared to other software. It provides faster replication and better security of information transmitted over the network. You can also create multiple replicas of the same database. Individual departments and sections of the same network can use these databases for faster resolution of client requests and faster replication.

◆ **Security APIs**. SEAM provides for the use of the Remote Procedural Call API that is provided by third-party software vendors. The procedure also provides facility for interoperability for future products that might be released by SUN. This interoperability is easily accomplished without performing any major modification to the software.

◆ **Improved security**. SEAM provides support for all the security-related services, such as NFS, FTP, `telnet`, and `rsh` commands. These services, when used with encryption, help you to ensure security of data and maintain data integrity. SEAM protects the network against snooping and sniffer attacks. Data can be easily and securely accessed by users from anywhere on the network.

SEAM follows the concept of Kerberos and is based on the ticket technology. Tickets are used to identify the user or the client computer on the KDC. When a client requests the service of a SEAM utility, a ticket is requested from the KDC. The KDC authenticates the credentials of the client and if the entry is found in the database, the client is issued a ticket. Since the ticket is issued to the client for a specific service, another user can't use the ticket, nor can the ticket be used to access other services. However, the same ticket can be used on another machine without the user needing to authenticate the credential again from the KDC.

Summary

In this chapter, you learned about Kerberos, its mechanism, and its features. You also learned about the limitations that have been addressed in the current version of Kerberos and the ones that still exist. Then you learned how to install and configure master KDC and slave KDCs. Finally, you learned about SEAM, which is the latest implementation of Kerberos.

Check Your Understanding

Multiple Choice Questions

1. When a client requests the KDC for access to an application server, what does the KDC return after authenticating the user's credentials?

   a. A session key

   b. A ticket and a session key

   c. An authenticator and a session key

   d. A ticket

2. Which component of the Kerberos mechanism stores information about the expiry date of the ticket?

   a. Ticket-granting ticket

   b. Session keys

   c. Granted ticket

   d. Authenticator

3. Which protocol is used in Kerberos for synchronizing the system clocks of all the servers?

   a. SMTP

   b. HTTP

   c. SNMP

   d. NTP

4. What is the recommended maximum time period for which you can use a password before it has to be changed?

   a. 8 days

   b. 90 days

   c. 7 days

   d. 30 days

Short Questions

1. In Kerberos, what are realms and how are they defined? Can you configure multiple realms on a single domain?
2. Explain the process of authentication on a KDC. How is a client provided access to an application server that exists on the network?
3. Explain cross-realm authentication and briefly explain the security risks.
4. What is a renewable ticket in relation to Kerberos?

Answers

Multiple Choice Answers

1. **b**. The KDC authenticates the client based on the information stored in its database. The database contains a list of all client keys available with the authentication server. The KDC then generates a session key and encrypts it using the secret key of the client. The newly created session key is used for creating a secure session between the client and TGS. The KDC also generates a TGT. This ticket is encrypted using the secret key of the TGS. Both the session key and the TGT are then sent to the client.

2. **c**. After the client has been authenticated, the TGT creates a granted ticket that contains information regarding the client computer's name, IP address, time-stamp, and date when the ticket expires. The ticket also contains the name of the application server to which the client requires access.

3. **d**. The easiest method for synchronizing the clocks is to use the Network Time Protocol (NTP) service. The service is built into the Solaris OE, and Solaris provides software for both the server and the client along with the system software.

4. **b**. The recommended time period for which a password can be used before it has to be changed is 90 days.

Short Answers

1. You could define a realm as a logical network. A realm is used to store information about different computer groups and user groups that exist under the same master KDC. Information can be stored in realms in either hierarchical or non-hierarchical format. In the case of nonhierarchical realms, you need to provide a link between both realms. Kerberos runs in a client/server model, where the KDC acts as the server and authenticates computers, users, and services that exist on the realm. This computer is known as the master KDC. You can also

have multiple slave KDCs for handling authentication services in case the master KDC goes down. Slave KDCs cannot perform the administration that is possible by a master KDC, but you can promote a slave KDC to a master KDC by changing its DNS entry. The user's Kerberos Principal contains information of every user and appears in the form of <username>@realm name. Although you can assign any number of ASCII values as the name of the Kerberos realm, an accepted practice is to use the domain name as the realm name. The only difference between the domain name and the realm name is that the realm name is always capitalized. For example, if the domain name is asc.org, then the Kerberos realm name will be ASC.ORG. In case you need to specify multiple realms for the domain, you should use descriptive names followed by the domain name, for example, LA.ASC.ORG, TX.ASC.ORG, and NY.ASC.ORG. You can maintain separate databases for all the realms that you implement on your network. You can also run three separate kadmin commands for each of the realms.

2. The process of authentication on a KDC can be divided into four steps. In the first step, a client requests the KDC to issue a ticket for accessing the TGS. The request is accompanied by the user's secret key. The KDC authenticates the client based on the information stored in its database and generates a session key S1 and encrypts it using the secret key of the client. The KDC also generates a TGT, which is encrypted using the secret key of the TGS. Both the S1 session key and the TGT are then sent to the client.

In the second step, the client computer decrypts the data packet it received from the KDC and retrieves the newly created session key S1. This session key is used to create an authenticator to request access to an application server. The authenticator and the TGT are sent to the TGS, which then decrypts the authenticator by using the session key S1 stored in the TGT. The TGS authenticates information stored in the authenticator. In case of authentic details, the TGS creates a new session key S2 and encrypts it using S1. It also creates a granted ticket that contains ticket related information. The TGS sends both the session key and the ticket back to the client after encrypting the ticket with the secret key of the application server.

In the third step, the client decrypts the message and retrieves the new session key S2. A new authenticator is then created and is encrypted using the session key S2. Both the authenticator and the session key are sent to the application server. The application server recognizes the client to be authentic because the session ticket is encrypted using the secret key of the application server.

In the fourth and final step, a secured connection is established between the client and the application server. The client is sure that the message, which it receives, originates from the server and the server is confident that the client, who sends the return message, is authentic. This is because both the messages are encrypted using the S2 key, which is only available with the client and the application server.

3. You can configure a Kerberos principal to authenticate another principal that might exist on the same realm. Similarly, you can configure Kerberos principals that are a part of one realm to authenticate principals that are a part of another realm. This concept is known as *cross-realm authentication*. You need to set up a connection between the two realms and create a cross-realm secret key for authenticating users from one realm attempting to connect to the other realm. In cross-realm authentication, there is a set path through which authentication takes place for all realms. Therefore, you need to move between realms until you reach the realm you require. The basic security risks are that both the realms trust the other realm's KDC not to issue cross-realm tickets to unauthenticated users. A safety feature is that a remote KDC can only issue a ticket for users that exist on its own realm and not to users of any other realm. This ensures that the user is at least an authentic user of the other realm. In addition in Kerberos V5, KDCs of remote realms are not trusted by default. You need to explicitly get into a trust relationship with each realm.

4. One of the problems related to Kerberos is that the tickets expire after a specific amount of time. Although the short lifespan of a ticket is deterrent for hackers gaining access to the ticket, there might be cases when you require the ticket for a longer time span. The concept of renewable tickets was introduced in Kerberos V5. Renewable tickets have a normal lifespan like conventional tickets. However, you can set the maximum time for which the ticket can be renewed. To create a renewable ticket, first, use the `-r` option with the `kinit` command to increase the life span of the ticket. The option takes the maximum amount of time for which you want the ticket to be renewed as the parameter. Then, use the `krenew` program to create the ticket. A renewable ticket is advantageous because even if a hacker gains access to a ticket, the hacker cannot renew the ticket after it expires. If the hacker tries to get the ticket validated from the KDC, the request is refused.

Chapter 9

In this chapter, you'll learn about network security and the network security tools available in Solaris. You'll begin by learning about firewalls and how they can be used to secure networks. The chapter will cover how channeling all data to pass through one point on the network helps to improve security. Then you'll learn about some TCP/IP security tools, such as SATAN, ISS, tcpflow, and tcpdump. You'll learn about some of the commonly used intrusion-detection systems available on Solaris, such as tocsin and Gabriel. You will also learn about SKIP and IPSec and how they can be used for ensuring security.

Network Security Overview

The Internet has become an integral part of our lives. You can sit at home and connect to a computer in the office. Along with all its advantages, the Internet exposes you to certain dangers. There is always the danger that hackers can gain access to the information stored on a computer on the network. They can also intercept the data packets that you send or receive. The information stored in these data packets can be manipulated. All these dangers have caused concern for network administrators. Administrators have implemented security measures to secure all information stored on either a computer or being transmitted from a computer. One such security measure is setting up firewalls on a network.

Firewalls

You could define firewalls as hardware or software components that are installed to protect a group of networked computers from hackers and other intruders. Firewalls can be installed on host computers, routers, or on other applications and act as a gateway for the entire network. All information entering or leaving the network is channeled through the firewall. Therefore, a firewall has two interfaces. One interface is directed towards the internal network that has to be protected, and the other, towards the external network from which the firewall has to provide protection. At the simplest level of implementation, a firewall could be a simple router that administers traffic between the internal network and the external network and enforces some access control policy over the traffic flowing in between the external and the internal network. An access control policy simply defines the direction of data flow to and from different parts of the network. It will also define what type of traffic is acceptable, assuming that other data types will be blocked.

A type of firewall known as a *packet-filter based firewall* is used for analyzing all traffic entering and leaving the network and for comparing each data packet against a set of rules. You'll learn about the different types of firewalls in a later section. The rules or access control policies are maintained on the firewall and determine what type of information can enter and leave the network. If the transmitted data packet contains information that is against the specified rules, the data packet is discarded. Firewalls log all attempts made by external users to access the resources available on the network. If a hacker is detected, the firewall alerts the administrator and can even counter attack most of the hacking process if properly configured. However this counter attack feature is supported only in the most advanced kinds of firewalls.

Firewalls can also filter data packets passing through the network based on the protocols used to transmit the packets. This task is known as *protocol filtering*. Information about the protocols that are allowed or denied access to the network is defined and stored in access control policies or rules files. Different types of protocols can be allocated to carry different types of information. For example, the FTP protocol can be used to carry plain data while the SMTP protocol can be used to send e-mails. You can also send data based on the specific attributes of data packets or their state.

The rules stored on firewalls also contain the IP addresses of computers that are allowed or restricted access to the internal network. When a firewall checks data packets, it also checks the IP addresses of the source and destination computers. This information is stored in the header information of the data packets. If the IP addresses are found in the restricted list, the data packets are not allowed to leave the network. If the restricted IP address file is empty, then the firewall automatically denies all data packets to leave the network.

All information that enters or leaves a network should pass through a firewall. However, a firewall cannot enforce this as a fundamental rule on the network. For example, a user might configure a modem on a client computer to easily bypass all the security measures implemented on a firewall and transmit data directly to the Internet. Because the client computer doesn't have security measures to check transmitted data, hackers can use this unsecured connection to gain access to the network. Therefore, it becomes the responsibility of network administrators to ensure that users do not have the right to install modems by themselves. Administrators can implement such security policies on the network to provide security. They can also implement authentication mechanisms for ensuring that only authorized users have the right to install.

Firewalls are essential for the security of a network. They need to be installed on networks even if only a single computer from the entire network connects to the Internet. Users who need to install modems on their personal computers also need to ensure that they have adequate security measures, such as personal firewalls, configured on their computers. Even a single computer that provides unsecured access to the Internet might provide hackers easy access to the network. Hackers can use simple hacking techniques, such as IP spoofing and network sniffers, to detect the passwords used by authentic users on the network. If hackers are able to gain access to a single valid user password, they can impersonate the user and decipher the other passwords used on the network. Therefore, it is critical to prevent hacker intrusion into a network.

Types of Firewalls

You can broadly categorize firewalls into four types depending on the technologies that are being used in order to control access over a network perimeter. They are:

◆ **Packet-level firewall**. This type of firewall is implemented at the network level in the OSI model. The firewall provides the security of information that is transmitted as data packets over a network. You can configure packet-level firewalls on either hardware, such as routers, or on software, such as packet filters. A router stores information about the IP address of machines that have the right to send and receive messages over a network. It also stores information about the port number and the protocols that are allowed on the network. Administrators can maintain separate rules files, known as *Access Control Lists* (ACLs), which contain information about the Source IP addresses, Destination IP address, protocols, and source and destination port numbers that should or should not be allowed access to a network. All assessment is made against the rules files. Therefore, when a router receives data packets, it filters the information based on the rules specified in rules files.

You can implement a packet-level firewall based on packet filters. Packet filters contain information regarding the different types of information that can be transmitted over a network. They sort all data packets based on the protocols used to transmit the data packets. After the data packets have been sorted, only the data packets belonging to specific protocols are transmitted to external networks. The advantages of using packet-level firewalls are low installation cost and insignificant effect on network performance. The firewalls can be configured as software on a particular OS, on routers, or they also come up as a separate hardware box with a high performance processor inside it and perform services such as NATing. Therefore, the security implemented by the firewall is almost transparent to the end user. However, the disadvantage of this type of firewall is that it is difficult to configure and vulnerable to IP spoofing attacks. Another disadvantage is that you cannot implement restrictions for individual users. There is also no logging or printing utility available with this type of firewall. This disadvantage makes it a poor choice in instances where you require logs to track intrusion or other errors.

 NOTE

Most networks consist of seven layers together known as the *OSI model*. The layers are application, presentation, session, transport, network, data link, and physical. Every layer in the model is responsible for a different set of clearly defined activities. A data packet must travel over multiple layers before it reaches its destination. Firewalls can be set at different levels. For example, you could configure a firewall at the network level or at the transport level.

◆ **Application-level firewall**. This type of firewall is implemented on the application level of the OSI model. It is typically used for monitoring and securing the services available on a network. For example, if you configure a firewall to allow only FTP traffic to pass through a network, all data packets that involve the use of other protocols, such as Gopher and Telnet, are denied access. The use of such a firewall is advantageous if you require the security of Internet-related services. For example, if some user requires access to FTP, you could configure the firewall to require authentication before allowing the user to access the service. You could also implement filtering based on commands. This is not possible in the other types of firewalls. You can also configure the availability of a service based on user details or based on the time of the day. The disadvantage of this type of firewall is that it is expensive and time-consuming to install. The use of this firewall can also affect network performance. It necessitates manual configuration on all client computers. All the information that passes through the firewall can be logged and filtered based on login information of users and the activities performed by them.

◆ **Stateful multilayered firewall**. This type of firewall is a synthesis of the other types of firewalls. The firewall can maintain state information, which is not possible in stateless router-based firewalls. The firewall overcomes the limitation of the previous two types of firewalls: data packets are analyzed based on their host and destination addresses and content. In the case of the stateful multilayered firewall, data packets are checked at the network layer. All the packets are sent based on the source IP address, destination IP address, port number, and protocols included in the data packets. The firewall expects a reply from the destination address regarding the number of data packets already received at the destination computer. It compares this information against the total number of data packets expected by the destination computer. This prevents the manipulation of data packets during transit.

◆ **Circuit-level firewall**. This type of firewall is used if you need to set up security for TCP or UDP connections. After a secure connection has been established, you can send and receive data over the connection without implementing further checks. This firewall is configured on the session level of the OSI model. It provides security of the authentication that takes place between the firewall and an external network. The firewall makes the internal network transparent to the external network and manages all data transfer. All data seems to originate from the firewall instead of from specific computers on the local network. This provides the advantage of anonymity to the local network at the same cost. The drawback of this type of firewall is that you cannot implement the scrutiny of individual data packets.

Requirements for Installing Firewalls

Before you begin to install a firewall, you need to decide the type of firewall that suits the security requirements of your organization. You also need to decide what services running on your private network require connection to an external network and need to be secured.

After the firewall has been installed, you need to ensure that the firewall is secure. This important task needs to be completed before you connect to the Internet, because once connected, it is difficult to control network traffic unless all security measures are in place. The first step to secure the firewall is shutting down all services. After shutting down, you should only start the services that are required on the server. This ensures that you have control over the services running on the firewall. Certain services are essential for the functioning of the firewall. You should ensure that if these services are started, they are configured to accept connections only from selective computers. Wherever possible, ensure that most of the services run on the private network behind the firewall. You should install only the applications necessary for the smooth functioning of the firewall. The risk of hacking is proportionate to the number of running applications you have on the firewall, because each application offers an opportunity for hackers to attack.

All software-based firewalls inherit the drawback of the operating system on which they are installed. Therefore all the options that make the OS vulnerable to attacks should be ruled out first by ensuring that the firewall PC runs the optimal required applications and services and all the latest patches have been installed.

In Solaris, you need to identify all the packages installed on the system and remove all unnecessary packages. Appropriate permissions are also critical for ensuring the security of a firewall. The `setuid` permissions for all root-specific applications should also be removed. Only the root account should have the right to perform administrative tasks. Files must be backed up and the checksum for all critical system files should be maintained. Maintaining checksums helps to check whether files have been hacked. It also provides a source of recovery if the server crashes.

The rules implemented on firewalls are an important component of firewall security. These rules decide which type of traffic is allowed on a network. As mentioned earlier, if a service is not explicitly allowed access, it is assumed to be denied access to the network. You also need to ensure that all cases of IP spoofing are detected when they occur and all data packets that originate from suspicious sources are automatically rejected.

Most firewalls also check for the port numbers of the source and destination computers before transmitting data packets. You need to implement different types of rules for managing data belonging to different protocols. For example, you would set different types of rules for allowing or restricting HTTP traffic. In addition, if data packets use FTP to move between networks, you would specify different rules for the data packets.

You can also use filtering applications, such as `ipfilter` and `ipchains`, for filtering out undesirable data packets from a network. One of the many packet-filtering applications available in Solaris is `ipfilter`. Because Solaris doesn't contain precompiled binaries, the application must first be compiled on the Solaris server. In most Solaris versions, the SUNWspro package is used for compiling the binary file. The ipfilter application contains two parameters, action and pattern. As the names suggest, the pattern parameter contains an example of what needs to be searched in data packets. If the search pattern is found, the action parameter provides details about what needs to be done with the respective data packet. The action parameter generally contains a port number and the value 0, drop, or 1. The value 0 implies allowing access, drop implies dropping a packet, and 1 implies denying access to the data packets.

The ipchains utility is used for creating filters. These filters, which are also known as chains, are implemented on a packet-level firewall. The firewall compares all incoming and outgoing data packets against the rules file and filters out all restricted data packets. You need to create different rules for each set of restrictions. For example, you could create a rule for preventing HTTP data packets from entering or leaving a network. You could create another rule for ensuring that a specific type of data packet is directed to a predefined port.

TCP/IP Security Tools

Many tools available in Solaris can be used to analyze TCP/IP data packets and detect intrusion. The following is a list of some of these tools:

◆ Internet Security Scanner (ISS)
◆ Security Administrator's Tool for Analyzing Networks (SATAN)
◆ tcpdump
◆ tcpflow

I'll discuss these in the following sections.

ISS

The *Internet Security Scanner (ISS)* is one of the most powerful Internet security scanners available in the market. It is flexible and can be easily ported to numerous platforms. It scans the network for weak points and alerts the administrator if any are found. The advantage of ISS is that it doesn't stop at the first weak point found, but performs a complete scan of the network. Hackers already know most of these flaws that the ISS finds. You might, therefore, wonder whether this application is of any use. The application detects all the basic security limitations of a network arising because of the implementation of wrong or incomplete security measures. These flaws are easily visible to hackers when they try to access the internal network from the Internet.

While implementing networks, the services of experienced hackers are used. This is because these people understand the importance of implementing proper security measures and know how to configure them.

How are hackers able to gain access to a network? The answer is simple. They attack the weakest link in the network. Because they know that most networks are secured from the entrance, they try to gain entry from the backdoor. These backdoors are the trusted computers or networks to which the primary network provides access. Most networks consist of many smaller networks or provide access to remote computers. Many of these remote computers might not be secured. Hackers can sniff out these computers and gain access to the primary network. Once hackers gain access to a system, they can gain control of other systems. It is against this kind of attack that ISS provides security. The scanner scans the network for all such weak connections or client computers and alerts the administrator if a flaw is found.

Table 9-1 lists some of the options commonly used with ISS.

Table 9-1 Options Available with ISS

Option	Description
-d	Specifies that the scan should ignore default logins. The use of default service accounts to log on to the network is not a security flaw. There is a flaw only if an account can be used without a password. In such a case, a hacker can log on as the service and use the gained rights to attain root permission. A good networking practice is to disable an user or service account until it is actually required.
-v	Ignores aliases in e-mail addresses. In case this option is not used, the scanner would check for all the users and their corresponding aliases on the host computer. The scanner also checks for all user accounts that have weak passwords and raises an alert for the administrator. Certain user accounts and aliases provide rights to users for overwriting system files.
-m	Ignores the checking of mail ports during scanning. If this option is not used, the scanner would also scan the mail port. The scan would return details regarding the hostname, the OS being used, and the version of the e-mailing service being used.
-y	Gains access to the pw command by using Ypx. Ypx is a program used for retrieving password information from ypserv. It is critical that you ensure that all unnecessary services are disabled on client computers. For example, if the Rexd command is running on a client computer, hackers can easily spoof password information and gain access to the server. They can similarly use the selection_srv service to gain access to user information and passwords. In the case of diskless clients, hackers can retrieve the name of a domain from the bootparm information.
-s	Specifies the maximum time to wait before scanning. The time is calculated in seconds.

Option	Description
-r	Specifies that the scanner should ignore all RPC calls. If the option is not used, the scanner uses the available RPC information to detect security loopholes that are otherwise undetected. The scanner retrieves all information about NIS clients, host computers, bootparams and NFS files. The command that the scanner uses for retrieving this information is `rpcinfo -p <hostname>`, where `hostname` is the server on which the command is run.
-f	Specifies that the scanner should ignore any instances of anonymous logging to the FTP port. If this option is not used, the scanner checks whether a user is able to log on to the network anonymously by using the FTP port. After the user logs on to the host computer, a hacker checks if the primary directory on the FTP site is writable. He checks this by creating a directory on the site. The hacker then writes to the `.rhost` file and adds entries that provide the user complete rights and access to the FTP site and the information stored in it. Because the FTP site is considered secure, it will contain a copy of all the user accounts that have the right to access the FTP site, creating another security loophole. Hackers can use this information to gain access to other computers on the internal network.
-p	Specifies that the specified port should be checked for all open TCP ports. If this option is used, the scanner checks the host computer for possible unsecured ports. It checks all the installed applications that might cause security risks.
-e	Specifies that only the directories that can be accessed by all the users should be logged. The log files maintained on the host computer contain information about all its clients and the directories exported from these clients. The `show-mount -e <hostname>` command is used to display a list of all exportable directories available on the host computer. Hackers can intercept this information and manipulate it so that the hacker's computer also appears to be a legitimate client to a remote host.
-o	Specifies a different log file for storing log information. By default, all log information is stored in the `ISS.log` file.
-q	Disables Quick Scan so that all hosts are checked. In Quick Scan, all hosts without names are not scanned. In normal scanning, the scanner searches a domain by looking for all listed addresses. If an address is found, it performs a more detailed search based on additional information.

The scanner checks the entire domain serially for any available hosts. When a host computer is found, all exposed ports are checked and all information returned by the host computer is displayed. The scanner begins by checking the Telnet port, because this is usually the most vulnerable port on a host computer.

Security Administrator's Tool for Analyzing Networks (SATAN)

Security Administrator's Tool for Analyzing Networks (SATAN) is used for scanning remote hosts. It is used for gathering information about network services and the resources available on the host machine. The need for the tool became evident when client computers were becoming dependent on the network for their security. If the network's security was compromised, all the client computers on the network were rendered vulnerable.

 NOTE

Some references indicate that SATAN stands for Security Analysis Tool for Auditing Networks. Therefore, either of these terms can be used while discussing SATAN.

SATAN helps administrators identify the common security flaws that exist on client computers and raises alerts for each flaw found. It also provides a detailed description about the cause and effect of the security problem and suggests solutions to resolve it. The solution may be making changes to the configuration file, installing patches, disabling a service, or restricting access to a service to a few users.

You have already learned about ISS, which is used for scanning remote hosts or the network. All security issues that are detected are immediately brought to the attention of the network administrator. SATAN also performs similar tasks, which include searching the network and Internet for weak systems, probing computers on the network, both internal and external, for vulnerabilities, and maintaining an exhaustive schema of content sensitive help. These features make SATAN different from most of the remote auditing tools commonly available. Other security auditing tools such as COPS need to run on the host server to be scanned. SATAN is a network security tools that can run remotely and can be used to scan any system on the network. The added advantage in using SATAN is that you do not need to have a user account or any privileges on the remote machine in order to scan it.

Most network services have some security flaws that cannot be easily detected. SATAN checks these services for improper setup or incomplete configuration. It also checks the services for known bugs or weak policies. Sometimes the security flaw of a network service relates to the policy implemented for the service. If the policy is incomplete or has certain shortcomings, the service cannot be fully secured despite implementing the best security measures. SATAN can either alert the administrator about these security flaws or implement a simple policy based on rules that help identify security-related problems. Although the tool is primarily used for detecting security-related problems, it can be used to retrieve important network-related information, such as a network topology, the hardware and software used, and the services running on a network. After the entire network-related data has been collected, the data and the rules used on a host computer are checked for trust and dependency relationships with other host computers. The check helps identify all the trust relationships that exist on the network and any flaw in network security that could arise because of these trust relationships.

The following is a list of some of the problems generally reported by SATAN. An unauthorized host could:

♦ Disable the access controls of the X server
♦ Use older versions of `sendmail` that would have security flaws that could be easily manipulated
♦ Access NIS password files
♦ Gain access to NFS system files by exporting them
♦ Use `portmapper` to gain access to NFS file systems
♦ Export NFS file systems by using unsecured applications
♦ Provide random access to files by using TFTP
♦ Provide access to anonymous users to write to the FTP home directory
♦ Provide shell access on remote machines to unauthorized users
♦ Provide REXD access to unauthorized users

Both administrators and hackers can use SATAN to retrieve information about a host computer. Administrators use the information to improve the security of the host computer. Hackers use it to hack the host computer to gain access to the other computers on the network.

System administrators who are responsible for ensuring the security of host computers primarily use SATAN. However, because the tool is freely available, it can be used by anyone who needs to check the security level of a computer and identify what needs to be secured. The tool lists the security loopholes that might have previously gone undetected. Because even hackers can use the tool to scan host computers for security flaws, administrators should use the tools before the hackers and plug all security loopholes.

SATAN is basically a targeting application that uses the `finger` utility to detect whether a host computer or a group of computers on a network are responding to messages. It prepares a list of host computers and sends the list to an engine that sends messages to the host computers and stores all the information they return. This task continues in a loop until all the host computers have been checked and their information is collected and stored securely. All the hosts are first checked for any previous attempts made by the tool to search them. If a host has not been checked before, all the services running on it are checked against a list of possible security shortcomings or bugs that could exist on the computer. After the check is complete, the host computer returns a set of information to the tool. This information contains the hostname, the result of the analysis, and any other relevant information found on the host computer. This information is then stored in a file and is used later for a complete analysis of the host computer for security flaws. Administrators can also view the result of the scan as a Web page. The Web page can appear in any of the commonly used Web browsers, such as Netscape, Mosaic, and Lynx. The data is divided into sections and the Web page contains a link to each section. Therefore, administrators can easily analyze and understand the vast data.

The basis of the analysis performed using the SATAN tool is trust. Trust becomes essential when a remote computer realizes the danger posed by a client who doesn't have proper authorization but can easily compromise the resources stored locally on the host computer. As trust is transitive in nature, there is always the possibility that a third computer that has not been secured will compromise the security of a host computer. A transitive trust relationship is created between all the three computers because the third computer trusts the unsecured computer and the host computer, in turn, trusts the third computer. This trust relationship can exist by adding the entry for the client computer in the .rhosts and hosts.equiv files. These files contain user information, and the passwords stored in these files can be used to provide access to users without authorization. Trust relationships can also exist between Web servers configured on different networks. If a host computer trusts another host, it is important that there should be proper authentication between the host computers. If a user attempts to log on to a remote host in the absence of proper authorization, a hacker can gain access to the user's information. If this happens, the hacker can use the information not only to compromise the host computer but also to gain access to other computers that exist on the network.

Most administrators are aware of the dangers of trust relationships. They implement security measures to protect networks against hackers. However, with the use of the Internet, the dangers of IP spoofing and account impersonation have grown. In the case of the Internet, you cannot ensure security by only securing the .rhosts and hosts.equiv files. Hackers can easily use trust relationships to their advantage by attempting to log on to the Web server by using the credentials of an authentic user whose user account exists on a remote server. As the user account doesn't exist on the Web server, the server assumes that the user has been authenticated on the remote server. The Web server only checks if the remote server is a trusted computer. If the remote server is trusted, the user is allowed access. Hackers use this vulnerability to gain access to the Web server and its resources.

SATAN is simple to use. You first need to edit the configuration file and specify any changes you require for the rules implemented on the Web server. The edit file will contain information about all the services that need to be checked and all the issues that need to be checked. Then you need to specify information about the target computer by using the SATAN `target` selection. You can run SATAN from the HTML interface or the command line. From the command line, the command is `satan <client.com>`. After the analysis is complete, all the information about the host computer is available in the SATAN Reporting & Data Analysis section. This section provides links to other subsections. There subsections provide a detailed report of the security vulnerabilities that might have been found in these sections.

An important point to remember is that `TCP wrappers` cannot be used along with SATAN. Therefore, before you attempt to run SATAN, you need to disable all TCP wrappers. After the analysis is complete, you can restart the wrappers. Although there are a number of files created and used in SATAN, the primary file is the configuration file that contains information about what needs to be checked on client machines. Another important file is the `config/*` file that SATAN requires for detecting other program files and detecting their default settings. SATAN uses the `bin/*` file for gathering information, while it uses `html/*` files for storing all the information generated by the tool. The `results/database-name` contains all the databases maintained by SATAN. There are three databases and each database is used for storing a separate kind of information. The following sections contain descriptions of these databases.

The all-hosts Database

The `all-hosts` database contains a list of all host computers detected by SATAN while scanning. It even contains information about host computers that were not checked during scanning. The database stores information about the host computers, such as the type of information they store. It also stores information about hosts that might not exist physically and the output returned by the `showmount` command. The database stores information in the form of an ASCII file containing six fields, and each field is separated by a pipe (|) symbol. The database stores information about the host computer's IP address, proximity to the target computer, and the attack level of the host. The database also contains information regarding whether subnet expansion is underway and the time when the scan needs to be performed.

The facts Database

The `facts` database stores information regarding all the information retrieved by SATAN. It is this data that is processed to create the final report that is displayed to the administrator or to hackers. The information available in the database is stored in the form of records and maintained in text files. All information is categorized into seven fields and each field is separated using a pipe (|) symbol. These fields are `target`, `service`, `status`, `severity`, `trusted`, `trustee`, and `text`. The `target` field contains the name of the host computer, which the scanner needs to analyze. This information can either be the FQDN number or the IP address of host computer. The `service` field contains the name of the SATAN tool that is used to analyze a specific service. The `status` field stores information about the current status of the connection. The status can be either reachable or timed out. The next field is the `severity` field that stores information regarding the level of seriousness of a security problem. The `trustee` field stores information about the computer that trusts another computer. The data is stored in two parts joined together by the @ symbol. The left part stores user information while the right part stores the name of the host computer. The `trusted` field contains the name of the computer trusted by the computer named in the `trustee` field. The entry in this field follows the same pattern as that of the entry in the `trustee` field. The final field is the `text` field that stores the messages that are displayed after the analysis is complete.

The todo Database

The `todo` database contains a list of all the hosts accessed by tools and all the queries executed on remote computers. The database stores information about the scans already performed on the host computer. All the information is stored in the form of records containing three fields. Similar to the other two databases, the fields of this database are also separated using the pipe (|) symbol. The database stores information about the name of the host computer, the name of the tool used on the computer, and the arguments used with tools.

Other files created by SATAN also store the information used and created by the tool. For example, the `rules/*` file contains a list of all rules used by SATAN to detect security flaws on client computers. The flexibility provided by these rules is one of the reasons why SATAN is so popular. The `src/*` file stores information about other programs and utilities supported by SATAN. These utilities provide SATAN with information about other security flaws and help gather information about the network.

Vulnerabilities in SATAN

As mentioned earlier, both administrators and hackers can use SATAN for entirely different purposes. Administrators use the tool for detecting security flaws on the host computer and to identify flaws in trust relationships that exist between the host computer and other computers. The tool can detect flaws that would normally go undetected by network administrators. Administrators can use this information to plug security loopholes. They can also ensure that only authorized users or computers are granted access to host computers.

A good network security practice is to run SATAN behind a firewall. This is a secure method because SATAN only checks the computers that have IP connectivity. The tool never ventures outside the firewall, and hackers cannot access the information returned by the tool. This rule also works on the assumption that IP_FORWARDING has been disabled on the client computer. It is important that you are careful about running SATAN behind a firewall. An IP_FORWARDING-enabled client computer that has the right to directly connect to the Internet is a security hazard. Hackers can use the computer to gain access to the information returned by SATAN. Another danger is that hackers can use the tool to gain access to the host computer to which they do not have any access rights. Hackers can easily use SATAN for spoofing and other hacking attacks because the tool works on the same principle that is used by other successful hacking tools.

It would be incorrect to say that SATAN is a security hazard. The tool has built-in security mechanisms to secure access. The first security mechanism is that it only accesses computers that are a limited distance away from the host computer or the subnet. This distance is known as the *proximity level* and is described as the distance between the host and the client computer. Every group of computers that forms a circle around the target computer is considered a proximity level. Therefore, if you set the proximity level as 3, then SATAN only searches all client computers that exist in the first three groups of computers around the host computer. However, each proximity level can contain numerous client computers, and the size of the search can grow to a large extent. Besides proximity levels, there are two other variables that can be used by SATAN to limit the scope of the search. These variables are $only_attack_these and $don't_attack_these. As their names suggest, the first variable is used to limit the search of SATAN to a limited number of clients, while the second variable is used for specifying the clients that SATAN should not check.

While scanning, SATAN maintains a status file that stores information about all the client computers scanned and any vulnerabilities found. The file, which is named status_file, stores the information along with the timestamp and the actions performed on the client machine. You could also use the -v option that specifies the verberos mode. In the verberos mode, all information appears at the command line along with other information relevant to the security of the network. Because the amount of information provided at the prompt is quite large, it is a good practice to store all the information in a file for future analysis.

Another recommended practice is to ensure that SATAN doesn't automatically scan a network to which you might not have permission. This is an unethical practice, and you need to ensure that you set the proximity level to a low value to ensure that only the client computers in the immediate vicinity of the target computer are checked. You can also set the $only_attack_these variable to narrow the list of clients that will be checked by SATAN.

You have already learned that hackers can use SATAN to detect system vulnerabilities. How can you differentiate between the probing implemented by you or a hacker? There is no simple answer. An attacklike situation can easily occur if two users run the finger utility or if TCP wrappers have not been disabled on host computers. In either of these cases, it might appear that a hacker is attempting to enter the network.

Nowadays, administrators have become knowledgeable and confident about being able to secure their networks from hacker attacks. Although hackers can use SATAN for nefarious activities, you need to remember that SATAN was primarily developed for ensuring the security of the network and detecting security flaws. If administrators use the full potential of the tool, they can easily secure their networks against hackers, who would not detect anything that is not already known to the administrator.

tcpdump

The tcpdump program is a powerful network-monitoring tool that is used for network analysis and diagnostics. The tcpdump is basically used to monitor and decode IP, TCP, UDP, and ICMP headers. The program sniffs the header information stored in the data packets being transmitted over the network. The program then statistically analyzes and prints the information in the data packets that match search criteria. This search criterion is provided in the form of a Boolean expression. You can also save the information to a file that can be later analyzed and reviewed. You can provide a file containing data to act as an input for the command. All information that matches the specified search criterion is displayed. The program examines numerous kinds of data packets such as IPv6, IPv4, ICMP, TCP, UDP, and SNMP. The tool is primarily used for detecting problems relating to network traffic and for monitoring network activities.

When the program is scanning a network to identify security problems, it can only be stopped if it receives a SIGINT signal or the -c option is used. The -c option is used to specify a limit for the number of data packets that the program can handle. If the limit is crossed, the program automatically terminates. After the program has analyzed the network, it prepares a report of its findings. The report contains information regarding the number of data packets checked and the number that matches the search criteria. The report also contains a count of data packets that were dropped due to a lack of disk space in the buffer. The following is the syntax of the tcpdump command:

```
tcpdump [-<option>] [-c count][-C <file_size>] [-F <file>]
[-I <interface>][-T type][ -w <file>][expression]
```

In the preceding code, the options indicate the different uses of the command. The -F option is used if you need to specify a file that provides the filtering expression. The -w option is used for storing the information retrieved by the program and storing it in a file. Table 9-2 contains a list of some of the other options that can be used along with the tcpdump command.

Table 9-2 Options Available with the `tcpdump` Command

Option	Description
-a	Converts a network address to valid hostnames.
-dd	Specifies that the program should dump data packets that match specified search criteria. The program dumps the data packets as C programs.
-ddd	Specifies that the program should dump data packets that match specified search criteria. Although the option might seem similar to the -dd option, in this case, the program dumps the data packets as decimal numbers.
-c	Specifies that the program should exit immediately after determining the total number of received data packets.
-C	Checks the file size of the text file before saving content to the file. If the size of the file exceeds the prescribed limit, the current file is closed and a new file is created to save data packet information.
-f	Prints the hostname of the external Internet address instead of its numeric version.

Option	Description
-F	Specifies a file name that will act as an input file for the program. This information acts like a filter, and all information found in the dat packets that match the search criteria specified is displayed.
-i	Specifies an interface that is used for listening for requests on the network. If this option is not specified, the program searches for the lowest numbered system interface available on the network.
-l	Specifies that the output of the program should appear at the command line. This option is particularly useful if you need to immediately view the output of program instead of storing it in a file.
-N	Specifies that the domain name should not be displayed without any qualification. Therefore, your domain name would appear as `sales` instead of `sales.asc.com`.
-O	Specifies that the program should not run the optimizer required for matching packet information with the search criteria. It is recommended that you use this option if an error exists in the optimizer.
-P	Restricts promiscuous mode on a computer. However, there can be other reasons for a computer to run in promiscuous mode.
-q	Removes protocol information from displayed information. This provides less but more concise information for analysis.
-r	Reads data packets from files. You can store all required information in simple text files, which can then be provided as parameters to the command.
-S	Prints the TCP sequence of numbers in absolute form instead of random form.
-s	Extracts more than the default amount of information from data packets. By default, you can extract 68 bytes of data at a time. Although 68 bytes of information is adequate for TCP and UDP data packets, the size might cause the program to shorten the protocol information provided along with a data packet. Data packets are truncated because a limited amount of space is available in their snapshots.
-t	Specifies that the program should not display the timestamp along with the other pieces of information.
-tt	Specifies that the program prints the timestamp without formatting.
-ttt	Inserts spaces between the different lines displayed in the output.

continues

Table 9-2 (*continued*)

Option	Description
-v	Specifies the verbose mode, where all the information retrieved by the program is displayed along with any errors encountered by the program. This option is also used to enable package integrity checks and ensure the authenticity of IP and ICMP header checksums.
-vv	Includes additional information that is not displayed with the -v option. This information includes the information retrieved from SMD data packets and NFS reply packets.
-vvv	Displays information about Telnet and SB services. The option also displays the information retrieved using the -X Telnet option.
-w	Writes the data packets directly to a specified file. This file can then be printed and analyzed.
-x	Prints data packets in hexadecimal format. The smallest portion of a data packet is printed.
-X	Prints information in hexadecimal and ASCII formats. This is particularly useful in cases where new protocols need to be analyzed.

The expression parameter that is used along with the tcpdump command is used to specify the data packets that need to be dumped by the program. If an expression is not specified with the command, all the data packets available on a network examined by the program will be dumped.

The program is basically used for measuring and monitoring the response time of network traffic and for calculating the percentage of data packets lost during transmission. The tcpdump utility is used for analyzing TCP/UDP connections and uses a special mechanism for opening and closing the connections. By measuring the time lag between the passing of data packets, the speed at which a connection is established can be determined along with the rate at which the data packets are being transmitted.

tcpflow

A UNIX-based program called tcpflow is used for capturing the data packets being transmitted as part of the TCP connection. The information in the packets is stored and later analyzed and debugged. Applications such as tcpdump return information about the various data packets being transmitted over a network. This information is generated and made available after the data packets have been transmitted. The tcpflow program, in contrast, provides information about the data packets currently being transmitted over a network. This data can be analyzed later. As the sequence of data packets is critical for their proper analysis, tcpflow maintains the records of data packets and the sequence of their transfer. The advantage of tcpflow is that it can easily retransmit data packets if there is a break in connection. However, the disadvantage is that the program does not understand IP packets and therefore cannot maintain their flow and sequence. The tcpflow program follows a packet filtering mechanism that is similar to the one followed by tcpdump. The tcpflow program is used for capturing all data packets transmitted to a specific network interface. You can also filter the returned data based on the security requirements of the network. The following command is used to detect and intercept HTTP data packets being transmitted and received by a computer:

```
sudo tcpflow -c port 80
```

Only users who have appropriate administrative access, such as root, can use the preceding command to retrieve the required information. The -c option is used to display the retrieved information in a terminal window instead of saving it in a file. As port 80 can only be used to retrieve HTTP data packets, the command displays all HTTP data packets being passed to and from the computer. You can also use tcpflow as a command-line utility.

IPSec

IPSec was first introduced with Solaris 8 and has been improved in Solaris 9. IPSec, or IPSecurity Protocol, is a layer of security implemented at the network layer. It is used for securing network communication. The standard is particularly useful in cases where Virtual Private Networks (VPNs) exist on a network and remote users are provided access to the private networks through public networks by using dial-up connections. The use of IPSec on VPNs is advantageous because the standard is compatible with both IPv4 and IPv6. This cross-platform compatibility helps migrate networks currently using IPv4 to IPv6. Another advantage of using IPSec is that the security-related modification made by the standard doesn't necessitate modifications on client computers.

IPSec provides two levels of protocols, Authentication Headers (AH) and Encapsulation Security Payload (ESP). AH is primarily used for authenticating the information sent by the sender, while ESP is used for providing support for both authenticating the sender and encrypting information. Depending on the protocols used, the specific information associated with the protocol is added to the information already stored in the header. These protocols can be used together or separately. The AH protocol is used for authentication and ensuring data integrity. The *Message Authentication Code (MAC)* is created using these services.

MAC is similar to a key and encrypts transmitted data by using a hash function. You cannot decrypt a MAC message without the use of the appropriate key. AH stores information in the header section of data packets and is used for creating the MAC. The content is encrypted using the secret key, which is transmitted between the sender and the receiver.

When the recipient receives the data packets, the receiver decrypts them by using the secret key and decrypts the MAC. If the MAC decrypted by the client doesn't match the one sent by the sender, the data packets are considered to be hacked during transit. In the case of ESP, using encryption provides the security of transmitted information. This protocol is generally used with the AH protocol for ensuring the authenticity and integrity of transmitted data. ESP provides security by encapsulating all transmitted information. However, it doesn't encrypt the IP header information stored within the data packets. For ensuring data authentication, a data packet is first encrypted and then used to create the MAC.

IPSec is primarily used for ensuring data authentication, integrity, and confidentiality. Both users and network applications can use IPSec without noticing any difference in performance. IPSec provides the security of existing network services.

Simple Key-Management for Internet Protocols (SKIP)

Sun provides numerous tools for securing remote access and ensuring Internet security. *Simple Key-Management for Internet Protocols* (SKIP) is one such tool provided by Sun-Screen. SKIP is one of the commonly used public-key cryptography software. It provides authentication of host computers and encrypts information by using multiple encryption algorithms.

The tool is transparent in its functioning to both the users and applications that use it. This is because SKIP works at the network level. It therefore becomes transparent to any application that is sharing information over TCP/IP networks. The application used could be a Telnet, FTP, or Web browser. Any two computers that use SKIP for authentication can also use it to encrypt communication by using IP. SKIP provides computers a secure channel for communication over an unsecured network such as the Internet. Therefore, SKIP provides network security without compromising or effecting user activity.

SKIP uses public-key cryptography for securing all communication over a network and for authenticating all traffic moving over an IP network. It is also used for ensuring the integrity and privacy of information transmitted over a network. Encrypting transmitted information ensures that the information is not tampered with during transit and cannot be viewed by unauthorized users. Using SKIP implies using sessionless protocols for establishing connections. It also involves exchanging automatic certificates and using the Certificate Discovery Protocol (CDP). The following is a list of some of the features provided by SKIP:

◆ Enables efficient and key management. It also provides a basis for creating a strong security policy.

◆ Provides support for the CDP.

- Provides support for using multiple name space identifiers.
- Provides for the use of access control methods that restrict access based on host-names or network addresses.
- Enables the automatic encryption and decryption of data packets by using encryption algorithms. This ensures the confidentiality of information transmitted over a network.
- Provides numerous utilities that can be used for ensuring security over a network.
- Provides ability to ensure the compression of data packets transmitted over a network. This ensures faster transmission of data between the computers on a network.
- Provides the services of the MD5 encryption algorithm for ensuring the security and authenticity of transmitted information.

When information needs to be transmitted between two host computers running SKIP, the tool creates a secret key by using an encryption algorithm and the current timestamp. Only the two computers sharing the information know this key. The sender divides the information into data packets and encrypts the data packet using the secret key. The sender then encrypts the key by using the current timestamp. Then SKIP is used to store the IP header information within the data packets along with information about the encryption algorithm used to encrypt the data packets. The header information also stores the encrypted secret key and the original IP data packets that have been encrypted using the secret key. When the data packets reach the destination computer, the receiver retrieves the certificate transmitted with the data packets and authenticates the client. The receiver then decrypts the secret key transmitted along with the encrypted data packets. After the key has been decrypted, it is used to decrypt the rest of the encrypted data packets. As the secret key is changed periodically, the secrecy of the encrypted data packet is maintained.

Intrusion Detection Tools

The use of networking and the Internet has increased the magnitude of business tremendously. Networking has not only brought buyers and sellers closer. It has also provided suppliers and business partners a means for faster communication.

However, with the increase in connectivity between users, there has been an increase in the vulnerability of the confidential data available on a private intranet. SUN provides numerous security products and services, some of which belong to third-party vendors, for ensuring network security. In the following sections, I will discuss some of the commonly available and regularly used intrusion detection tools.

tocsin

From the range of intrusion detection scanners available in Solaris, tocsin is an intrusion detection scanner that is used for scanning networks for flaws. Although the application performs a function similar to the one performed by klaxon, it is used for scanning a network. You only need to run tocsin on one client computer in a subnet to detect intrusion attempts in the entire subnet. The tocsin application is available with Solaris and uses packet filtering to identify port-scanning attempts. It has been designed specifically to monitor and detect TCP SYM hacking attempts. The scanner tracks all SYN data packets transmitted between the host computer and the port exposed on a server. If the client receives an answer, then the TCP service is available, otherwise, the server doesn't provide the service. All messages received by tocsin are logged in the LOG_AUTH or LOG_NOTICE log file by using the syslog utility available in Solaris.

Gabriel

You learned about SATAN and how you can use it to detect system vulnerabilities. You also learned that the tool is freely available over the Internet and even hackers can use it to detect system vulnerabilities. Gabriel was developed to protect a network against the danger posed by SATAN. The tool keeps a constant check over a network and raises warnings for the administrator if it discovers any network intrusion or a threat of a hacker attack. Gabriel works like SATAN and detects all network search programs before they can begin to sweep the network and gather any security-related information. When Gabriel detects an intrusion, it e-mails the report directly to the administrator. The advantage provided in the current version of Gabriel is that it uses other technologies besides e-mails to alert administrators of intrusion attempts. This is unlike the previous versions of Gabriel, where the alert mechanism was confined to e-mail, which could be easily overlooked or missed. You can configure Gabriel to raise alerts by using page messages, phone calls, or alert messages. Another advantage of Gabriel is that it can be used for detecting intrusion throughout a network and provides centralized administration for an entire network. One computer handles the tasks of the Gabriel administrative software. One machine in each of the subsections of the network is identified and loaded with the client software.

This client machine is responsible for handling the administration of the entire section besides performing its normal tasks. The client machine monitors all network traffic passing through the section and reports any sign of intrusion to the central server. The server then raises an alarm and alerts the administrator. An advantage of using Gabriel is that you do not need to install client programs on all the machines on a network. You only need to install the client software on selective computers. Another benefit of Gabriel is that the operating systems running on the client computers and on the other computers on the network do not need to be the same. For example, a client computer running Solaris can also be used to administer computers running Windows NT.

Gabriel is also easy to install and configure. It is a freeware program that can be easily downloaded from the Internet and installed by administrators to protect networks. Both the server and client programs provide a configuration script that only needs to be run on the client and the server, respectively. You can also download the source code if you want to customize the software according to the needs of your organization. The package is available with all its binary files precompiled and ready for installation.

The client computers need to send messages to the server at predefined intervals indicating that they are still functioning and capable of raising alarms. You can test the package by using the test scripts provided along with the package. Gabriel doesn't affect the performance of the client computer. Once installed, it regularly sweeps the network to detect traces of hacking attempts and sends periodic reports to the server. The Gabriel package has minimal dependence on the environment and is not affected by any changes made to the environment variables. However, there is a warning. As the package is primarily written in C, you need to ensure that you do not install other packages such as PEARL that require the use of similar packages or libraries.

You need to install, configure, and test the server part of the Gabriel package before you install the client portion. The `install_gabriel_server` script is provided along with the server section, which automatically installs the package on the server computer. Similarly, the `install_gabriel_client` script is used to automatically install and configure the client software. After installation, the client software begins to scan the network for intrusion. If the network is small, you can install the server and client programs on the same computer. Otherwise, you need to designate another computer as the client and run the script on the computer. After the server has been installed, you need to make changes to the configuration files and add information specific to your network. The configuration files also contain information about how alert messages need to be sent to the administrator. After you have saved the changes made, all the changes are immediately implemented. The `gabriel_tester` script can be used to test if the package has been correctly installed. This script also works in case no scanning program is running on the network. However, you should run the script for detecting intrusions from another computer because the server cannot detect any intrusion that occurs on itself. You need to run the `gabriel_server` program on the server to raise the error and send an administrative alert. Based on the settings of the configuration file, the administrator is either e-mailed, phoned, paged, or shown an alert message.

Gabriel can be used to detect SATAN intrusion by detecting sweeps made by probing applications that try to identify the services running on the host computer. The client program examines all data packets sent across a network, regardless of the type of data carrier. For example, the client program can be used to examine all transmitted TCP, UDP, or ICMP data packets. However, if the client program tries to examine an entire data packet, it would be overwhelmed with the amount of data it needs to check. Therefore, the client only checks the connection information of the data packets.

The client program creates entries for each data packet. Each entry contains information regarding the source IP address, the destination IP address, the type of service, and the timestamp, recording the time when the packet was analyzed.

The `gabriel_client` shell script is used for accessing different types of client programs. Client computers periodically check the connections database to determine whether any program has recently requested the use of a number of services for which the program did not have appropriate permission. The activities of this program are analyzed, and if any suspicious behavior is identified, its next transaction is tracked. If the program is found to be involved in intrusion and hacking activities, the client computers automatically report this to the server. The server then sends an alert to the administrator.

Summary

In this chapter, you learned about network security and the various tools available in Solaris for ensuring network security. You learned about firewalls and how they can be used for implementing security on the network. The chapter also covered some of the commonly used TCP/IP security tools available in Solaris, such as ISS, SATAN, tcpdump, and tcpflow. Then you learned about IPSec and SKIP. Finally, you learned about some of the intrusion detection tools available in Solaris, such as tocsin and Gabriel.

Check Your Understanding

Multiple Choice Questions

1. Which database available in SATAN is used for keeping track of the host computers that have been scanned and the progress of scanning?

   a. all-hosts

   b. todo

   c. facts

2. In which type of firewall can you implement filtering based on commands?

   a. Packet-level firewall

   b. Application-level firewall

   c. Stateful multilayered firewall

   d. Circuit-level firewall

3. Which two log files are used for logging all the messages received by tocsin? (Select two.)

   a. LOG_ALERT

   b. LOG_AUTH

   c. LOG_NOTICE

   d. LOG_WARNING

4. Which option available in the tcpdump command should be used for checking the size of the text file before saving its content to a file on the host computer?

   a. -O

   b. -X

   c. -F

   d. -C

5. Which option available in the tcpdump command should be used for specifying that only the domain name should be displayed without any qualification?

   a. -a

   b. -t

   c. -N

   d. -q

6. Which option available in the ISS utility should be used for specifying that the scanner should ignore instances of anonymous logging to the FTP port?

   a. -f

   b. -y

   c. -r

   d. -s

Short Questions

1. Does the use of IPSec make the existence of firewalls redundant?

2. Explain the difference between packet-level firewalls and application-level firewalls.

3. Explain how SATAN works.

4. Discuss the various scripts used while configuring Gabriel.

5. Briefly explain what SKIP is.

Answers

Multiple Choice Answers

1. **a**. The `all-hosts` database contains a list of all the host computers detected by SATAN. It even contains information about the host computers that were not checked during scanning. It reveals the type of information stored on the computers. It also stores information about hosts that might not exist physically.

2. **b**. The application-level firewalls can be used for implementing filtering based on commands. This is not possible in any other type of firewall.

3. **b, c**. All messages received by tocsin are logged in the `LOG_AUTH` or `LOG_NOTICE` log file by using the `syslog` utility available in Solaris.

4. **d**. The `-C` option is used to check the file size of the text file before saving content to the file. If the size of the file exceeds the prescribed limit, the current file is closed and a new file is created to save data packet information.

5. **c**. The `-N` option is used to specify that the domain name should not be displayed without any qualification. Therefore, the domain name would appear as `sales` instead of `sales.asc.com`.

6. **a**. The `-f` option is used to specify that the scanner should ignore any instances where an anonymous logging to the FTP port has taken place. If this option is not used, the scanner checks if a user is able to logon anonymously to the network by using the FTP port.

Short Answers

1. IPSec creates a layer of security implemented at the network layer and is used for securing network communication. IPSec is used for host authentication and encryption. Firewalls are used for securing a private network against Internet attacks without using any form of authentication or encryption. Firewalls are only responsible for ensuring the integrity and secrecy of information being transmitted between two host computers.

2. Packet-level firewalls are used for administering data packets entering and leaving a network. You can check the content of the data packets by using packet-level filters or by implementing filtering at the router level. The packet filters analyze each data packet based on certain predefined rules. If the content of the data packets matches the rules, the data packets are allowed to enter or leave the network. It the content of the data packet doesn't match the set rules, then the data packets are rejected and sent back to the original sender. If filtering is implemented on routers, the data packets are checked against a set of ACLs that determine which network addresses can send or receive data packets. Application-level firewalls are used for monitoring and securing services avail-

able on the network. You can also implement filtering based on commands. This is not possible with the other types of firewalls.

3. Most network services have some security flaws that cannot be easily detected. SATAN checks these services for improper setup or incomplete configuration. It also checks the services for known bugs or weak policies. SATAN is a targeting application that uses the finger utility to detect whether a host computer or a group of computers on a network are responding to messages. It prepares a list of the host computers that are responding and sends the list to an engine that sends messages to the host computers. SATAN then stores all the information returned by individual host computers. This task continues in a loop until all the host computers have been checked and their information is collected and stored securely. All the hosts are first checked for any previous attempts made by the tool to search them.

If a host has not been checked before, all the services running on it are checked against a list of possible security shortcomings or bugs that could exist on the computer. After the check is complete, the host computer returns a set of information back to the tool. This information contains the hostname, the result of the analysis, and any other relevant information found on the host computer. The information is stored in a file and is used later for a complete analysis of the host computer for security flaws. The result is displayed as an HTML Web page to the administrator. The Web page can appear in any of the commonly used Web browsers, such as Netscape, Mosaic, and Lynx. Because the data is divided into sections and the Web page contains a link to each section, administrators can easily analyze and understand the data despite its vastness.

4. Gabriel was created for protecting networks against the programs that probe them in an attempt to detect flaws. The tool keeps a constant check over networks and raises warnings for administrators if it discovers any network intrusion or a threat of hacker attack. When Gabriel detects an intrusion, it e-mails the report directly to the administrator. The server portion of Gabriel needs to be installed and configured before you can set up the client section. The install_gabriel_server script is provided along with the server section that automatically installs the package on the server computer. Similarly, the install_gabriel_client script is used to automatically install and configure the client software. The client constantly scans the network for any sign of intrusion and raises an alert if an intrusion is detected.

After the server has been installed, you need to make changes to configuration files and add information specific to your network. After you have saved the changes, they are immediately implemented. The gabriel_tester script can be used to test if the package has been correctly installed. This script functions effectively even if no scanning program is running on the network. You need to run the gabriel_server program on the server to raise an error and send an administrative alert. Based on the settings of the configuration file, the administrator is either e-mailed, phoned, paged, or shown an alert message.

5. Simple Key-Management for Internet Protocols is one of the many tools available for securing remote access and ensuring Internet security. The tool uses public-key cryptography for ensuring security by encrypting the information transmitted between two host computers. SKIP also authenticates the host computers before establishing a connection. The tool is transparent in its functioning to both the users and applications that use it. This is because SKIP works at the network level. It therefore becomes transparent to any application that is sharing information over TCP/IP networks. The application used could be a Telnet, FTP, or Web browser. Any two computers that use SKIP for authentication can also use it to encrypt communication by using IP. SKIP provides computers a secure channel for communication over an unsecured network such as the Internet. Therefore, SKIP provides network security without compromising or effecting user activity. The process of using SKIP includes using sessionless protocols for establishing connections. It also involves the use of exchanging automatic certificates and using the CDP.

Chapter 10

The use of Internet for e-mail and other services has become an immensely popular, integral feature of both the personal lives of individuals and the business world today. Consequently, the need for ensuring the security of the information exchanged or the transactions carried out using the Internet has also gained great significance. If you obtain certain information from the Internet or send an e-mail to a user on remote network, you need to ensure its security. This chapter deals with the requirement of securing Web and e-mail services. It also deals with measures you need to implement on the Web and on e-mail servers to prevent hackers from gaining access to the network. While hackers are blocked from gaining access to the internal network, you must ensure that authorized users have free access to the Web and e-mail services.

Web Security Overview

The use of the Web or the Internet has brought with it advantages as well as disadvantages. The disadvantages are mostly attributable to the lack of proper security on Web servers. Unsecured Web access presents a grave danger to networks and their legitimate users.

Web administrators are responsible for ensuring the security of the Web servers. They must first secure their own Web server before connecting it to the Internet or to the rest of the network. External users can also gain entry inside the network through the Web server. Due to lack of adequate security, if hackers gain entry to the network along with the external users, these hackers can break the security implemented on the internal network. The Web server is responsible for ensuring the security of information passing through the network. The security risks from the Internet that a Web administrator faces can range from pranks by hackers who want to deface your Web site, to hackers who try to hack into the confidential information stored on your network.

Sometimes even the software that you have installed on a Web server is itself prone to security limitations. Therefore, it is a recommended practice that only the necessary software be installed on the Web servers. This, too, is not a completely effective solution since the Web server itself may contain certain security loopholes that cannot be easily identified by the Web administrators. Even the CGI scripts that are executed on the server might contain bugs that may cause security breaches. Therefore, the only solution seems to be to restrict access to the Web server.

However, as the Web server is a connection between the internal network and the Internet, it is very difficult to determine the optimum level of connectivity that needs to be provided. If the security measures implemented on the Web servers are not properly configured, it can render useless the best security measures implemented by a firewall. If the security on the firewall is rendered useless, then the internal network cannot be secured against hackers. This problem is further aggravated when the internal network comprises several subnetworks. Each subnetwork might have its own set of users and group accounts. The Web server needs to provide Internet access to all users on the internal network, irrespective of which subnetwork they belong to. This might lead to utter confusion, since the administrator needs to authenticate users belonging to different networks. Each group of users would have its own set of access rights. Following are some of the potential hazards of the Internet that might affect users on the internal network:

◆ **Active X controls**. A security-related problem is the presence of Active X controls in Web pages. These controls could be potential viruses or scripts run by hackers to gather information from your network. Clients who access the Internet might download these Active X controls along with the Web pages. Since the Active X controls are hidden with the Web pages, they can easily avoid detection by the firewalls. Active X components, therefore, provide hackers with an easy access to the internal network.

◆ **Cookies**. Certain Web components, such as cookies, collect information regarding the users' surfing habits and system information. The information gathered during a particular session is lost once the session is over and cannot be transferred to another session. This stateless session may make the Internet access appear secure, but it is a major drawback if you want to implement an e-market where the actions performed by users during one session need to be retained for future sessions. Although this information is gathered to customize Web pages according to user preference, hackers can also use the cookies to gain information about the user's computer. In such a case, cookies are an excellent choice for storing information. When the browser connects to a Web site for the first time, it stores a cookie sent by the Web server, which is used for storing information relevant to the Web site. This information can then be used across sessions. As a security precaution, domains on cookies cannot be set as the top-level domains of an external network. For example, you cannot set the domain for a cookie as .com, .org, or .edu. Cookies are conventionally used to store information about your computer. This information can then be used by Web sites to customize the content of their Web pages based on your requirements. Besides containing information about your Web preferences, cookies also store confidential information about your computer, such as the IP address, computer name, the operating system running on your computer, and the type of browser. Hackers can use this information to gain access to your computer. However, browsers such as Internet Explorer and Netscape Navigator provide options that can be enabled for alerting you if cookies try to store confidential information. You can either refuse all cookies or manually delete the cookies. A disadvantage of this method is that certain Web sites will continuously ask you before storing cookies, even if you refuse them the first time. Since most cookies are harmless, you could allow them to be stored on your computer but should also implement restrictions on the information they can collect.

NOTE

A cookie can also be termed as an information gathering mechanism that is sent by a Web server to a client computer. The cookie is stored on a Web browser and can be used later to retrieve information about the computer. This practice not only saves time but also reduces overheads. The browser is able to store specific information about a transaction between a server and a client.

♦ **TCP/IP protocol**. Security of information transmitted in the network and between the internal network and the Internet is important. The TCP/IP protocol has many shortcomings. This protocol is commonly responsible for transmitted information over the network. Hackers can use the shortcomings to hack any information sent over the network. They can also hack information transmitted between a user on the internal network and a Web server kept on a remote location.

You could implement many types of security measures to ensure security. Some of these measures can be implemented on the client computers, while others need to be implemented on the Web server. I'll discuss more about these measures in the following sections.

Client-Side Security

You can implement different types of security measures for ensuring user privacy and the integrity of information stored on the network. You can:

♦ Implement security measures for protecting users from viruses and other spoofing software

♦ Configure the browser not to send client information to external programs without first obtaining consent from the users

♦ Implement Web security policies that restrict access to the Internet to specific users

♦ Restrict the kind of information users can access from the Internet

All these measures help ensure the security of information downloaded by users from the Internet.

Since IP spoofing and social engineering are common occurrences on large networks, cryptography may be resorted to for ensuring security of transmitted information. You can encrypt all information that needs to be shared between computers using a secret key that is known only to the sender and recipient of the information. The effective use of cryptography and a strong security policy implemented on the Web server are interdependent. Even if you use the latest and the most effective cryptographic techniques for encrypting information, it would be worthless if you do not have a secure Web server. If hackers are able to get past the security on the Web server, they could also break through the encryption mechanism. For example, there are numerous encryption mechanisms such as, PKI and PGP, that are available in Solaris and which you can use to encrypt information. For more information about encryption refer to Chapter 2, "Introduction to Cryptography."

Hackers can also use packet sniffers and IP spoofing applications for retrieving information about users. For example, if a user submits a Web-based form, hackers can intercept the information and read it if it is not encrypted. Secure Sockets Layer (SSL) is one of the ways to ensure the security of information as it is passed from the user to the remote server. SSL can also be used for implementing authentication of both the sender and the receiver, thereby providing security.

Server-Side Security

You can also implement certain security measures on the Web server. These measures help protect the server from hackers who might attempt to engage in Denial of Service (DoS) attacks. You can implement firewalls and make sure that all security measures are implemented on the Web server. Hackers will then be unable to gain access to the network. Firewalls form the first level of security to protect the internal network from the hazards of the Internet. You have already learned about firewalls in Chapter 9, "Securing Networks." Packet filtering is used on routers for examining TCP and UDP data packets and for providing access based on a set of rules. Since the implementation of firewalls is relatively inexpensive and does not affect network performance, it is an excellent choice for ensuring security of information. However, the implementation of firewalls is a complex process, because it involves the knowledge about the network protocols, data transport mechanisms, and the use of application protocols for the proper configuration of firewalls. IP spoofing is another hazard faced on Web servers. Hackers can use the shortcoming of IP for gaining access to the data packets transmitted over the network. Using user authentication mechanisms in addition to TCP authentication can prevent IP spoofing. Firewalls also provide security against these attacks.

Another method for configuring security on the Web server is to control access to the resources based on different criteria. For example, you could restrict access based on individual users. Every user on the network is assigned a unique username and password. When a user needs to be authenticated on the network, the user has to provide both the appropriate username and password. You could restrict access to resources available on the network based on this information. You could also restrict or provide access based on the domain name. The IP addresses of all computers on the network are unique. This property of IP addresses can be used to restrict or allow access to information or resources available on the network.

Securing Naming Services

The security of naming services is an important but neglected facility on a server. Most of the time, the services are clubbed together and are not secured effectively. Administrators are often apprehensive about making any major change to the files related to these services. Administrators fear that if the files are modified, the service might not function correctly, or else the modifications might create a security loophole. You need to remember that the naming services are as secure as the servers on which they are installed. Therefore, just as you need to ensure the security of servers, you also need to ensure the security of the naming services.

Ensuring DNS Security

The purpose of DNS is to resolve queries by clients and other servers regarding IP addresses. Since IP addresses are just a series of numbers, they are difficult to remember and are easily forgotten. Users on the networks prefer assigning and using proper names for all the computers and servers available on the network. On the other hand, the computers identify each other based on their IP addresses. Therefore, you require a DNS server to act as an interface between the users and the servers. When a client needs to communicate with a server, the client writes only the computer name. The DNS server then converts this name to the appropriate IP address. This information is maintained in a database stored on the DNS server. The IP address is then used to track down the appropriate server. The same process is followed when a user needs to connect to a Web server over the Internet. The DNS server can also be used to resolve the names of Web servers. The database maintained on a DNS server contains a list of registered domain servers available on the network and their corresponding computer names. It also stores the computer names of all the client computers available on the network and their corresponding IP addresses. If the main domain contains a group of subdomains, all the computers installed in each subdomain are registered, along with the information about the domain to which they belong. Each domain on the network contains a primary domain server. This domain server is responsible for maintaining the list of IP addresses and their corresponding computer names. Each domain might also have a set of secondary domain servers, which contain the IP address of the primary domain server. The secondary domain servers periodically replicate the information stored on the primary server and maintain an updated copy of this information. The secondary domain server can, therefore, take on the responsibility of resolving name queries whenever the primary server crashes or is unavailable.

DNS resolves queries about computers available on the network based on two configuration files. These files are the /etc/nsswitch.conf and the /etc/resolv.conf files. The /etc/nsswitch.conf file contains information about the services that should be used to gather information about hostnames, password files, and group files available on the network. This file also stores information about the various directory services available on the network. Typically, the entry in the file states that when an IP address needs to be resolved, it must first be checked in the `/etc/inet/hosts` file and then checked in DNS. Figure 10-1 shows a typical `nsswitch.conf` file.

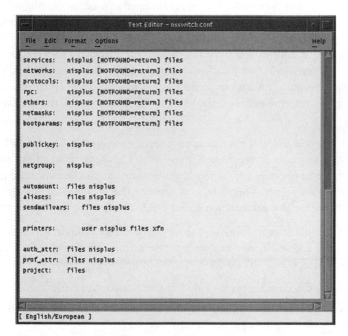

FIGURE 10-1 *A sample* `nsswitch.conf` *file*

The `/etc/resolv.conf` file, on the other hand, is used only for the purpose of DNS and provides information regarding the domain that should be checked to find information about the queried address. The file contains information about the name of the servers and the corresponding IP addresses. The entries provided in the file are also used for providing information about partly resolved domain names. For example, in the domain `sales.asc.com`, if you need to search for the IP address of the server named `north.sales.asc.com`, you can also send the query as `north`. The DNS will search for the entry containing the name `north` and display its IP address.

DNS has certain limitations against which you need to provide security. The computer names and the IP addresses of computers on the internal network can easily be queried from the Internet. Therefore, you need to ensure that you do not provide a specific name for your server that may become an easy target for hacker attacks. For example, the DNS names of the servers on the internal network are specified as `sales`, `finance`, or `accounts`. Since the names of the server define the function the server performs on the network, these servers are easily visible to Internet users. Therefore, these servers would be the first choice of hackers who want to hack information available on your network. A feasible solution to this problem is to use *split-horizon* DNS addresses. In this architecture, the publicly available computers and other network components are defined on a DNS domain that can be accessed for the Internet, while all the elements that pertain to the internal network and need to be secluded from all external contact are configured on another internal DNS domain. This ensures that the external DNS computer forwards all external queries that it receives to the internal DNS server. The internal DNS server then resolves the request for the IP address and passes it back to the external DNS server. The external DNS server then sends the query back to the client who had requested it. This ensures absolute security, because if a hacker needs to gain access to the IP information about the computers on the internal network, the hacker will need to crack the security of two computers.

Berkeley Internet Name Domain (BIND) also contains a security feature called the `allow-query` function, which is available in the `named.conf` file. This feature was first introduced in BIND version 8 and provides the facility to determine which clients should have the right to query the named server. Therefore, you can use the function to allow computers to query the DNS server for information about other client computers or servers.

Zone transfer is used for replicating information from the primary domain server to the secondary domain servers. However, you can restrict users from obtaining information from the primary source computers. You could:

◆ Use the `xfernets` directive that is provided in the `named.boot` file

◆ Bind also uses a key ID in its configuration files. This key id is used for authentication and authorization on a particular name server.

◆ Use the `allow-transfer` option to specify the domain hosts or networks that have the right for zone transferring from other domains

◆ Configure Internet firewalls for restricting all TCP traffic originating from the internal network to the Internet

The firewall ensures that no zone transfer can occur between the internal DNS server and the Internet. Firewalls also help in regulating traffic between the internal DNS server and the external DNS server.

Other methods of securing DNS are using BIND, using the *domain information groper (DIG)*, and disabling the process of caching. You will learn about BIND in the following section. The DIG is used with a DNS server for analyzing client computer-related problems. It is also an excellent tool to retrieve information about DNS from named servers. This command is used if you know the IP address of a computer and need to find out the computer name, or vice versa. You can also retrieve information about the computer such as the operating system it is running or the services available on it. It is basically a DNS debugging tool that is used to resolve client related queries. These queries could be specific to the local network or to the Internet. You can also disable the `nscd` cache for improving the performance of the DNS server.

BIND

BIND is a naming service that is used along with DNS. BIND is used to provide an implementation of the various components of the DNS. It is used to set up the DNS server, has a library to resolve addresses, and provides different tools that can be used for ensuring that DNS works in an appropriate manner. Introduction of version 8 of BIND has made it very easy to identify name servers. Earlier, most name servers were identified based on their roles on the network. These servers could be set up either as the primary or the secondary DNS servers. The primary server was responsible for storing the zone databases, and the secondary servers read the zone information from the information stored on the primary server. This concept changed in BIND 8, where the concept of the master server was introduced. The servers transparently provided name-resolving facility to the clients. This also improved the efficiency of the DNS servers. Previously, administrators who needed to provide DNS service to clients on the external network had to configure an external server for handling all the name queries. This affected the performance of the clients who had to connect to the remote server over a WAN link. With the use of BIND on an internal nonregistered server, this problem was solved. Clients could resolve their name queries locally in the network, without needing to connect over the WAN. Since the server is not registered as a name server in the zone, it can only resolve the requests of clients belonging to the specific zone. This removes the danger of external clients belonging to other zones connecting to the server for name query resolving. Every remote client computer in the zone has to be configured to point to the server, which responds to their requests and resolves all name queries.

DNS servers cause certain security risks, and BIND can provide protection against these risks. For example, if hackers are able to gain access to the DNS server, they have complete access to all the hosts and router addresses available on the server. They also have information about all the computers available on the network, along with their names, location, and IP addresses. If the DNS server crashes, the internal network will be cut off from the Internet since no addresses will be resolved. DNS also provides the facility of resolving e-mail addresses, but if the server is down, even this facility would not be available. Another danger is that hackers could set up a fake DNS server on the network. In the absence of the original DNS servers, all the clients on the network would consider this server to be authentic and request the server to resolve computer names. This fake server could then disperse misleading DNS information about your network to the Internet. A fake DNS server could send fictitious e-mail that would seem to originate from your network. Hackers could also easily manipulate the content of e-mails being sent from the network. If the firewalls implemented on your network also use the DNS for name resolution, the fake DNS server could compromise security on the firewall.

Another requirement of DNS is to provide users on the external network connection to other servers available in the domain, such as FTP, Web servers, and mail servers. Since the clients cannot be directly resolved on these servers, hackers cannot detect and connect to these servers. Therefore, both the internal as well as external zones are divided into two separate sections, each section containing its own naming service. However, with the increase in the size of the internal network and the creation of extranets, the external clients require access not only to the public services but also to other services available on the internal network. BIND is used to allow a single naming server to provide DNS facility for clients both on the internal and on the external network. BIND basically resolves the client requests based on the address of the client computer.

BIND is used to provide DNS facility on a wide number of naming servers on the Internet. It provides a strong and secure architecture on the existing naming service used in an organization. The revolver library contained in BIND contains certain APIs that can be used for interpreting the domain names into their corresponding Internet addresses and for providing a link between the application requiring the naming service and the naming server. Following are some of the security measures that you can implement to ensure security on the DNS server:

◆ **Minimum privileges**. Run BIND with a limited number of privileges. This ensures that even if hackers are able to gain access to the information stored on the server, they would not have the appropriate access rights. The best option is to create a new user and group account to run BIND. This user and account information should be specified as command-line options when executing BIND.

◆ **Latest version**. Install and use the latest version of BIND. This ensures that you use the latest security fixes and implement the best possible security on the network.

 TIP

The version number is hard-coded in the BIND code. If you have the source code, you can replace code with a fake version to mislead hackers. You can also configure BIND to enable version requests from specific addresses only. Hackers need to know the version before they can launch an attack.

◆ **Separating resources**. Ensure that the Internet DNS used on the network is exclusively dedicated to the service and, therefore, cannot be used by other services. If the server is dedicated to only one service, only a limited amount of software needs to be installed on the computer. This not only saves installation time but also makes it more secure. Restrict local logins by users on the server to ensure that hackers cannot log on as local users and try to exploit the vulnerability of the software loaded on the computer.

◆ **Controlling transfer of information**. Impose restrictions on the amount of information that can be transferred between zones. BIND should be configured to disallow zone transfer except to authorized servers. Use transaction signatures and restrict persistent queries to provide this control over accessing resources.

◆ **Backup DNS**. Install a backup DNS server that would take the responsibilities of the primary DNS server in case it crashes. This also ensures that all the requests for name and e-mail address resolution can be queued up and resolved once the server is back online.

◆ **Maintaining logs**. Maintain logs of all activities that occur on the server and raise an administrative alert if anything suspicious is detected. Regularly monitor the server for any changes.

◆ **Isolation services**. Also run BIND in isolation so that if the service is compromised, the bind daemon cannot access the other services or the security of the computer.

You can easily install and configure BIND on you naming server. First, compile BIND on the primary host computer. Normally, you would not have a compiler on a hardened Solaris computer running DNS. Next, copy the BIND files onto the DNS server and install them. Finally, make certain configuration changes to your DNS data files to ensure that BIND runs properly on the server. Also, create a user and group account that will be explicitly used for administering BIND, and set up appropriate file access permission for the files. You might need to make certain changes to the configuration file `named.conf`. Some of these configuration changes are as follows:

◆ Since BIND stores all process numbers based on a `pid-file` command, the user account requires the appropriate read and write access permissions for the file.

◆ The file contains information regarding the location where BIND needs to search for its data files. This information is stored in the `directory` entry.

◆ Since BIND provides a flexible logging facility, you need to provide support for logging by adding the log information in the configuration file.

◆ You could also use Access Control Lists (ACLs) for specifying which servers are restricted and which are allowed to transfer information across zones. If the service of ACLs is used correctly, it becomes difficult for hackers to identify the complete structure of the network.

You could also configure BIND to resolve queries received from specific hosts by using the `allow-query` option. A suggested practice is to restrict global access for the entire network and then provide access to specific zones that need to access the Internet. You can also configure the Internet servers to accept only recursive queries from valid DNS servers and not directly from the Internet. Recursive queries provide DNS clients with the facility to query the DNS server IP information for which the client does not have explicit rights. Normally, the DNS server would retrieve the appropriate information and cache it. However, if you restrict the recursive queries, you would improve the performance of DNS servers and also ensure that the server provides the latest information when queried.

Ensuring NFS Security

The *Network File System (NFS)* is another service that needs to be secured and has to be constantly monitored for limitations. NFS security is compromised mostly in cases where external users have to be provided access to resources on the internal network. NFS is basically a service that is used to create a directory structure on a computer. The uniqueness of this service is that the created directory structure only exists virtually on the client computer and actually exists on another computer. Therefore, NFS is literally invisible to the users, who believe that they are working on the local computer when their files are actually stored on an external computer. All the commonly used file commands can be used to work with these files.

When a client is working on a file that physically exists on another computer, the client is said to be working in a *share*. Share is the name given to the task of providing another computer the right to access and store information on your own computer. The `share` command is used for allocating the directories available on the server. You can restrict the right to access these shares and also restrict the users who can mount the NFS directory. The syntax of the `share` command is as follows:

```
share -f FStype -o options -d description <path>
```

One of the most common security limitations associated with NFS is that the share can be accessed by anyone without any restriction. Another problem related with security is that each user would use one copy of the directory structure on the client computer. Therefore, there are multiple shares available of the same directory structure. Hackers could use any of these shares to gain access to the confidential information stored on the master computer.

Generally, NFS answers all requests originating from the UDP port. However, to improve security, you can configure NFS to respond only to requests originating from privileged ports. Privileged ports are ports from which only the root account can send requests.

NFS shares provide four levels of authentication. These levels are as follows:

◆ **Secure RPC AUTH_KERB**. This authentication level is available in Kerberos and is used for authenticating users. The authentication level provides interoperability with all the other authentication features available in Kerberos.

◆ **Secure RPC AUTH_SYS**. This is the default authentication mechanism in which all the group IDs, user IDs, file permissions, and directory permissions are transmitted over the network without being encrypted. You do not need to be authenticated by the administrator to access the information. This is the most commonly provided authentication option in most of the versions of Solaris. However, it is also the most insecure.

◆ **Secure RPC AUTH_DES**. AUTH_DES is another authentication level available in Solaris Secure RPC. The level provides security of information transmitted over the network by using a combination of secret key and cryptography technique.

Although it is not commonly used on UNIX platforms, it is used on Solaris for security.

◆ **Secure RPC AUTH_NONE**. AUTH_NONE is the basic RPC mechanism without the use of any of the user authentication mechanism. It is used to perform the common tasks on a computer, such as checking the system date. The level ensures security by charting the NFS client IDs with the user ID none. The user account none is a default user account that exists on the NFS server.

E-Mail Security

E-mail is another area where network administrators need to ensure security. Hackers can use the known limitations of the e-mail application to exploit information transmitted over the network. If e-mail is not configured correctly, it can lead to other potential security problems. E-mail consists of both hardware and software components. We will be discussing these components in the following sections.

Software Components for E-Mail

The process of sending e-mail involves writing not only the e-mail but also other components that take the e-mail from the sender to the recipient and at the same time ensure security. In Solaris, the process of sending and receiving e-mail involves three components working together. These components are the *transport agent*, the *delivery agent*, and the *user agent*. A detailed description of these agents follows:

◆ **Mail transport agent**. The mail transport agent acts as a post office for the e-mails sent over the network. The agent is responsible for routing all the e-mails and for resolving e-mail addresses. The transport agent first picks up the e-mail message from the sender's mailbox. The agent then resolves the recipient's e-mail address against the list of available e-mail addresses stored on the DNS server. The agent then selects an appropriate delivery agent that can take the e-mail to the recipient's address. The mail transport agent is also responsible for managing e-mails received from other transfer agents. The protocol that is generally used for transporting e-mail messages is the Simple Mail Transport Protocol (SMTP). This messaging protocol is a TCP protocol and is generally assigned port 25 for sending and receiving e-mail messages.

◆ **Mail delivery agent**. The mail delivery agent acts as an interface between the sender of the message and the transport agent. In Solaris, the most commonly used mail delivery agent is **UNIX-to-UNIX Copy** (UUCP). This agent uses the uux command to send and receive e-mails. Solaris also contains a delivery agent called mail.local that is built in the software. This is the default agent in case no other delivery agent is installed on the computer.

◆ **Mail user agent**. The mail user agent provides an interface between the recipient and the mail transport agent. The program provides an interface for users to read, write, and store messages sent and received by a user. Solaris, by default, contains some built-in user agents that it uses for managing e-mails received from other users. These user agents are the `mail`, the `mailx`, and the `mailtool` programs. The `mail` and the `mailx` programs are standard GUI-based programs that are available with the Common Desktop Environment (CDE) program. The `dtmail` is the GUI version of the mail program and is used for composing, sending, and receiving e-mails. Figure 10-2 shows a default `dtmail` mailbox. All the e-mails received by a user are stored in the user's mailbox. The user's mailbox is located in the `/var/mail/userid` folder. The userid folder contains an individual folder for every user who has an account on the computer. The user agent program sends e-mails by establishing a connection with the `sendmail` program running on the mail server. This connection is established by using the SMTP messaging protocol. The secured connection is then used for sending the message data packets.

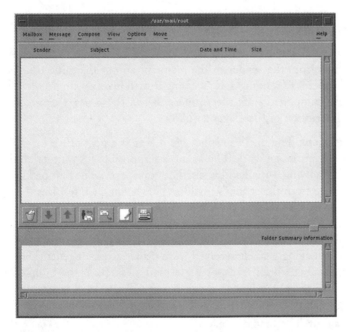

FIGURE 10-2 *A default* `dtutil` *mailbox*

Some hardware components also form a part of the e-mail system. The following section discusses these components in detail.

Hardware Components for E-Mail

Like the software components, the hardware part of e-mails also requires three components. These are the *mail host*, the *mail server*, and the *mail clients*. You can also include a mail gateway in case you need to configure e-mail facility for external users. The following sections discuss each of these components in detail:

- ◆ **Mail server**. As mentioned earlier, all e-mails sent and received by a user are maintained in the user's mailbox. The mailbox can be stored either on the local computer or on the mail server. A mail server maintains the mailboxes for all users as simple text files and stores them in the `/var/mail` directory. Each user is assigned a separate directory for storing personal e-mail. The same directory structure is followed irrespective of whether the folders are maintained on the local computer or on the mail server. The mail server receives mail from all the clients and queues it for delivery. After the e-mails have been queued, the sender's responsibility is over. The mail server first checks whether the recipient is available to take delivery of the message. If the recipient is not available, the e-mail is stored on the server until the recipient logs on to the network and can deliver the messages. The name of the mail server that is responsible for resolving the recipient's address and ensuring that the e-mail receives the current destination appears in the From field. In case the user folders are maintained on remote computer, clients using NFS can use the `vfstab` file for maintaining the `/var/mail` directory. If the folder can't be maintained on the local computers or NFS can't be used, the users can log on to the mail server to read and send their e-mails. By using a mail server for managing e-mails for multiple users, since all the e-mails are received and sent from one central location, it becomes easier to ensure security and take backup of the e-mails. Though the same advantage of centralized storage can become a disadvantage in case the server crashes, the advantage of easy administration, centralized security, and simpler backup facility easily outweighs the disadvantage.

- ◆ **Mail host**. The main responsibility of the mail host is to handle all e-mails whose e-mail addresses cannot be resolved. A server can be designated as a mail host by adding an entry in the `/etc/hosts` file on the local computer. This entry would contain the IP address of the computer prefixed by the word `mailhost`. You could also make changes to the `main.cf` file, which is also available on the mail host computer. You could configure the mail host either on a computer that has a mode and provides PP connections or on routers that provide connection between the local network and the Internet.

- ◆ **Mail client**. The mail client program is used for interfacing with the mail server and sending and receiving e-mails from it. The client program is mostly used when the user directories of the e-mail users are not maintained on the local computer. These mail clients are also known as *remote clients*. Remote clients are enabled by default and details about them are stored in the `/etc/mail/subsidiary.cf` file. The user writes the e-mail and sends it. After the user has sent the e-mail, it becomes the responsibility of the client mail programs to ensure that the e-mail reaches safely to the server. It is also the client mail program's responsibility to periodically check with the mail server if any mail addressed to the client has been stored on the server. If any new e-mail is found, the client program is responsible for ensuring the safe retrieval of the e-mail from the mail server and displaying it to the client. You need to ensure that the details of the mail clients appear in the `/etc/vfstab` file and point to the user account stored on the mail server. You also need to ensure that the alias used for the client is the same as the one specified on the mail server.

◆ **Mail gateway**. As mentioned earlier, the mail gateway is used if you need to provide e-mail facility to external users. The gateway is used for ensuring security of all messages sent and received from the external network. The gateway provides secure connection between two networks. It also acts as an interpreter in case both the networks are using different messaging protocols. If the address specified in an e-mail does not belong to the domain, the mail gateway is responsible for resolving the address and searching for the address on the external network. The gateway communicates with the mail servers of external networks and attempts to search for the e-mail address. If the address is not found, the gateway returns the mail back to the mail server. The mail server then sends the message back to the original sender in the form of an error message. The easiest way to set up a gateway is to configure it on the firewall or any computer that can directly connect to the Internet.

E-mails are an excellent method of sending and receiving information. However, there are certain limitations in e-mails against which you need to provide security. In the following section, I will discuss these limitations in detail.

Limitations in E-Mail

Most software has certain limitations that exist in the software itself. Some of these limitations are caused by incorrect installation or the lack of proper security measures being implemented. Irrespective of what caused the limitations, they are most commonly the reason why many attacks on security are successful. Having identified the limitations that exist in the software, hackers use them to manipulate the software to suit their purposes. One example of such software is e-mail that is used for communication between users.

Today, all businesses and individuals heavily depend upon e-mails, which are the major carriers of viruses and a cause of network vulnerabilities. Attachments sent along with e-mails are perhaps one of the most common means for spreading viruses. Users forward many of these seemingly harmless attachments since they receive them from friends or people they know. However, what people fail to realize is that hackers can easily intercept these attachments and supplement them by adding malicious code or viruses. When these attachments are opened on a client computer, they infect every computer the client accesses. Some of the viruses contained in the attachments are so powerful that they replicate their content and send e-mails to everyone in a user's address book.

One of the possible solutions is to delete all e-mails that you receive from unknown users. This may sound like an extreme step, but it is one of the ways to ensure that the e-mails that you receive do not have any harmful content. Another method is to scan the content of the message before opening any attachment. This ensures that you know the purpose for which you received the e-mail and the attachment. There are certain types of files, such as executables, that you need to prevent users from executing.

sendmail

The most commonly used mail transport agent available in Solaris and which has been in use since 1979 is, sendmail. Initially, it was a very rigid application and required quite a number of modifications. However, it has grown and has undergone many modifications. Today, sendmail is widely used for administering e-mail services on UNIX, Linux, and Solaris computers. It is used for sending e-mail messages to single or multiple recipients. After the e-mail is dispatched from the client computer, sendmail takes the responsibility of routing the messages over all the required networks. The utility does not take the responsibility of providing the users an interface for typing and creating their messages. The sendmail utility is only responsible for taking the e-mail from the sender and ensuring that it reaches the recipient. It does not use flags for marking the beginning and the end of the message. The utility copies all the information available in the mail file and sends it to the specified address. The utility also resolves the address based on its syntax and content. If the specified address is local to the current domain, it is searched and resolved, otherwise the address is sent to the mail gateway that resolves all external addresses. The local addresses are maintained in a separate file along with their aliases. The sendmail program can use different types of communication protocols to transmit the message, such as TCP/IP and UUCP. Following are some of the features available in sendmail:

◆ Acts as a mail router that collects mail from the user agent, decides on the best route for delivery, modifies the header information of the message and includes information about the delivery agent, and finally dispatches the message using the appropriate delivery agent.

◆ Provides facility for routing mail over multiple networks, uses network gateways for resolving addresses belonging to external networks, and uses aliases and forwarding of messages on the local network.

◆ Provides support only for text files and cannot handle binary files unless the file is part of the message and is stored as a uuencode file.

◆ Does not contain any GUI-based software for reading and maintaining e-mails.

◆ Provides support for both types of addressing, either the Internet style where both the username and the hostname are provided, or the UUCP style of addressing.

◆ Provides reliability and can be trusted to deliver all messages it is entrusted with.

◆ Can be used to send e-mails to networks containing multiple network types or multiple connections to a single type of network.

◆ Stores and uses the configuration information in separate files instead of compiling the information directly into the message.

◆ Reuses the software currently available and installed on the computer instead of installing its own software.

◆ Provides support for specifying customized messages that users can use, if required. For example, users can specify an auto-forwarding header for messages containing specific words in their subject.

◆ Groups multiple mails to a single address and sends them together. This helps reduce network traffic.

◆ Allows users to maintain their personal address lists that the users can customize without affecting the aliases used over the network.

Table 10-1 lists the options that you can use with the sendmail program.

Table 10-1 Options Used with sendmail Program

Option	Description
-Btype	Specifies the body type that can be used in a message. The default message body types are the 7BIT or the 8BITMIME.
-ba	Sets the program into ARPNET mode. In this mode, all lines of messages in the text should end with CR-LF. The names of the sender and the recipient are retrieved from the From and Sender fields.
-bd	Runs the program as a daemon. The program runs in the background and attempts to listen to all SMTP connections received on port 25. This port is reserved for only receiving and sending SMTP data packets.
-bD	Runs the program as a daemon but in the foreground.
-bh	Displays and prints information retrieved from the persistent host status database.
-bH	Detects and purges all entries in the persistent host status database that are either obsolete or expired.
-bi	Initializes the information available in the aliases database.
-bp	Displays all the mail queued on the mail server in the form of a list.
-bs	Provides standard input and output facility by using the SMTP protocol. It provides facility to manipulate body text that is compatible with the SMTP protocol.

Option	Description
-bt	Runs the application in address test mode. In this mode, all the steps involved in reading the address and parsing the information are listed. This option is generally used when you want to debug information available in the configuration tables.
-bv	Verifies the names specified in the From and Sender fields. The option does not provide the facility for gathering information or for delivering the actual message. This mode is generally used for validating user information and for retrieving information from the mailing lists.
-C file	Specifies the path to another configuration file instead of the default file used by sendmail. You can customize the configuration file and maintain multiple copies that suit different requirements. However, a drawback in using this option is that sendmail cannot be run as a root in case a different configuration file is used.
-dX	Used in the debugging mode and for specifying the debugging value as X.
-F<fullname>	Accepts the full name of the sender in the message. This name is then mapped by sendmail to the appropriate e-mail address. However, this name should exist in the records of the sendmail list.
-F<name>	Specifies the name of the sender in the e-mail. The same information is also used in the header in case the header part is missing when the e-mail is submitted to the mail transport for sending it to the recipient. The information is also used to notify the sender in case the message cannot be delivered or if a read receipt has been requested. The option should only be used by the root account, daemon, or any other trusted user account.
-G	Specifies the gateway that is used to handle external e-mail addresses.
-hN	Specifies a value for the number of hops that an e-mail takes to reach its destination. A hop is a computer in-between the sender's and recipient's computers that is used for relaying the message further. The hop number acts like a counter and increments its current value every time the e-mail reaches another computer. There is a maximum value set for this counter and when the counter reaches this value, an error is raised and the sender is informed that the e-mail did not reach its destination.

continues

Table 10-1 (*continued*)

Option	Description
-i	Specifies that dots appearing in-between the message should be ignored. This is because sendmail does not maintain a flag about where the message begins and ends. It only copies the message from the beginning of the file until it encounters the last full stop.
-L\<tag>	Specifies a tag value and sets the identifier used in the syslog message along with the tag.
-N dns	Sets a delivery notification message for the dsn. This value can be never in case you do not require notification or can be multiple values. Each value in the list should be separated by a command. These values can be success, delay, or failure.
-n	Disables aliasing.
-p	Specifies a protocol that needs to be used for transmitting a message. You can use any of the commonly available protocols, such as UUCP or TCP/IP. You also need to specify the hostname along with the protocol. For example, TCP/IP: hostname.
-q[time value]	Sets a time period when all the saved messages in the message queue are processed. If a time period has not been set, the message is processed only once. The value for the time period is specified in as w for weeks, d for days, h for hours, m for minutes, and s for seconds. If the option is used, then sendmail runs in the background.
-qI\<substr>	Specifies a string that you need to search for in all the messages. The value contained in substr would appear as a part of the queue ID.
-qR\<substr>	Specifies that only the tasks whose recipient information contains th substr as its part should be performed.
-qS\<substr>	Specifies that only the tasks whose sender information contains the substr as its part should be performed.
-r\<return>	Specifies a limit on the amount of the original message that should be returned in case the sent e-mail bounces back. If the parameter passed with the option is full, then the entire message is displayed. Otherwise if the specified value is hrds, then only the header information is returned.

Option	Description
-t	Specifies that the recipient information should be stored along with the messages. This information is retrieved from the To, Cc, and Bcc fields. In the case of the Bcc fields, this information is deleted immediately after the e- mail has been sent.
-V \<envid\>	Retains the original envelop IDs. This information is used across SMTP servers that provide support for DSNs. It is also used to send back messages not conforming to DNS standards.
-v	Specifies the verbose mode where all the relevant information is displayed on the screen. It is also used for displaying alias information.
-X	Specifies that all information about e-mail traffic needs to be logged into a particular log file. This information can always be used for debugging mail-related problems. However, this should be the last option, because the mailing application should report and fix all bugs. This option is used to store all the data relevant to the e-mails.

Now that you know about the various options available with sendmail, I'll discuss the types of sendmail users.

sendmail Users

There are basically three types of users maintained in sendmail. They are:

◆ **DefaultUsers**. This user account is used by the mailer service running on the computer. If any specific user is not using the mailer service, then you can consider it being used by the DefaultUsers. This user account uses a specific user ID called mailnull. The sendmail application uses the getpwnam() function during startup to retrieve information about the mailnull account. This information is stored in the /etc/passwd file. The sendmail application also uses the DefaultUsers account in case it needs to perform certain activities as the root.

◆ **RunAsUser**. If the sendmail program starts as root, it only has a link with the SMTP socket. However, later you can run sendmail as a different user after providing appropriate permissions. Therefore, the RunAsUser user account is used by sendmail after the SMTP connection has been established. This is the default user account for the root and is mostly used by the root account. If the application logs on using another user ID, the rights associated with the user ID are also implemented. This user account is mostly run on a firewall where security of the sendmail application needs to be ensured.

◆ **TrustedUser**. In most circumstances, the sendmail application doesn't trust any other user account except the root. This user account is generally used for running scripts that need root-level trust rights but should not be run using the root account. The user account provides trust relationships with maps, aliases, and other security-related information that is specific to the root. Since the sendmail application can also be run by the root account, you need to be careful while using the TrustedUser account. You need to ensure that you do not accidentally log on as root.

You can implement certain security measures with sendmail. I'll discuss some of the most commonly used measures in the next section.

Security Measures in sendmail

Following are some of the security issues that you need to secure against in sendmail:

◆ **Sendmail restricted shell**. You can restrict the number and type of programs that can be executed in the aliases, include, and .forward file by using the smrsh or the sendmail restricted shell. This is useful in cases where you do not want the user to perform certain actions and execute specific files. You also need to ensure the security of the queue directory since sendmail runs as root. This is also one of the reasons why the queue directory should be owned by the root. You can ensure further security on firewalls by configuring their setting to give access only to SMTP service.

◆ **File and directory modes**. File and directory modes are an important consideration for security. If these modes are not adequately secured, then they can cause security-related problems. Users, if provided appropriate rights, want to install numerous applications on the computer. Some of these programs might be potential security risks. Similarly, even the manufacturers of operating systems apply only the bare minimum or incorrect security permissions for their software before shipping them to the customer. Therefore, it is critical that you keep a regular check on the files and directories permissions related to the programs used with sendmail.

◆ **Using SafeFileEnvironment**. This environment variable can be used to specify the location where the mailboxes need to be maintained in the file system. This option performs a similar function as that performed by the smrsh command. The only difference is that in this case, it is done to write the information in the user directories. The SafeFileEnvironment option uses the chmod command to change the file access permissions and to change the access rights for the files. For example, you could restrict the write permissions of users to their individual home directories. However, in case you require a stronger authentication mechanism, you can use AUTH_DH.

◆ **Using aliases**. Most users prefer to migrate their aliases from one version of sendmail to another. This is a security risk because there can be a number of false entries in the current version of aliases file. If the same file is migrated to the new version of sendmail, then all the false entries are also included in the new version. Hackers can use these entries to manipulate information and e-mails being transmitted over the network. Therefore, it is a recommended practice either to create the alias list again for every version or to check the list before migration for any false or unnecessary entries.

 TIP

You might also consider using Qmail instead of sendmail. Qmail has been designed and coded with sound security principles in mind.

You can also ensure security by implementing file access permissions and by imposing restriction on certain types of users from accessing the service.

File Access Permissions and Restrictions

The most critical files and directories in sendmail whose security is of utmost importance are the /etc directory, mail configuration file, and the mail queue directory. You need to restrict the access permission to the mail queue directory to the file owner by specifying the rights as 777. This implies that only the file owner, who is generally the RunAsUser, has full permission while no one else has any permission. This file is stored in the /var/spol/mqueue directory. Next, the security of the mail queue has to be ensured. In case of this directory, the access rights are specified as 755. This means that the directory owner, who is generally the root, has full permission while everyone else has read and execute permissions. The mail queue information is stored under /, /var, and the /var/spool directories. Since the /etc folder contains the passwd file, its access permissions should also be 755. The root account generally owns the folder, but sometimes a sysadmin group can also own it. The configuration file needs to be accessible and modified by the TrustedUser account. However, since the user account can be easily used to log on as the root, it is a security risk. Therefore, you need to set the access permission for the /etc/mail directory as 755. This means that the file owner, who is the TrustedUser account, has full access permission while everyone else has only read and execute permission.

The sendmail.cf configuration file is also an important file used for configuring sendmail and contains settings for the sendmail program. Therefore, you need to set the file access permission for the file as 644. This means that the file owner, which is generally the TrustedUser, has full permission while everyone else only has read permission.

> **NOTE**
>
> Sometimes manufacturers or some administrators specify the access rights for the mail queue directory as 777 to avoid access problems. Since this is not only incorrect access permission setting but also a potential security hazard, you need to periodically check the access permissions for these directories.

Following is a list of some of the restrictive file access permissions you can implement on the file system to prevent the possibility of future attacks:

◆ You should not access .forward files that provide links to other files.

◆ You should not read files that are set as writable for the group and other accounts.

◆ You should not read directories that are set as writable for the group and other accounts.

◆ You should not read files in directories that are set as writable for the group and other accounts.

There are numerous other file access restrictions that you can use along with sendmail. This is why you need to implement multiple level of checks for the files and directories. In this way, if one level of check fails, the next level can secure against the limitation.

Summary

In this chapter, you learned about ensuring the security of Web and e-mail services. You learned about the various measures you can implement on a Solaris Web server for ensuring security. The chapter covered securing DNS and NFS servers and implementing BIND. You also learned how to implement security on e-mails and the various components involved in setting up an e-mail service. Finally, you learned about the sendmail utility, which is one of the most commonly used e-mail services in Solaris.

Check Your Understanding

Multiple Choice Questions

1. Which option available in the sendmail utility will you use if you need to specify that all saved mails should be processed after a specific interval of time?

    a. `-qR <substr>`

    b. `-qS <substr>`

    c. `-q [value]`

    d. `-ql <substr>`

2. Which option available in the `sendmail` utility will you use if you need to specify that the `sendmail` program should run in the background as a daemon and should listen for all SMTP connections available at port 25?

    a. `-bd`

    b. `-bD`

    c. `-bH`

    d. `-bH`

3. Which of the following statements are true?

    Statement A: You can configure `sendmail` to restrict the type of programs that can be executed in its files.

    Statement B: When upgrading to the most recent version of `sendmail`, it is advisable to migrate the aliases used in the previous version to the new version for better security.

    a. Both A and B are correct.

    b. A is correct while B is incorrect.

    c. A is incorrect while B is correct.

    d. Both are incorrect.

4. Which of the following statements are true?

    Statement A: You should restrict the access permissions to the mail queue directory to only the file owner, who is generally the RunAsUser.

    Statement B: You need to provide full access permission for the `/etc/mail` directory to the TrustedUser account.

    a. Both A and B are correct.

    b. A is correct while B is incorrect.

    c. A is incorrect while B is correct.

    d. Both are incorrect.

5. What is the default authentication level set for NFS shares?

    a. Secure RPC `AUTH_DES`

    b. Secure RPC `AUTH_KERB`

    c. Secure RPC `AUTH_SYS`

    d. Secure RPC `AUTH_NONE`

Short Questions

1. What are cookies, and what are the various security risks that they might cause?
2. What is BIND, and what are some of the measures you can implement to ensure its security?

Answers

Multiple Choice Answers

1. **c.** The `-q[value]` option is used to set a time period when all the saved messages in the message queue are processed. If a time period has not been set, the messages are processed only once. The value for the time period is specified as `w` for weeks, `d` for days, `h` for hours, `m` for minutes, and `s` for seconds. With the use of this option, `sendmail` runs in the background.

2. **a.** The `-bd` option is used to run the `sendmail` program in the background as a daemon. The program attempts to listen to all SMTP connections received on port 25. This port is reserved for only receiving and sending SMTP data packets.

3. **b.** You can restrict the number and type of programs that can be executed in the `aliases`, `include`, and `.forward` file by using the `smrsh` or the `sendmail` restricted shell. This is useful in cases where you do not want the user to perform certain actions and execute specific files.

   Most users prefer to migrate their aliases from one version of `sendmail` to another. This is a security risk, because there can be a number of false entries in the current version of an aliases file. If the same file is migrated to the latest version of `sendmail`, then all the false entries are also included in the new version. Hackers can use these entries to manipulate information and e-mails being transmitted over the network. Therefore, it is a recommended practice either to create the alias list again for every version or to check the list before migration for any false or unnecessary entries.

4. **a.** You need to restrict the access permission to the mail queue directory to only the file owner by specifying the rights as 777. This implies that only the file owner, who is generally the RunAsUser, has full permission while no one else has any permission. This file is stored in the `/var/spol/mqueue` directory. The configuration file also needs to be accessible and modified by the TrustedUser account. However, since the user account can be easily used to logon as the root, it is a security risk. Therefore, you need to set the access permission for the `/etc/mail` directory as 755. This means that the file owner, who is the Trusted-User account, has full access permission while everyone else has only read and execute permission.

5. **c**. The Secure RPC AUTH_SYS security level is the default authentication mechanism in which all the group IDs, user IDs, file permissions, and directory permissions are transmitted over the network without being encrypted. You don't need to be authenticated by the administrator to access the information. This is the most commonly provided authentication option in most of the versions of Solaris. However, it is also the most insecure.

Short Answers

1. Cookies are a mechanism to gather and store information about a computer. Generally, when a browser connects to a Web site, it establishes a new session with each new connection. The information gathered during a particular session is lost once the session is over and cannot be transferred to another session. This stateless session may make the Internet access appear secure, but it is a major drawback if you want to implement an e-market where the actions performed by users during one session need to be retained for future sessions.

   Cookies are conventionally used to store information about your computer. This information can then be used by Web sites to customize the content of their Web pages based on your requirements. Besides containing information about your Web preferences, cookies also store confidential information about your computer, such as the IP address, computer name, the operating system running on your computer, and the type of browser. Hackers can use this information to gain access to your computer. However, browsers such as Internet Explorer and Netscape Navigator provide options that can be enabled for alerting you if cookies try to store confidential information. You can either refuse all cookies or manually delete the cookies. A disadvantage of this method is that certain Web sites will continuously ask you before storing cookies, even if you refuse them the first time. Since most cookies are harmless, you could allow them to be stored on your computer but should also implement restrictions on the information they can collect.

2. BIND is a naming service that is used along with DNS to help DNS in resolving names of client computers. BIND follows the server-client model, where the servers transparently provide name-resolving facility to the clients. This also improves the efficiency of the DNS servers. With the use of BIND on an internal nonregistered server clients could resolve their name queries locally in the network, without needing to connect over the WAN. Since the server is not registered as a name server in the zone, it can only resolve the requests of clients belonging to the specific zone. This removes the danger of external clients belonging to other zones being able to connect to the server for name query resolving.

   You can implement some of the security measures available with BIND for ensuring security on the DNS server. For example, you need to ensure that you install and use the latest version of BIND. This ensures that you use the latest security fixes and also implement the best possible security on the network. You must also run BIND with a limited number of privileges. This ensures that even if hackers are able to gain access to the information stored on the server, their access rights would still be limited. You can also implement restrictions on the amount of information that can be transferred between zones.

Other measures for ensuring security are:

◆ Use of transaction signatures.

◆ Use of transaction signatures.

◆ Dedicate a server to only handle Internet DNS.

◆ Maintain logs of all activities that occur on the server.

◆ Raise administrative alert if anything suspicious is detected.

◆ Regularly monitor the server for any changes.

◆ Install a backup DNS server that would take the responsibilities of the primary DNS server in case it crashes. This also ensures that all the requests for name and e-mail address resolution can be queued up and resolved once the server is back online.

◆ Run BIND in isolation so that if the service is compromised, the bind daemon cannot access the other services or the security of the computer.

Appendix A

Best Practices

In this appendix, I'll discuss certain best practices to be kept in mind while dealing with Solaris security.

Protecting Web Servers

This section deals with protecting servers used for FTP or any other anonymous service. You can protect servers permitting anonymous access by isolating the file systems where anonymous access is permitted from the other file systems where strict access controls are placed. You can perform this isolation by creating different partitions or logical volumes for anonymous access control. The virtual root that is used by the anonymous Web or FTP users as the root should be placed one level down in the file system hierarchy. Make it a practice to explicitly deny access to the root of the file system where anonymous access is allowed. You can set permissions to permit anonymous access only from the virtual root in the anonymous file system container. In case you plan to offer anonymous FTP services to untrusted clients, you might consider using a dedicated, standalone system placed in its own Demilitarized Zone (DMZ).

All of these tips help prevent anonymous users from accessing a root of the logical drive, which provides access to the entire file system. Following these tips restricts an anonymous user to only those containers where such access is allowed, thereby protecting the sensitive parts of the file system.

Debugging sendmail

You can debug sendmail by connecting it to port 25 of the specified machine. After it is debugged and you get the following output, you know that sendmail is running properly, as shown in Figure A-1.

You might want to expand addresses while debugging sendmail. This can be done by using the expn SMTP command. You can also use the HELP SMTP command to identify the commands supported by a sendmail host.

Debugging sendmail becomes easy if you run sendmail in verbose or debug mode. The -v flag indicates the verbose mode. You can use debug level 0.1 by specifying the -d0.1 flag. You can test address rulesets and how an e-mail is being routed by using debug level 21.12 marked by the flag -d21.12.

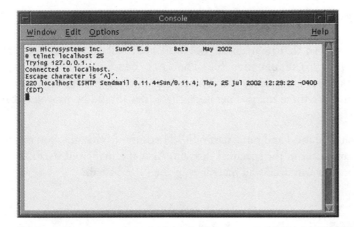

FIGURE A-1 *Output of the telnet command verifying that sendmail is running properly*

Enabling and Disabling the Solaris Basic Security Model (BSM)

If you wish to use the auditing facilities in Solaris, you must enable BSM before proceeding further. BSM can be enabled or disabled by using two scripts defined in the /etc/security directory. These scripts are bsmconv and bsmunconv. The bsmconv script is used to enable BSM and the bsmunconv script is used to disable BSM. Note that you need to restart your machine for BSM to take effect. If you execute the bsmconv script without any options or arguments, BSM is enabled on the host computer and on all diskless clients connected to the host computer.

Securing a Solaris Server

You can improve the security of a Solaris server by implementing different security aids in the server configuration. You can install the latest recommended patches from the Sun-Solve site. You can also install any intrusion detection system, such as Snort, that contains a huge database of exploits. Snort takes up limited resources for its use. It logs all the alerts raised in the syslog file. You can install and configure SWATCH for monitoring the log files generated by the Snort alerts.

You can also install a packet filter, such as an IP filter, that acts as a firewall to the server. A set of rules that denies the incoming packets except the ones that offer specific services, as defined by you, should be defined for this packet filter. You can also install Yet Another Solaris Security Package (YASSP) to improve the default file system permissions.

Configuring NIS Maps for Security

NIS should be configured so that its maps are not available to all networks. This can be done by using the `/var/yp/securenets` file. The `/etc/passwd`, `/etc/shadow`, and `/etc/inetd/netmasks` files are used by NIS for its maps. Any user with login access to the system can read and use these maps. Therefore, these files should be moved out from the `/etc` directory.

The root account should be local and not a part of NIS because if NIS fails, you can never log in as root to any computer in the specified domain. Also, if a malicious user intercepts the root password, the user can access all machines in the NIS domain.

Detecting Intrusion Attempts

You might be faced by intrusion attempts in your network. You can protect the network by detecting these attempts before they harm the other systems on the network. A hacker can enter your network by attempting port scans. Data collected from using scanners such as SATAN can be used for identifying weak points in the network. Port scans indicate an attempt to connect to different ports. Using SATAN, a hacker can identify the ports or services open for intrusion. To detect these attempts, you can build systems that alert you if a hacker attempts to connect to a specified port. You can use `TCP wrappers` for wrapping insecure ports in your system. These wrappers raise e-mail alerts that inform you in case of an intrusion attack. You can also use router logs that log the different intrusions to your system. You can also build an Access Control List (ACL) on your router that lists the ports or systems to be denied access to. You can implement any intrusion detection system dependent on the type of intrusion method used.

You should be careful before reacting to an intrusion attempt. The intrusion attempt might not be deliberate. It could be an accident. A user could be confused and access your system or misspell the URL. It might also be possible that the source IP address was changed by the user. Therefore, although your log shows that three different computers have accessed a specific port, only a single computer whose IP address was changed might do it. Maybe a specific system is being used as a launching point for an attack. You must gather as much information as possible before getting back to the user of the attacking system. Identify the source address from the logs and identify the person responsible for the attack. This can be done by using the `whois` database or the `dig` and `nslookup` methods. Finally, notify the person you identify of the attack.

Restricting Access to Network Services

You can restrict access to FTP or Telnet services for a set of user IDs or to users over the network. You can limit access to these services by using UNIX groups or Solaris Access Control Lists (ACLs). You can use Role-Based Access Control (RBAC) to restrict access to these network services for certain users. By using RBAC, you can create a role that has access to execute the Telnet or FTP commands. Users can then be assigned these roles.

You can limit access to users who cannot log in by using the FTP protocol. This can be done by removing these users or by not adding entries of users in the /etc/ftpusers file. You can also restrict hosts and domains to connect to Telnet or FTP services by using TCP wrappers.

Checking for Changes in the System

You can find out if someone has been tampering with your system by checking the changes made to your system. The things to compare in the system are modification dates, file ownership, protection, and inode numbers. To access these system properties, use the ls command with the -lsid option. This combination displays inode number, file size, owners, modification dates, and protection modes. Create a file that contains the correct output and then compare this file with the data generated by the ls command with the -lsid option. However, to avoid confusion, you must update the file with the original data if you make any changes to the system.

Protecting File Systems and Files

You must audit your systems to check whether they are secure or not. Sun provides you with Automated System Enhancement Tool (ASET) for auditing systems. ASET is a set of administrative utilities that help in improving security of a system. System administrators use ASET to check system file settings and the contents of system files. ASET works in three security levels, namely low, medium, and high. ASET checks and reports potential security weaknesses without making any modifications when operating in low level. ASET modifies few system files settings and parameters in order to restrict system access, thereby saving the system from security attacks when operating in medium level. When operating in high level, many more restrictions are placed in system access.

Another tool for auditing file systems is Advanced Intrusion Detection Environment (AIDE). This tool compares the properties of files and directories with the original information stored in a database. If any changes are made to files, these changes are flagged and logged. This tool also has the facility of optional e-mail reporting. You can also use the `find` tool to audit the file system.

You can also use a set of scripts called *fix-modes* for increasing the security for the filesystem modes. The increase in security is possible by removing world and group write permissions for all files or directories that are listed in the `/var/sadm/install/contents` file.

Using the Nessus Security Tool

Nessus is a security scanner tool that audits a given network to check for vulnerabilities. Crackers who can misuse them can explore these vulnerabilities. This tool checks for all the vulnerabilities in a network and generates an HTML-formatted report of the vulnerabilities along with their fixes. It runs on all versions of Windows, Solaris, Linux, and MacOS X systems.

Setting Firewall Resources

Consider a situation where your organization does not have the hardware and software resources for setting up a firewall. However, setting up a firewall is very necessary. Certain firewall resources can help build an effective firewall in your organization network: IPFilter, Firewall Builder, and Isba.

IPFilter is a software package that provides firewall and Network Address Translation (NAT) services. Using this package, you can pass or reject data packets passing through multiple interfaces. IPFilter also sends errors for rejected data packets. It performs NAT for all data packets entering the network and leaving it. It also uses redirection technology to set up transparent proxy connections.

Firewall Builder is based on an object-oriented GUI scheme. It consists of a set of policy compilers for different firewall platforms. By using Firewall Builder, users create a policy file containing rules that consist of `abst` or `pract` objects representing network objects and services, such as routers, networks, protocols, and firewalls. Users can edit the policy files by using drag-and-drop operations because it is based on a GUI interface.

Isba is also a graphical tool and a firewall ruleset builder. It is used to edit IPFilter rulesets and manage IPFilter firewalled hosts. The hosts, interfaces, and services are treated as objects and can be assigned names. The rules generated by Isba are displayed in columns according to types, which can be interfaces, actions, and hosts. Both Isba and IPFilter contribute in maintaining the flexibility and readability of firewall rulesets.

Securing NIS

NIS is insecure and does not provide a very strong authentication service. For completely secure services, you can choose from LDAP or NIS+. But you can also secure NIS to make it fault tolerant. The method for securing NIS consists of two steps:

◆ Read the main page of the securenets file and store the file on the NIS master machine in the /var/yp directory. You should ensure that no user tries to access this NIS information form the master computer.

◆ Set an NIS client as an NIS secondary and the securenets file to contain information that allows each NIS client to retrieve information from itself only.

This method ensures that no computer other than the NIS clients can access any NIS data. It also ensures that no client is dependent on another for NIS information and allows for fast retrieval of information.

Securing the System from Trojan Horses

A Trojan horse is a virus program that attacks a system but appears normal to the system user. The administrator should provide suitable access permissions for superusers of the system. When you become superuser by using su, the PATH variable is set as follows:

```
PATH=/usr/sbin:/usr/bin
```

Malicious users can easily modify this PATH string and add the path for a Trojan horse. When you login as root by using su, the shell reads the su script stored in the /etc/default directory. This script defines the SUPATH variable that controls the value of the PATH variable when you become a superuser. You need to uncomment the line describing the SUPATH variable and change its value. Some Host Intrusion Detection Systems (HIDSs) can look for Trojan code that has been planted on the system.

Setting Resources for Using the Automounter

The automounter is used with NFS to automatically mount and unmount directories on the network whenever the need arises. Before using the automounter, the network should be up and running with NIS+. The machines on the specified networks need the default auto_home and auto_master maps defined in the /etc directory.

Before using NIS+ with the automounter, create and update the NIS+ automount maps. The auto_home map contains a list of usernames, the server, and the path for each user's home directory. The auto_master maps contain names of maps, mount points, and optional mount options. Besides these maps, you can create additional maps that provide access to source files, project files, and manual pages.

Improving Fault Tolerance

Solaris 8 has introduced a new feature called IP Network Multipathing. This feature allows for the fail-over of NICs automatically. It also routes the outgoing connections over various NICs. However, to configure this extension, you need to add parameters, such as interface identifiers to the /etc directory. After this new feature is configured, the in.mpathd file retrieves the private addresses on the cards. It then transfers the current connections to other NICs in the same physical interface. The IP Network Multipathing technology protects you from cable failure, switch port failure, and NIC failure.

Securing Solaris by Disabling Ports

To secure Solaris, users can disable ports without affecting the functionality of the system. In such cases, it is usual that users overlook the syslog port. However, in Solaris 8 this port can be disabled without affecting its functionality by modifying the /etc/init.d/ syslog rc script, and adding the -t switch. After disabling the port, you must execute the start and stop commands to initiate the system with the change.

Running Fewer Services

If the inetd services on your system are not configured properly, they can affect your system security by introducing security loopholes in the system. Generally, network services are initiated by the inetd daemon service. These services are configured according to the rules specified in the /etc/inetd.conf file. The default configuration file in Solaris starts up many unnecessary services that are highly susceptible to security attacks. The most susceptible services used by hackers are rpc.cmsd, sadmind, and rpc.ttdbserverd. These services enable buffer-overflow attacks that allow compromise of the targeted systems by using the remote root.

Using the chown Command

To change the ownership and group of files or directories, provide separate commands, such as chown and chgrp. However, you can use just one chown command with a colon between the owner's name and the group name.

Users do not require root access for giving access to files by using the chown command. To enable, add the following statement in the /etc/system file.

```
set rstchown=0
```

You can change the preceding code statement to disable the root access functionality by using the following command:

```
set rstchown=1
```

Inserting Current Date in an E-Mail Message

You can send an e-mail message from UNIX with the date and time specified. If the system is slow, it displays a delayed timestamp in the message. However, by using the following code statement, you can have a real timestamp with your mail.

```
date ¦ mailx-s 'Testing time stamp' norman@asc.com
```

Securing Deletion of Files

Imagine if a user with root permissions executes the rm * command; all your data will be lost even without bothering you with a prompt. To minimize these errors, create files in directories with >i. This enables the system to display a prompt before deleting the specified file.

Displaying the Access, Modification, and Creation Times for a File

There are no UNIX commands available that can display the access, modification, and creation times for a file in one step. However, it is possible to display all three by using the following command:

```
$ truss -vlstat -tlstat ls -l [file name]
```

Recovering the /etc/path_to_inst File

Generally, it is a good practice to create copies of system files to avoid problems during a system crash. However, the /etc/path_to_inst file can be recovered during system bootup. This can be done by specifying the -a option at the bootProm. When the system starts, you'll be prompted for recovery of this file.

Appendix B

FAQs

Q. Differentiate between public key and symmetric cryptography.

A. Public key cryptography is also known as asymmetric cryptography and uses a set of private and public key pairs to encrypt and decrypt messages. A public key is normally used to encrypt messages. You can decrypt the message by using only the associated private key. It is not very easy to decipher the private key if you are able to access the public key. Therefore, you can distribute the public key to various users.

On the other hand, symmetric cryptography uses a single key for encrypting and decrypting messages. Unlike public key cryptography, you cannot share this secret key with everyone. Only the users who are intended to encrypt or decrypt the message have access to the secret key. The drawback of using this cryptography is that the secret key needs to be transmitted over a secure channel, because there is always a possibility of the secret key being intercepted if transmitted over an insecure channel. This drawback is covered by the usage of public key cryptography where you do not need to transmit the secret key.

Q. What are SHA-1 and DSA?

A. Secure Hash Algorithm (SHA-1) was developed by the National Institute of Standards and Technology (NIST) and is used to create message digests. Digital Signature Algorithm (DSA) was also developed by NIST and is used to create digital signatures.

Q. What is a Certificate Authority (CA) and why do you need one?

A. A CA is a package that stores public keys in a directory. A CA authenticates the credentials of an entity. The private keys are not stored and are handled by the users at their end. The public keys are used to generate signatures, encrypt documents, and verify that the documents have not been changed during transmission. The public keys are stored in certificates that are signed by the CA. The signed certificates are stored in the X.500 directory.

A CA helps in providing encryption, authentication, and integrity. It is a good practice to incorporate a CA in your organization as a solution for security issues.

An internal CA is used to issue certificates to internal employees. A third-party CA is used to facilitate transactions (normally e-commerce transactions) between two parties.

Q. What are CRLs?

A. Certificate Revocation Lists (CRLs) represent a certificate list that contains invalid certificates whose private keys are either lost or stolen. Certificates are added to CRLs if the private key is mishandled. The respective user of the key informs the CA administrator for the same.

Q. **Public keys are stored in certificates. How do the users store their private keys?**

A. The private key is stored on the user's system hard disk. The key is stored in DES-encrypted format and can be decrypted only after the set password is provided. Consider a situation: A user logs on to multiple systems, but the private key is stored on one system only, thereby posing a problem. This problem can be solved by using a private key server, which is provided by the Distributed Computing Environment (DCE). The user simply needs to log in to the DCE, and the private key server encrypts and delivers the private key to the user. If the user is using another machine, the user simply needs to log in to the private key server.

Q. **When do you use smart cards and tokens?**

A. Smart cards and tokens provide the user's private keys even if the user accesses the private key from multiple locations. For authentication, users insert their smart cards into an appropriate card reader.

Q. **What is the need for PGP?**

A. PGP stands for Pretty Good Privacy. It is a program that encrypts and decrypts data. PGP uses the RSA public-key encryption process. Various people who wish to secure their confidential data and messages can use PGP. PGP is based on public key cryptography. While using PGP, the software generates two keys, a public and a private key. The private key remains with you, whereas you can distribute the public key. It is almost impossible to decode PGP.

Q. **Explain the term LDAP.**

A. LDAP stands for Lightweight Directory Access Protocol. It is a descendant of X.500, which is the OSI Directory Access Protocol. This protocol provides access to directory services. Directory services are databases that are read more often than are written to. Therefore, it is used for providing access to directory information. Information can be stored in an LDAP server, from where it is accessible to applications, mail servers, or Web servers.

An LDAP entry is a record in the LDAP database and consists of attributes and values. All LDAP entries are identified by their unique names called distinguished name attributes. Distinguished name is referred by the mnemonic dn.

Q. **Compare LDAP and RDBMS.**

A. LDAP is a communication protocol. Therefore, you can communicate with a relational database management system (RDBMS) by using LDAP. LDAP servers are configured for read access and provide a faster read operation than RDBMS servers. Users who need information such as names and phone numbers of employees prefer an LDAP connection to an ODBC connection to the RDBMS.

Q. **Define LDIF.**

A. LDIF stands for LDAP Data Interchange Format. The data exchanges between the client and the servers are in LDIF.

Q. **What is NIS+?**

A. NIS+ indicates Network Information Service Plus. It is a default naming service for Solaris. NIS+ fills the loopholes formed by NIS. NIS+ implements security through an authentication method. Users have the standard login and password to access the system. In addition, they have a secure RPC password or network password, which accesses NIS+ for the new security implementation. By default, the login password is same as the network password, therefore, after logging in, a user has access to the NIS+ security features. If the two passwords are different, the user needs to use the keylogin facility to get access to NIS+.

Q. **What are the different types of problems faced by NIS+?**

A. The different types of problems faced by NIS+ are authentication problems, performance problems, irregular problems, and missing information from tables.

Q. **What is SSH?**

A. SSH stands for Secure Shell. SSH is a program that can log on to a remote computer in a network. It can then execute commands on this computer and files from this system to another. SSH provides strong authentication and secure communication over an unsecured network connection. This program has replaced the rsh, rcp, and rlogin commands. These traditional commands were susceptible to different types of attacks. If a user had root access to computers on a network, by using these commands, the user could gain unrestricted access to systems. These commands were also maintain a log of user-sensitive information, such as passwords, which is avoided by SSH. SSH is transparent to users because of the creation of remote X sessions.

Q. **What is SSH based on?**

A. SSH communications are based on IDEA or cipher algorithms, such as DES, Triple-DES, blowfish, or TSS. The keys used for encrypting data are transmitted by using RSA. The data generated by this key exchange is destroyed periodically after an hour. The RSA keys are used for authentication and encryption. Authentication protects the system against DNS and routing spoofing, whereas encryption protects against IP spoofing.

Q. **From where can I obtain the SSH program and how do I install it in my system?**

A. You can get SSH from the ftp://ftp.cs.hut.fi/pub/ssh/ site. Unpack it by using the following command:

```
tar zxvf ssh-1.2.20.tar.gz
```
Change the directory to `ssh-1.2.20`. Read the INSTALL file and follow the directions in it.

Q. **List the attacks avoided by SSH and those that are not avoided.**

A. SSH protects against the following attacks:

◆ IP source routing attacks, where a host computer pretends that the IP data packet comes from a trusted source computer

◆ IP spoofing attacks, where a remote host delivers packets that pretend to be delivered from a trusted host

◆ DNS spoofing attacks, where attackers fake name server records

◆ Attacks posed due to the passwords or other sensitive data being interpreted by intermediate hosts

However, if an attacker has gained access to a computer as root, the effect of SSH is subdued. On the other hand, security by SSH is rendered ineffective if an attacker has access to a user's home directory.

Q. **Can I legally use SSH?**

A. SSH 1.2.20, a part of UNIX, can be distributed freely but cannot be sold as a separate part or project. The earlier versions of SSH were less restrictive. The MS-Windows version of SSH by Tatu Yloenen is a licensed commercial product. There are countries where encryption procedures cannot be used legally if they are not accompanied by a special permit.

SSH uses the RSA and IDEA algorithms, which are patented in the United States and other countries. SSH can work without the IDEA algorithm also. You must have a license to use IDEA commercially.

SSH was written outside the United States. Once SSH is imported in the United States, it is a criminal offense to export SSH software outside the United States.

Q. **How is SSH administered?**

A. Using RSA host authentication, a client connects to a remote host. However, for authentication to be successful, the server needs the client's public key. For administering SSH it is very important to manage the host keys. These keys can be automatically collected by using the `ssh-keyscan` and `make-ssh-known-hosts.pl` utilities. These utilities enable you to write scripts for verifying public keys. These utilities are susceptible to man-in-the-middle attacks. Therefore, if users have changed their public keys or new computers are running the SSH software, the administrators should contact the user concerned to avoid these attacks. To avoid these attacks, a fingerprint scheme is proposed for the next version release.

Q. **I can see cleartext on the Net even if I use SSH. Why?**

A. It is most likely that you are viewing a `rlogin` or X session on the computer where you run the SSH software. You can check whether the packets are actually SSH by checking their port number because SSH listens on port 22.

Q. **Why does SSH hang while working in Solaris 2.5?**

A. This is because of a problem with the Solaris shared library code. This code causes some name server functions to hang. You can rectify this problem by getting the 103187-02 patch.

Q. **What does the following statement signify: "Warning: remote host denied X11 forwarding"?**

A. This warning indicates that X11 forwarding is disabled in the remote host. The warning is also displayed if the `xauth` command or X11 libraries are not located during server compilation.

Q. **Why does SSH not function properly for multihomed hosts?**

A. You need to check whether the `gethostbyname()` method returns a complete listing of the possible IP addresses. Your system may not be configured to search for all IP addresses.

Q. **How do I disable network root logins to implement security?**

A. Enable the CONSOLE line in `/etc/default/login`. Disable the use of FTP by root by adding `root` to `/etc/ftpusers`.

Q. **How can I modify file permissions to enable a higher level of security?**

A. In Solaris, the `fix-modes` program modifies system, directory, and file permissions, therefore making it difficult for nonroot users to convert to root or for nonroot users to modify files.

Q. **How can you stop the usage of unnecessary accounts?**

A. Unnecessary accounts, such as `sys`, `nuucp`, `listen`, or `uucp`, can be avoided by removing or locking them. These accounts can also be commented out. They can also be blocked by putting `NP` in the `password` field of the `/etc/shadow` file.

Q. **How can I disable the NFS service?**

A. You can disable the NFS server daemon by renaming `/etc/rc3.d/S15nfs.server`. You can also prevent a computer from posing as an NFC client by renaming `/etc/rc2.d/S73nfs.client`. You can disable NFS exports by removing the `/etc/dfs/dfstab` file.

Q. **How can device permissions be modified?**

A. The devices associated with login, such as monitor or keyboard, can be assigned permissions. These permissions are specified in the /etc/logindevperm file. The permissions in this file can be modified based on the requirements. To ensure that only a single user accesses removable media, such as floppies or tapes, you can use the allocate and deallocate commands.

Q. **Is rpcbind a secure program?**

A. Standard rpc is not secure. The rpcbind program allows rpc callers and rpc service providers to locate each other. The rpc program uses AUTH_UNIX authentication. This indicates that the program depends on the remote user's UID and the remote system's IP address for identification. However, both of these are susceptible to change. You can disable rpc on Web servers, mail servers, or FTP servers by renaming /etc/rc2.d/S71RPC. You must ensure that none of the facilities are affected if you disable rpc.

Q. **Does EEPROM improve the security of your system?**

A. EEPROM does not completely secure your system. It can be replaced if someone has physical access to your system. If the computer's EEPROM is replaced, the host ID is also changed. Therefore, you can verify that no EEPROM is replaced by maintaining a list of host IDs of your computers and checking this list against your computers occasionally.

You can password-protect all EEPROM commands by setting the EEPROM security mode to command by using the following code statement:

```
ok setenv security-mode=command
```

Q. **How can I securely use NFS?**

A. You should not run the NFS mount through rpcbind because the mount daemon treats the request as local and allows it. You should install the latest Sun rpcbind patches to disable forwarding. You should use secure-RPC with NFS. Your access list contains available IP addresses. Any computer using any of these IP address is allowed access to NFS. It is good practice to disable NFS because NFS traffic is represented in cleartext and susceptible to snooping attacks.

Q. **How can anonymous FTP service be used securely?**

A. Although Solaris 2.5 ftpd contains most of the configuration directions, few are missing. These are that you should make sure that the file system containing FTP is not mounted with the nosuid option. No files under the FTP service should be owned by FTP itself.

Q. **How can I disable the automounter?**

A. To disable the automounter, remove the /etc/auto_* configuration files. You can also disable it by disabling the /etc/rc2.d/S74autofs.

Q. **Are there any risks involved in using dynamic routes?**

A. Computers using dynamic routes are susceptible to receiving incorrect routes. These incorrect routes can disable the connectivity to remaining networks. Therefore, it is advisable to use static routes rather than dynamic route-receiving daemons like in.routed and in.rdisc.

Q. **Can syslog provide more effective and relevant information?**

A. Generally, syslog provides minimal information related to login operations. The /etc/syslog.conf file should be modified such that syslog can contain more relevant and important information. The security-related information should be placed in a file and the file should be encrypted.

Q. **What happens if code is executed in a stack? How can this be avoided?**

A. Many security loopholes can be posed on a system if the code executes in a stack. These loopholes perform operations that overflow a buffer such that it writes in the stack space. The space generated can then hold the malicious code to be executed. As a result, malicious code is executed on your system. You need to add the following entries to /etc/system to avoid this:

```
set noexec_user_stack=1
set noexec_user_stack_log =1
```

The first statement prevents code execution on the stack. However, if a program was written to perform this, it would crash because you have negated this option. Therefore, care should be taken with the first statement. The second statement creates a log to track the stack status.

Q. **How can TCP sequence prediction attacks be avoided?**

A. You can avoid TCP sequence prediction attacks by setting the TCP_STRONG_ISS variable to 2 in /etc/default/inetinit.

Q. **Define Kerberos.**

A. Kerberos is a network authentication protocol. It is based on secret key cryptography. It provides strong authentication for client/server applications. The word Kerberos is derived from Greek mythology. It is the three-headed dog that guarded the entrance to Hades.

Kerberos was created by MIT and solves many of the network security problems that arise when a client needs to send the identity information over an unsecured channel to the server. The client and server can prove their identity securely by using Kerberos. This protocol can also be used to encrypt communication form the client to the server and vice-versa.

This protocol is available free of cost from MIT with a copyright permission notice. MIT provides this protocol in source form so that users can read the code and use the protocol only if they trust it.

Q. **Which is the latest version of Kerberos?**

A. The latest version of Kerberos 5 is 1.2.1.

Q. **What is SASL and how is it related to Kerberos?**

A. SASL stands for Simple Authentication and Security Layer. It is a protocol framework for providing different authentication mechanisms to client and servers. A SASL profile specifies the protocols such as SMTP, POP, or IMAP that are used to encapsulate SASL messages. SASL mechanisms specify the various authentication schemes. An example of such a mechanism is GSSAPI. Kerberos is one of the standardized mechanisms for GSSAPI. Protocols using SASL for authentication also support Kerberos through GSSAPI.

Q. **Where is the `kadm5.acl` file located and what is it used for?**

A. The `kadm5.acl` file is located on the KDC host. It is used to control access to the Kerberos database. The exact location of the file is specified in the `kdc.conf` file.

Q. **What is the use of `krb524d` daemon?**

A. The `krb524d` daemon converts a Kerberos 5 service ticket to a Kerberos 4 service ticket. The krb524init program and the AFS-Kerberos 5 Migration Kit mainly use this daemon. You need to run this daemon on the KDC or grant it access to keys for the service principals whose tickets are to be converted. To use `krb524init`, you need to run `krb524d` on your KDCs. After you have gained a V5 TGT, run `krb524init`. Your V5 TGT is converted to a V4 TGT, which can be used by V4 applications.

Q. **How is the AFS Kerberos different from the normal Kerberos?**

A. AFS stands for Andrew File System. The AFS Kerberos was created by using Kerberos 4 papers. AFS Kerberos uses the RX protocol to communicate between clients and database servers. These database servers can be compared to KDCs in normal Kerberos. The AFS clients destroy the TGT after getting an AFS service ticket.

Q. **What is ASN.1?**

A. ASN.1 stands for Abstract Syntax Notation One. It is used for describing abstract types and values. Using this notation, you can create format for complex objects by collating simpler types. Kerberos 5 uses ASN.1 and Distinguished Encoding Rules (DER) to encrypt and decrypt all the message of Kerberos. You need to use ASN.1 only if you are adding to the Kerberos protocol.

Q. **What is the difference between TGT and TGS?**

A. TGT stands for Ticket Granting Ticket and TGS stands for Ticket Granting Service. The TGT is a Kerberos ticket for TGS. While authenticating a user to Kerberos, the user requests the authentication service on the KDC for a TGT that is encrypted by the user's secret key. When interacting with a Kerberos service, the user uses the TGT to interact with the TGS running on the KDC.

TGS verifies the user's identity by means of TGT and grants a ticket for the desired service. With the usage of TGT, a user need not enter a password to connect to a Kerberos service.

Q. Explain the concept of forwardable, renewable, and postdatable tickets?

A. A Kerberos ticket contains the encoded IP address of the client that is used by KDC and application servers to verify the client address. A client can request for a TGT to be marked as forwardable in Kerberos 5. The administrator of KDC decides whether a forwardable ticket is to be granted to the requesting client or not. To mark a ticket as forwardable, the `TKT_FLG_FORWARDABLE` flag is set in the flags field of the ticket. Using this forwardable ticket, the user can request for a new ticket with different IP address. Tickets in Kerberos are valid only for a specified time period. They ultimately expire. A short life span is preferred so that if a ticket is stolen it cannot be misused. However, in Kerberos 5 there is the concept of renewable tickets. These tickets have expiration times and a maximum renewable lifetime. You can renew a renewable ticket by requesting KDC for a new ticket with an extended lifetime. You have to renew a ticket before it expires. A renewable ticket can be renewed multiple times until it exhausts its maximum renewable lifetime.

Consider a situation when a user needs a ticket to be valid in the future. This was made possible in Kerberos 5 with postdatable tickets. These tickets are invalid when delivered to the user. They become valid later. The user needs to send a postdatable ticket to KDC for validation during the valid lifetime of a ticket.

Q. What type of resources are needed for implementing KDC?

A. First, you will need a dedicated machine for KDC to run on. The machine needs to be very secure because the database on the machine is very sensitive and if mishandled, your entire realm would be affected. This can be done by allowing clients to login only through the console. If the machine is down, all Kerberos services are rendered ineffective. Running KDC requires little memory and CPU usage. Taking regular backups of KDC is important because if any data is lost, a lot of time and effort goes into restoring KDC to its initial state.

Q. How can I configure the admin server to reject certain passwords?

A. You need to define a variable called `dict_file` in the realms section of the `kdc.conf` file. This variable contains a list of passwords not permitted in the system.

Q. Explain v5passwdd.

A. The v5passwdd daemon implements the Kerberos 5 password changing protocol. Kerberos 5 clients, such as the MIT Win32 Kerberos client and few Xyplex terminal servers, use this protocol. To run this daemon, you need to create a `changepw` principal as specified here:

o changepw/YOUR.REALM@YOUR.REALM

Then, set the `DISALLOW_TGS_REQ` and `PASSWORD_CHANGING_SERVICE` attributes. The principal's key needs to be added to the admin keytab. Finally, start the v5passwdd daemon by using the following command:

o v5passwdd -port 464 -T /path/to/admin/keytab

Appendix C

Other Security Tools

In this appendix, I'll cover certain additional security tools in Solaris. These include Yet Another Solaris Security Package (YASSP) and Toolkit for Interactively Toughening Advanced Networks and Systems (Titan). YASSP is a tool for Solaris administrators with which they can secure a Solaris host. Titan is a host-based security tool. It is used to improve or audit the security of a UNIX system. It is freely available. Another interesting fact is that TITAN was released much before YASSP.

Yet Another Solaris Security Package (YASSP)

System administrators can use YASSP to implement security hardening on the system. It consists of the SECclean package and a set of other packages that are optional. The YASSP project was started in 1997. The project was initiated to implement exposed Solaris servers. YASSP was created to fulfill the weaknesses in the default installation of Solaris servers. In the default installation, the logging process is not consistent. The system does not display any default security messages for users trying to use the system. Above all, the system is configured to run almost all network services. This exposes the system to vulnerable security attacks because any host can request for a network service from the specified server. The services provided by a computer should be controlled by its owner. YASSP can be used on Solaris 2.6, 2.7, or 2.8 architectures to secure servers.

Certain rules that were kept in mind while creating the YASSP package:

◆ YASSP follows the Sun standard rules and is closely integrated with Solaris. If Sun's standard rules are not present for a particular module, YASSP provides administrators with the facility to exploit different choices of their own.

◆ YASSP is created to run on a minimal installation. Its core is written in Bourne shell by using sed and awk.

◆ YASSP can be installed and uninstalled without affecting the integrity of the system. It does not modify or remove any configuration files during uninstallation. Moreover, any changes done by the YASSP package can also be undone.

◆ YASSP, by default, installs the components that it considers secure. The default configuration is again reviewed and modified after YASSP package is installed.

Your system becomes secure and closed by using the YASSP package because of installing SECclean. Specifically, SECclean turns off all network services in /etc/inetd.conf and disables nonessential services started from /etc/init.d. The default SECclean configuration hardens the servers by shutting out services, resulting in a secure and closed server.

But you need to reconfigure the SECclean configuration for implementing end user workstations. SECclean hardens Solaris servers by performing certain tasks. Some of its tasks include:

- ◆ Controlling startup scripts through the `/etc/yassp.conf` file.
- ◆ Deleting unnecessary files, such as `etc/auto_home`, `/etc/auto_master`, and `/etc/dfs/dfstab`. There are many more files it deletes that are not specified here.
- ◆ Shutting down the available network services by using the `/etc/inet/inetd.conf` file.
- ◆ Enabling banner files, such as `/etc/motd`, `/etc/issue`, and `/etc/ftp-banner`.
- ◆ Changing the default environment setting to secure your system. The default environment variables that it changes are specified in the `/etc/yassp.conf` file.
- ◆ Enabling a standard syslog configuration by using the `/etc/syslog.conf` file.
- ◆ Controlling access to certain system commands, such as `etc/pam.conf`, `/etc/hosts.equiv`, `/.rhosts`, `/etc/default/login`, `/etc/cron.d/at.allow`, `/etc/cron.d/cron.allow`, `/etc/default/sys-suspend`, `/etc/dt/config/Xaccess`, `/usr/dt/config/Xaccess`, and `/etc/ftpusers`.
- ◆ Controlling RPC services.
- ◆ Checking network stack performance and security tuning. For example, YASSP provides increased resilience against DoS attacks. It also activates logging at the kernel level with a parameter change in /etc/system.
- ◆ Enabling package database correction, therefore implementing security.
- ◆ Changing filemode for security purposes.

In addition, YASSP provides an encrypted data channel by using the SSH protocol. It provides integrity checks by using tripwire, version control for system files, and log rotation by using `PARCdaily`, `GNUrcs`, and `GNUgzip`.

More about SECclean

SECclean implements security in a Solaris system by adding, modifying, or deleting files. The files are categorized in different groups based on these operations. The startup files are Bourne shell scripts that control run level changes. Each run level has an `rc` script associated with it, which is stored in the `/sbin` directory. The startup files are also called run control scripts and are stored in the `/etc/init.d` directory. SECclean treats startup files with special attention. You are already aware that the state of a system must not change after the installation and uninstallation of SECclean. Therefore, all file information, such as owner, group, permission mode, file contents, and file package must be saved after SECclean installation so that the system state can be restored during uninstallation.

These restoration or backup procedures are not defined by default and have to be decided by the user. The `cleanlib.sh` library provided by the Bourne shell provides file backup and restoration functions. SECclean uses these functions for file backup and restoration. Some of the functions provided by the `cleanlib.sh` library are:

◆ The `Save_and_move_file()` method moves the specified file and its information into a backup area and unregisters it from the package database.

◆ The `Backup_user_file()` method copies the specified file and creates a new path for the file in a given backup directory.

◆ The `Restore_RC()` method restores a startup link from the saved information and updates the package database.

◆ The `Restore_file()` method restores a file from the saved information and updates the package database.

◆ The `Install_file()` method installs a file and maintains a copy of the file to track it for modifications.

◆ The `Install_RC_file()` method installs a startup script and creates associated links under the `/etc/rc[0-6S].d` directories.

◆ The `Disable_RC()` method removes the links to a startup script and maintains a backup of all package information.

◆ The `Disable_Init()` method looks for any registered link to a startup script. If it is found, it calls the `Disable_RC()` method for each of these links.

◆ The `Init_preremove()` method initializes the value for the backup directory that contains files modified since YASSP installation.

◆ The `RCconfized_Init()` method modifies a startup script by using the `/etc/yassp.conf` file. It also modifies this file for every startup script it changes.

◆ The `DE_RCconfized_Init()` method undoes the modification done by the `RCconfized_Init()` method.

Files for modification are defined as a part of the `sed` class in SECclean. No method needs to be invoked for file modification. Everything is taken care of by the associated `sed` scripts. To delete a file, you can use the `Save_and_move_file()` method that saves the current file and package information and moves it to the package save directory and unregisters it from the current package.

The administrators can control startup scripts by setting the starting point of a script. They must set the shell variable in the `/etc/yassp.conf` file to `YES`. The name of the shell variable is same as the name of the script, with all nonalphabetic characters removed and all remaining characters capitalized. This entire operation can be performed by the `RCconfized_Init()` method.

All information associated with a startup script is backed up and deleted by using the `Disable_Init()` method. This method, starting from the name of the startup script contained in the `/etc/init.d` file links to the script in the `/etc/rc[0-6S].d/` directory, records all the links and the package information associated with the links. This method is used to delete or replace a startup script. In addition to file management, SECclean performs other tasks, including operating system cleanup, user backup, and password file cleanup.

After a Solaris installation, you might find that the Solaris components are not in perfect harmony with each other. This could be due to many reasons, such as files being modified during installation or files not being registered correctly. However, SECclean can rectify these inconsistencies by using an OS-dependent shell script.

SECclean provides a copy of the tree of files to provide more information to the system administrator. Using this information, the system administrator can observe the files that were changed and how it was done. The password file is checked and cleaned up by using the `clean_passwd` script of SECclean.

Now let's observe the installation process of the SECclean component.

SECclean Installation

SECclean uses the preinstall and postinstall procedure scripts for installation. The preinstall script determines the directory in which SECclean component will be installed. By default, SECclean is installed in the `/opt/local` directory. If the directory cannot be changed to the `/opt/local` directory and the `/usr/local` directory exists, the `/usr/local` directory is used. But the `/opt/local` directory exists as a symbolic link to the `/usr/local` directory.

After the installation path is decided, the preinstall script initializes the shell variables, namely $SECBCK and $CLEANUPDIR. The pathname where the user-convenient backup is created is stored in the $SECBCK variable. This variable stores the default value of `/yassp.bk`. The path where the scripts and binaries related to operating system cleanup are installed is stored in the $CLEANUPDIR variable. The $CLEANUPDIR variable stores the default value of `/var/sadm/clean-up`.

Then the preinstall script defines four shell variables, namely $RCCONF, $NRC, $SD, and $SA. These variables are stored in the $PKGSAVE/.PROC_Init_Var file. The $RCCONF variable stores an exhaustive list of startup scripts. The $NRC variable defines the startup script that you want to replace with your own OS-dependent version. Generally, the `inetsvc`, `inetinit` and `networks` scripts in Solaris 8 are used by this variable. The $SD variable specifies the list of files to be deleted. The $SA variable specifies the list of variables to be replaced. Finally, the preinstall script decides the user convenient backup position.

After the preinstallation phase, you can install the SECclean component. In the installation phase, all objects defined in the SECclean package are installed. Objects corresponding to files that need to be replaced are installed with a name prefixed by SECclean_. Objects dependent on operating system version or on host architecture are installed by using the operating system version or architecture as suffix. Finally, in the installation phase, all sed scripts associated with objects part of the sed class are executed modifying the targeted file.

The postinstall script is the last to be executed in the installation phase. The postinstall script disables startup files by invoking the Disable_Init() method. The files listed in the RCCONF variable are modified by using the RCconfized_Init() method. A sed script is generated and applied to these files. The yassp.conf file is generated by gathering static information and information about startup files present in the system. The deleted and replaced files are backed up and moved out by using the Save_and_move_file() method. SECclean closes and validates the removals done to the package database.

Next, the SECclean package objects are sorted out. The correct version of files dependent on an operating system version or machine architecture is stored and the remaining versions are deleted. The package database is closed after package information is updated. The files to be replaced that are installed with the SECclean_ prefix in their names are renamed their original names. The new inetinit, inetsvc, and networks startup scripts are installed. Links to these scripts are created from the appropriate /etc/rc[012].d directories. The SECclean database is closed to validate these changes. Security tuning is then performed for the /etc/system file, depending on the operating system version. The password file is cleaned up by calling the clean_passwd script. Finally, operating system cleanup is completed.

After the completion of the preceding phases, the SECclean component is installed. Besides the SECclean component, YASSP installs other tools, such as GNUrcs, GNUgzip, WVtcpd, SSHsdi, and PRFtripw. The GNUrcs component eases version control of your files. The GNUgzip component helps in file compression. The WVtcpd component provides TCP wrappers for users who need to run RPC. The SSHsdi component provides secure ID support. The PRFtripw component provides integrity checking tools.

Toolkit for Interactively Toughening Advanced Networks and Systems (Titan)

Titan is a set of programs that strengthens the security for a UNIX system by fixing potential security problems. It is written in Bourne shell. The set of programs consists of a master script that controls the execution of other small scripts. It is a simple tool and checks whether the system adheres to its security policy or not. UNIX is a complicated system and is difficult to secure. Features of Titan help in securing the UNIX system. Titan minimizes the entry points in the system. It improves the network and local security, prevents the effects of DoS attacks, provides better logging and auditing features, and enforces the system's operation as per the given security policy.

Titan was built around certain design goals:

- ◆ Titan should be simple and easy to install.
- ◆ The source code for Titan is freely available, enabling users to be aware of the methods and functions running on their machines. The users have full access to the code.
- ◆ Titan is modular and extensible. You can either add or remove shell scripts from Titan without affecting other programs.
- ◆ Titan assists in the creation of a system policy to regulate security of a system. This helps in maintaining a consistently secure system.
- ◆ Titan can be used frequently to secure your systems.

However, Titan does not solve all your problems. It does not attempt to fix the security issues raised by CGI programs. It is very difficult to write programs that detect and prevent all security issues raised by these programs. Titan also does not control the problems associated with secure software distribution or updates.

Titan fulfills the preceding design goals by preventing the effects of various DoS attacks. It shuts down various vulnerable entry points in the system, improves the level of logging and auditing features, and defines and maintains a system security policy.

Titan is very simple to use and easy to run. However, you need to use it continuously to maintain security of the system. To decide whether it fits into your system security policy or not, you should first read the Titan documentation and examine its source programs. You should back up your system before running Titan on your computer. You should also examine your system security after installing Titan and observe whether the security is strengthened and Titan has overcome the flaws of the earlier used security tools or not. After Titan is installed, you need to continuously monitor the security of your system.

After Titan has been initially installed on your system, you need to run it in the `verify` mode periodically. You should also provide strong authentication services to your system. Data should be encrypted before being transmitted across the network. Titan is extensible; therefore, you can add modules based on your security requirements.

Features of Titan

This section covers the changes that Titan makes to your system to implement security. You can enhance the Titan security implementation by adding new features or tests.

As discussed earlier, the `rc` shell scripts consist of startup services that start executing at boot time without your prior knowledge. Titan disables such services, which could pose vulnerable attacks to the system. Examples of such services are `automounter`, `lpsched`, `dmi`, and many more daemon services. Titan disables these services by either commenting them out or moving them from the `rc*` directories.

Titan also controls the general system configuration by checking whether the security mode is set in your system's EEPROM. You should always set the EEPROM password because Titan does not set the password. If the password is not set, an attacker can set a password for your system's EEPROM and halt the system. You would need a new EEPROM to reinstate your system.

Titan also controls the file and directory permissions by using `umask`. Titan ensures that the root uses a file creation mask, 022, which provides better security than the default one. By doing this, all system daemons create files with more secure file permissions. An attacker can exploit the security of the system by locating a file or directory that a privileged user is about to access or execute and obtain additional privileges to the system. Titan avoids such situations because it has three modules designed for this purpose.

NFS always supports an insecure port range. Titan modifies this by setting the privileged port definition of all the ports above 2050. This can be done by using the following parameters:

```
ndd -set /dev/udp udp_smallest_nonpriv_port 2050
ndd -set /dev/tcp tcp_smallest_nonpriv_port 2050
```

The ping echo command opens up the system for DoS attacks. To avoid this, Titan modifies your system so that it can avoid broadcast ping requests. This prevents attackers from entering your system by issuing a `ping -s` command. Titan modifies the system by using the following parameter:

```
ndd -set /dev/ip ip_respond_to_echo_broadcast 0
```

Titan also modifies the configuration files for a better security implementation. A few examples of configuration files that it modifies are `inetd.conf`, `sendmail.cf`, `nsswitch.conf`, `syslog.conf`, and `ftpusers`.

The `inetd.conf` file contains the default Internet services that are unnecessary or vulnerable to attacks. Titan removes or blocks such services in this file. Titan enables the privacy flags in the `sendmail.cf` file with the `goaway` option. It also disables EXPN and VRFY and sets the `sendmail` logging at a realistic security level. The security of the `nsswitch.conf` file is very important. An NIS or NIS+ entry in this file provide an attacker control of the important files that are trusted by your system to a remote system. If the local system does not have enough knowledge about the remote system, the remote system could pose a threat to the security of the local system. Titan solves this problem by building a minimal `/etc/nsswitch.conf` file by using the `/etc/nsswitch.files` sample file. Titan edits the `syslog.conf` file so that the console `auth` notice messages are logged to a file. The `ftpusers` file contains the usernames that are not allowed to use the

FTP service. Titan further adds system users, such as `root`, `lp`, and `bin`, to this file, thereby restricting these users from the FTP service.

Titan also strengthens the password and authentication services on your system for enhanced security. Network naming services such as NIS, NIS+, and DNS are insecure for the system and must be avoided. Titan disables these services from the `/etc/nss-witch.conf` file. Titan creates a `/var/adm/loginlog` file that logs more than five failed login attempts. Titan also modifies the `/etc/passwd` file. It removes or enables the system accounts that are not used or are not intended to be used. It can also set passwords to protect these system accounts.

It is recommended to run all modules defined in Titan. However, there are situations when such strong security measures are not recommended. Titan provides a single configuration file from which you can run all the different modules. Titan also creates a `/etc/issue` file that contains a warning stating that a user should not tamper with the system. The contents of this file appear on the login prompt.

Implementing Titan

Titan is a collection of Bourne shell scripts. The first script to be run is the `Config` script that determines the OS type and version of your system. It also helps in creating links to the other modules in Titan. This script has very little user interaction. The user just needs to provide the `-i` and `-d` flags. The `-i` flag indicates the install operation and `-d` flag indicates the deinstall operation. Titan can operate on the fix, verify, and inform modes. Titan uses the fix mode to create a secure system by editing and fixing the system. Titan in fix mode informs you of the changes it is making to the system. The verify mode does not modify the system; instead, it informs you of the changes to the system when in fix mode. The inform mode only echoes the operation of all functioning modules.

By default, the Titan program runs all the programs in the module directory with the same mode. You can create a customized policy that does not run all modules or you can remove the modules from the module directory. Every Titan module supports arguments from a given set. This set contains three arguments, namely `-f`, `-v`, and `-i`. Each of these represents the Titan modes. By default, Titan runs the modules in alphabetical order.

All Titan scripts are commented so that it is easy for the users to understand their operations. Each script is defined by a similar code, as follows:

```
#
umask 042
# This tool suite was written by and is copyrighted by Brad Powell , Matt
# Archibald, and Dan Farmer 1992, 1993, 1994, 1995, 1996, 1997, 1998
# with input from Casper Dik, and Alec Muffett.
#
# The copyright holder disclaims all responsibility or liability with
```

```
# respect to its usage or its effect upon hardware or computer
# systems, and maintains copyright as set out in the "LICENSE"
# document which accompanies distribution.
```

After this, the scripts set the path and verify whether the program is being run by root.

All Titan scripts contain three methods: intro(), check(), and fix(). The check() method is invoked if the Titan script is run in the verify mode. This method checks whether the specified Titan fix is needed by the system or not. The method returns appropriate output stating whether it passes the check. The fix() method performs the associated Titan fix to the system. All Titan modules return 0 if the module was successful and a nonzero value otherwise.

When creating your own Titan modules besides the built-in ones, you can start with the ${Titan-HOME}/arch/sol2sun4/src/stubs/skeleton script. Your module should be built around the fact that it accepts three arguments: -i, -v, and -f. It should be designed so that it outputs a success or failure notice as well. Notice that your Titan module will run as root and will modify the current system. Therefore, be very careful in the commands that you define in the module because a single erroneous command can lead to either a system hang-up or a system crash.

Appendix D

Disaster Recovery

In current times, all organizations are to a large extent dependent on IT for most of their tasks and services. There are situations when the normal functioning of organizations is affected because of factors beyond their control. These events upset even the most meticulous planning that IT might have performed while setting up the affected organizations. Such events are called disasters.

It is not practical or realistic to prepare in advance for disasters that do not cripple your entire system. However, you do need to set the functioning of the system in such a way that the system can continue to operate, albeit in a limited way, when such disasters occur. This is done by formulating and bringing together appropriate disaster recovery plans and procedures. Disaster recovery plans aim at recovering the important system functions in a short span of time. The plans have to be made well in advance. A disaster recovery plan typically consists of a list of actions that need to be performed before, during, and after a disaster occurs. The process of creating a disaster recovery plan is called *disaster recovery planning*.

Disaster recovery planning is essential for all organizations, as the time lost in system recovery leads to loss of revenue and can affect your customer relations. Serious problems may arise if the disaster causes loss of business information.

Organizations store a large amount of data, which needs to be available round the clock. This calls for IT-enabled databases in the organization system. As data needs to be accessible around the clock, the systems become more vulnerable to attacks. Natural disasters such as earthquakes, fire, or floods can destroy business data and utilities that affect the normal functioning of businesses. Manmade disasters, such as war or terrorism, also affect organizations by restricting their business activities.

Hardware failures, too, can cause disasters, such as disk failures, cable faults, power breakdowns, or faulty adapters. Some disasters can be caused by human failures, such as a UNIX administrator inadvertently deleting all files while backing up the server.

Data loss can also occur in case of power or system failures. An Uninterrupted Power Supply (UPS) should be configured so that the administrators can successfully shut down the UNIX servers. System users can also lead to data loss, because of poor system documentation, lack of training, or poor attention to details.

Therefore, it is very important to plan for recovery of data in case of disasters.

Disaster Recovery Planning

Should a disaster occur, it is important that the organization is made operational in the shortest possible time. A team of well-trained, experienced hands should be formed to effectively implement recovery procedures. The aim is to restore the critical business processes of the organization.

Special attention needs to be paid to the file system design. You need to check how the servers and other systems are designed. It should be possible to differentiate between the home directories and the directories where applications and other tools are stored. All this information is important and is needed during system recovery. If the system is not structured properly and files are randomly distributed, it will be very difficult to recover such a system. To avoid such a situation, you should install all tools and applications on a centralized server and the NFS—mount the server directories on local client machines. You should not alter the contents of the /usr/bin and /usr/sbin directories. Instead, put the local tools in a directory such as /usr/local/bin. You should not store the local tools configuration files in the /etc directory. Instead, store them in a different directory. Finally, you need to segregate the OS partitions and the ones used for home directories and applications.

It is a good practice to build file systems by using the -v option with mkfs. This helps in making a hard copy of the mkfs session, which can be used in times of disaster recovery. One important point that must be considered while taking backups is the *time to recovery*. It should be possible to effect recovery in a reasonable timeframe. A backup is of little use, if it cannot be restored in time. Apart from the conventional tape backups, various technologies such as remote mirroring could be considered.

Another important aspect of disaster recovery is system backup. It is very important to back up all crucial data so that it can be easily restored during disaster recovery. You should also ensure that all the backups are working. Administrators should randomly examine backup media to check whether the restore software can copy the contents back to the system. You need to examine backup run logs to check that the backups are working properly. Periodical audits need to be performed on the backup system configuration to check that all systems are being backed up consistently. The possibility of natural disasters ruining a data center and backup tapes cannot be ruled out. Therefore, backup media should be stored on an offsite location.

Another important aspect in system recovery is that of the presence of release media. You should always have two or more sets of release media for every Solaris version. Another set of release media for each Solaris version needs to be stored with the offsite backup tapes.

Administrators must be adequately trained in the recovery system. Server recovery tests should be conducted at periodic intervals. The test can be done by cloning the server and then practicing system recoveries on the clone. You should back up the production server twice and make sure that the backup sets are readable. Practice rebuilding the clone from scratch. Finally, you can verify that the clone is working fine by performing regression testing on the server clone to check whether it is providing all services.

It is very important for effective system recovery to maintain logbooks. These logbooks help in system recovery by determining file system customizations, various OS versions and their install options, disk partitions, and device addresses. The logbooks should contain all system construction details. It is a good idea to maintain a local archive of all Solaris patches to rule out the possibility of the Internet being down during system recovery.

You should provide appropriate hardware and software service agreements that match your organization's business needs. The different types of service agreements are carry-in, cross-ship, on-site repair, and replacement services. The carry-in service indicates that the failed system should be taken to a service depot, and cross-ship service indicates that the vendor should send a replacement system to the customer before receiving the damaged system from the customer. Even though you have hardware and software services available, it is a good idea to keep spare hardware crucial for the running of the system. You can build a system to provide spare parts. The spare system can either be a development or test server. The spare system should not be invested with all system resources; instead, it should contain only the minimum crucial services required for running the system.

Certain business tools have licensing agreements that restrict the movement of software from a spare system to the actual system. The best solution for this is to have a spare PROM for every server. This allows administrators to move software packages attached to a specific host ID from one server to another. Another important thing to keep in mind is that systems with similar host IDs should not run concurrently. A spare PROM should be used only if the system with similar host ID is not running.

It is very important to have detailed recovery documentation available for the disaster recovery plan to be successful. The documentation should provide detailed server architecture, offsite storage media recovery, backup and recovery procedures, and other operational procedures. Ensure that there are no version problems in documentation. This can be achieved by destroying all old copies of documentation. A list of passwords should also be available, but this list should be securely stored.

An alternate solution to recover a failed server is to recover important parts to other servers until the failed server is reinstated. However, this is possible only if servers run below their hard disk capacity. It is recommended to have enough spare disk space so that crucial data needed for the execution of a failed server can be stored in the neighboring server.

It is essential to ensure availability of the recovery personnel during time of a disaster. A disaster may strike at any time. The designated recovery personnel may not be able to reach the site quick enough to launch the recovery operations. Therefore, everyone in the UNIX team should be aware of how to recover systems. Members of the recovery team should be authorized to access offsite storage media and should be entitled to make certain emergency purchases in times of disasters. You need to ensure that the recovery personnel are available and can be contacted through pagers or cell phones so that they can reach the disaster site as fast as possible. You should always have a backup plan in place to avoid delays in startup of recovery operations. A backup team should always be there in case the original recovery personnel cannot be contacted.

Besides the internal UNIX teams, you require support from other people. For instance, you need to coordinate with the team that supplies power backup and air-conditioning to the organization. There should be backup available for UPS and air-conditioning systems. Computer equipment is prone to damage by natural disasters. Close liaison with hardware suppliers helps in obtaining quick replacements of urgently needed parts and assemblies.

Index

A

A&M University, 170
access
  based on user accounts, 18
  times, displaying, 313–314
access, securing
  to physical devices and files, 17–18
  remote, 23–25
Access Control Lists (ACLs), 70, 252
  Key Distribution Center and, 238–240
  using, 174–177
access control models
  Discretionary Access Control (DAC), 84–85
  Mandatory Access Control (MAC), 9, 84
  Role-Based Access Control (RBAC), 9, 69–84
access control tools, 208
  Crack, 212–213
  rpcbind, 210–211
  TCP wrappers, 209–210
access permissions, 3
  assigning, 160–165
  sendmail, 299–300
  types of, 157–159
  viewing, 159–160
account module, PAM, 52
accounts, removing unnecessary, 60–61
ACLs. *See* Access Control Lists
action, 133, 134
Active X controls, 279
addif, 128
Address Resolution Protocol (ARP), 128
administrative rights, 97
Administrative Roles tool, 74
administrators, 13
  roles, 72
admintool
  adding groups using, 196–198
  adding users with, 195–196
  tasks performed by, 194–195
Advanced Encryption Standard (AES), 38
Advanced Intrusion Detection Environment (AIDE),
    309–310
AES. *See* Advanced Encryption Standard
AFS. *See* Andrew File System

agent log, 145
AIDE. *See* Advanced Intrusion Detection Environment
algorithms
  effectiveness of, 34
  types of, 34–47
aliases, 98, 298–299
all-hosts database, 261
Andrew File System (AFS), 323
application-level firewalls, 253
arp, 128, 129
ARP. *See* Address Resolution Protocol
ASET. *See* Automated Security Enhancement Tool
asetenv, 115
ASET Internal Environment Variables, 115
ASN.1 (Abstract Syntax Notation One), 323
assigning access permissions
  chmod command for, 160–164
  numerically, 164–165
asymmetric cryptography, 34, 38–39
asymmetric encryption, 33
at command, 60
attacks
  Denial of Service (DoS) attacks, 4, 186–187
  handling malicious, 188–190
  ID spoofing, 185
  man-in-the-middle, 187, 204
  network sniffing, 185
  password, 186
  secret key, 187
  service-layer, 185–186
  TCP hijacking, 187
  types of, 184–187
attributes, LDAP, 106
audit_class, 66
audit_control, 67
audit_event, 68–69
auditing
  See also logging; syslog (system log)
  flags, 65
  implementing, 64–65
  objective of, 63–64
  preselection mask, 65
  principles of, 64
  terminology, 65
  trails, 65

GAME DEVELOPMENT.
IT'S SERIOUS BUSINESS.

"Game programming is without a doubt the most intellectually challenging field of Computer Science in the world. However, we would be fooling ourselves if we said that we are 'serious' people! Writing (and reading) a game programming book should be an exciting adventure for both the author and the reader."

—André LaMothe,
Series Editor

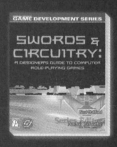

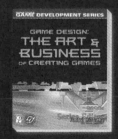